The Sociology of Money

THE SOCIOLOGY OF MONEY

Economics, Reason &
Contemporary Society

Nigel Dodd

CONTINUUM · NEW YORK

1994
The Continuum Publishing Company
370 Lexington Avenue
New York, NY 10017

Printed in Great Britain on acid-free paper.

Library of Congress Cataloging-in-Publication Data

Dodd, Nigel, 1965–
  The sociology of money:
  /Nigel Dodd.
        p.   cm.
    Includes bibliographical references and index.
    ISBN 0–8264–0637–8 (hc)
    1. Money.   I. Title.
  HG221.D53   1993
  332.4—dc20   93–34177
                                                        CIP

Contents

Preface

A book about the sociology of money might reasonably be greeted with scepticism. Existing sociological analyses of money are relatively insubstantial. Few social theorists have taken up money as an object of study in its own right, merely employing it as a means of exemplifying or extending other aspects of their work. A coherent sociological approach to money would be something of a novelty. The persistent inattention of sociologists towards money stems partly from a failure to recognize its importance as a consequential social institution. The uses made of money, the institutions associated with its control and acquisition, and the ideas people have of its nature and functions, are compelling features of contemporary life. On these grounds alone, there is no intrinsic need to justify a sociological examination of money. But there are further, conceptual reasons for writing a book about the sociology of money. Existing monetary theories tend to be derived from a set of assumptions about the nature of money and the types of social action with which its use is associated which are untenably narrow. The form of reasoning underlying these assumptions is restrictive when trying to understand how money is used and perceived in all but the most specialist arenas. It is open to question whether it can lead to a completely persuasive explanation of how money works at all. The purpose of this book is to examine and where necessary reformulate such assumptions in seeking out an incisive route for the sociological analysis of money and monetary relations. But for reasons I shall be exploring in the book, monetary analysis should not occupy a subsidiary position as a specialism in social theory in the way that the study of economics seems so dryly disconnected from most of the significant concerns of sociologists in general. The study of the nature of money, of its role in social, political and cultural life, and of how and why people perceive and use money in the present day crystallizes many of the issues – structural, cultural and epistemological – that are at the heart of contemporary social theory. Monetary analysis in social theory should not aim merely to make the study of money, finance, consumption and investment more palatable from the point of view of sociologists. It can on the contrary play a major and constructive part in deepening and enriching understanding of the core theoretical and empirical difficulties, and not least the relation between them, faced in social theory today.

Two major criticisms of extant monetary theories are crucial to the arguments pursued in this book. First, many of the assumptions regarding the rational behaviour of individuals in economics are empirically groundless and analytically unsustainable. It is customary to suggest that these assumptions are confined to the economy and not intended to be applicable to the rest of society. But this understanding of economics has never been far-reaching enough. Economic reasoning underpins a form of knowledge which has dominated the sociological analysis of modern society. But the supposition that individuals maximize cannot withstand closer inspection even in the one area of human activity to which it should most convincingly apply, namely the transaction of money. I do not intend to suggest that economic action is basically irrational rather than rational, but that the opposition between rationality and irrationality which has informed monetary theory, and indeed analyses of the distinctive character of modernity in sociology, is fundamentally misconceived. Second, anthropological findings regarding the nature and functions of pre-modern money rely on a naive and over-simplified account of modern forms of money. There is little doubt that these findings could be usefully applied to contemporary monetary forms and institutions, yet *prima facie* acceptance of what economists have had to say about money in the present day precludes many of the potential insights which such an application should provide. It is wrong to draw a clear distinction between pre-modern and modern money, at least within the terms of reference that anthropologists and economists have tended to employ. Taken together, these criticisms suggest that the sociological analysis of money should not confine itself to the margins of what is essentially an economic domain, concerned with the examination of why markets malfunction or investors misbehave. I have something distinctive to say about money which is directed towards the core, not the periphery, of monetary theory: to the relationship between money and rational human activity; to the reasons behind the demand for money; to the operation of markets and the role of money within them; to the dynamic relationship between national monetary control and international monetary integration; to the importance of culture for the operation of money in different societies and different periods of history; and to the methodological and epistemological problems inherent in monetary analysis.

The book is divided into two parts. The first part contains discussion of work by major social theorists on money. The category 'social theorist' is loosely defined, including political economists such as Adam Smith and Karl Marx and legal theorists such as Georg Knapp as well as writers conventionally linked with sociology and social theory. All the writers discussed none the less have in common a view of money which depends on analysis of social relationships and institutions beyond the scope of economics alone. They are divided into four groups according to the dimension of society highlighted in their work: political economy (chapter 1), the state and legal system (chapter 2), culture (chapter 3) and communicative processes within the social system (chapter 4). The second part of the book is devoted to integrating and extending themes and debates discussed in the first part. Strengths and weaknesses of the various approaches to money will have been pinpointed, and their implications will now be more fully explored from the point of view of contemporary social theory. The main issues here will concern the politics of financial and monetary integration (chapter 5), developments in consumption and investment behaviour highlighted in recent theories of postmodernity (chapter 6), and the relationship between high modernity, trust and rationalization (chapter 7). Finally, I draw the arguments of the book together by outlining a fresh and distinctive approach to monetary analysis in sociology (chapter 8).

There are several people who have helped, advised and supported me at various stages in writing this book. In particular, I should thank Anthony Butler, Mike Clarke, David Frisby, Tony Giddens, Lesley Glassington, Alex Goold, Geoffrey Ingham, Phil Joyce, Nik Kokosalakis, Jeanette Robey and Anna Wynne. In addition, I should like to thank my colleagues and students in the Department of Sociology at the University of Liverpool for their flexibility and encouragement. In the interests of all concerned, the customary disclaimer applies.

Introduction: On the Nature of Money

On 16 September 1992, turbulent speculation with currencies inside the European Exchange Rate Mechanism (ERM) led to the withdrawal of sterling from the system. Its depreciation was virtually instantaneous. Monetary authorities in Britain had instigated unprecedented rises in interest rates, twice on the same day, in a psychological strategy to counter speculation. This was not only politically untenable but unsuccessful. Open market operations by the Bank of England to buy sterling and maintain its exchange rate required a loan of £7.25 million in addition to the use of around £7 billion or one-third of foreign reserves.[1] In similar operations in support of sterling, the Bundesbank and Bank of France employed an estimated £2 billion of reserves.[2] These operations were insufficient to counteract the quantity of sterling being sold on international markets in financial centres across the globe. The French and German central banks were later engaged in intervention to counter massive speculation on the French franc, respectively employing an estimated FFr50 billion, or one-half of foreign reserves, and between DM10 billion and DM30 billion, in order to do so.[3] During the same period, the Italian lira required official devaluation, and later temporary suspension from the system, in order to maintain its position within the ERM.

The infamy of this episode perhaps owes more to the dramatic pattern of events rather than to any serious assessment of their long-term significance. Yet the unfolding of events, particularly the attention given to the crisis through media coverage and in everyday conversation, is indicative of some of the more important features of money and monetary systems in the late twentieth century. The crisis was generated by a complex range of psychological factors and actual incidents: long-term weakness of key macroeconomic indicators in Britain; ambiguity in the outcome of a French referendum on the Maastricht Treaty on European unification held on 13 September 1992; persistent uncertainty regarding the implications of the negative result of the Danish referendum held on the same issue several months earlier; a smaller than hoped for cut in interest rates by the Bundesbank; leaked statements by officials of the Bundesbank critical of decisions taken by the British Treasury and central bank; and consistent doubt over the capacity of the British Chancellor to resist the devaluation of sterling, thereby under-pinning the commercial attractiveness of its sale on currency markets. The morbid title given to the episode, Black Wednesday, indicates its instant absorption by monetary folklore, expressing a sense of super-stition and helplessness towards the behaviour of markets by turns deified and condemned as forces beyond the control of individuals and governments.[4] But the immediate and long-term impact of any currency crisis, transmitted across sectors of the international economy, is indisputably real, not only for the activities of corporations and government but in relation to everyday life: business survival, unemployment, pension and investment funds, the price of imported and exported goods, government expenditure on everything from health and education to welfare and defence, the cost of housing, and tourism. It would be misleading to suggest that such problems derive solely and directly from the handling of money. But the specific pattern of these consequences, the rapidity of their occurrence and the scope of their implications, certainly does owe much to the present-day organization of money, to the institutional, technological and political arrangements designed to ensure that it works. These consequences are also indicative of the rise of monetary and financial markets to an internationally exposed and politically consequential status which is without precedent.

Yet for academic and political purposes, money remains embarrass-ingly elusive. Lack of comprehension regarding how money functions and lack of competence regarding its administration and control are not especially new. The task of pinning money down, whether as an object of study or as an instrument of economic policy, has rarely been achieved with lasting success. Yet there is something uniquely modern about how the unfortunate consequences of major transactions can affect the lives of non-participating individuals some distance away, often to their sole cost and bewilderment. Money serves as a bridge between transactions which take place in different locations and at different points in time, distances which have been stretched as monetary networks have developed towards the present day. These networks rely on trust between people who may never come into contact with each other, trust derived from a range of rational and not-so-rational dispositions, a complex intermeshing of calculating expectation, confidence, habit and even faith. When confidence in money is high, not only in what it is but what it appears to enable us to do, money can symbolize a sense of boundless good fortune which seems unreal or mythical. When confidence breaks down and these dispositions are undermined, the transmission of grief through money can be penetrating and swift, a grief which in its intensity not only mirrors its opposite pole but shows it up for what it was. But such extremes in our perceptions of money should not be treated as inconsequential failures to understand what money really is, how it really works. They should not be defined away as fictions which have no part in monetary analysis. They are on the contrary integral to the operation of money, highly consequential features of the cultural conditions which make the existence and circulation of money possible.

Contemporary monetary networks are remarkable for the complexity of technological, institutional and social mechanisms necessary for them to operate at all. But they are also compelling for their fragility. Structural tension within contemporary monetary networks has an extensiveness and circularity from which it can seem difficult to escape. Uneven or high inflation, eroding the value of money, occurs widely in the present day, partly but by no means solely because of the intrinsic lack of resistance of inconvertible paper money to excesses of production and supply. For the same reason, hyperinflation is a uniquely modern phenomenon. Monetary grief in a contemporary context has a range of further and interconnected causes, however, none of which can be separated out as singularly responsible. For significant periods in the twentieth century, the rapid or uneven depreciation of money has resulted from strain or breakdown of international regimes designed to link or even fix exchange rates as a foundation for stable trading relationships. Breakdown has sometimes resulted from errors or deviations in monetary policy by governments and central banks. It has more frequently stemmed from tensions between incompatible policies oriented to changing international circumstances and diverging national aims. Currency regimes have also been undermined, often at the same time, by the gross corrosive effect of massive professional speculation. Telecommunications networks linking financial institutions enable the information conveyed through speculation to be transmitted instantaneously. Such instantaneity makes this apparently distant and curiously insular, self-perpetuating activity difficult to constrain or supervise. Yet its consequences can be uniquely far-reaching, affecting the lifestyle and livelihood of individuals in ways which, even when readily discernible, are rarely easily understood by those individuals themselves. This is especially so where they have apparently contributed nothing to the misfortunes to which they regard themselves as subject. The strategic importance of the financial centres in which professional speculation takes place means that national governments are in any case reluctant to commit themselves fully to seeking out more effective means of regulation and supervision. It is precisely this dilemma which helped generate the constitution of present-day currency regimes in the first place, as an attempt by governments and central banks to institute a co-ordinated counterweight against speculation. This paradox is illustrated by the uneven development of the ERM. Following the breakdown and eventual collapse of the other major postwar currency regime, Bretton Woods, the ERM originated as a flexible system of exchange rates known as 'the snake'. The regime was designed to hold currencies in constant relation to each other rather than allowing them to fluctuate as dictated by international trade and money markets. The snake was established in April 1972 amongst the nine member states of the European Economic Community. Britain and Ireland had left the scheme by May of that year. Denmark left and later rejoined. Italy withdrew in February 1973. France opted out in January 1974, opted back in during July 1974, and opted back out again in March 1976. The system was formalized as the European Monetary System (EMS) in March 1979, centred around the parallel basket currency, the European Currency Unit (ECU). The unsteady development of this scheme throughout the 1980s owed much to currency speculation in international markets facilitated by regulatory changes, particularly in Britain, to enhance the freedom and scale of operation of such markets. The events leading up to Black Wednesday were perhaps inevitable in the light of the confusion of market-oriented and regime-centred policies implemented by the British Treasury and central bank.

Difficulties in monetary policy do not stem merely from a combination of technical incompetence and political contingency, although these are undoubtedly important features of the protracted efforts of governments to control and administer money. The periodic disappointments of policy-makers in respect of money are linked inextricably to the problems faced by scholars in the formulation of monetary theories. Failure to define money satisfactorily renders its measure and control mostly a matter of educated guesswork and psychological gerrymandering, a craft rather than a science. But despite the volume of literature on money, no completely satisfactory definition exists. Whether monetary policy is taken to be a matter of controlling the money supply directly or responding to monetary signals in implementing macroeconomic policies, the need to know what money actually is has self-evident importance. As

I shall try to demonstrate in this Introduction, defining money is a less simple matter than it first seems. The functions of money as characterized by economists are partially fulfilled by other, non-monetary instruments. In practice, this has meant that substitute forms of money can be produced which evade restrictions imposed as part of monetary policy. Technological developments in the major financial centres, in conjunction with regulatory changes which have opened up the range of activities in which non-banking institutions can engage, have made this process of substitution increasingly easy and, from the point of view of policy-makers, increasingly problematic. Whether substitution is driven by commercial ends or designed specifically to evade restriction, its consequence is obfuscatory: money cannot be defined in terms of a particular set of named assets; nor can it be defined by association with specific institutions, such is the range of services which can fulfil a monetary role in the context of the economy as a whole. These are some of the most fundamental reasons why monetary policies, or the monetary framework in which macroeconomic policies are implemented, can have such awkward but unintended consequences as uneven inflation or volatile exchange-rate parity. Establishing a rigorous definition of money, applicable over time, may not necessarily provide an exhaustive solution to all such outcomes. But it certainly is a necessary component of any such solution. Indeed, the persistent absence of such a definition suggests that the assumptions underpinning what we think we have known about money are in need of reappraisal. The task of reappraisal is not, however, simply a technical matter concerning the formulation of better monetary policies, nor even a substantive question of arriving at a better understanding of money itself. These questions are important but do not exhaust my objectives in this book. Existing approaches to monetary analysis have been derived from a form of reasoning which has fundamentally shaped our understanding of the distinctive features of modernity. Reappraisal of the assumptions underlying these approaches therefore has far-reaching theoretical implications.

Most definitions of money tend to reveal as much about the interests of the theorists who formulate them as they do about money itself. This is partly because of the close orientation of monetary theory to practice: the utility of a definition of money for policy-making or professional speculation is frequently the sole test of its precision. The more serious difficulty, and this is where social theory has to come in, is epistemological. Most accounts of the nature and functions of money tend to strive either for detailed descriptive accuracy or for a level of abstraction suitable for analytical modelling. Neither approach is without its problems. A descriptively accurate definition will focus on the physical and symbolic properties of monetary objects. But this has restricted analytical value, often providing little more than a statement of the obvious and only a limited basis for generalization. A definition of money formulated for analytical purposes in economics will usually include a list of standard functions. But these tend to be empirically indifferent, insensitive to important differences between actual monetary forms. This can have confusing consequences for monetary policy, to the extent that policy-makers are uncertain as to what instruments should and should not be treated as money for purposes of control. Conventionally, the empirical and analytical approaches have been separated, applied respectively to pre-modern and modern money. Separation along these lines is misleading, over-emphasizing differences between pre-modern and modern money while under-emphasizing variations within each category. Ideally, a definition reconciling empirical and analytical aims should be possible. As far as empirical study is concerned, it seems unquestionable that any approach to monetary analysis should incorporate a set of interpretative techniques with which to understand and account for the various ways in which money is perceived and utilized, whether by policy-makers and professional speculators and investors or by individual savers and consumers. But this does not call for a less rigorous analytical approach to monetary analysis, rather a different kind of rigour.

Monetary Objects and Monetary Functions

How, then, might one approach the question of an adequate definition of money? The problem, as I shall argue here, is not that nobody knows exactly what money is, but that monetary theorists have been convinced that they do. Such conviction has been based, however, on an understanding of the characteristics of particular forms of money rather than on the essential features of money in general. This is a vitally important distinction for the arguments I shall be developing in this book. One way of breaking this down, which also may illuminate contemporary difficulties over monetary policy, particularly those concerning the measure and control of the money supply, is briefly to examine the definitional problems which in my view arise in the literature concerning earlier monetary forms. A simple test for any definition of money is to ask whether it helps distinguish between money and non-money. Such a straightforward task is woefully beyond the definitions conventionally used and accepted in studies of pre-modern money. As these studies show, a wide range of objects such as livestock, staple products and ornamentation serve as money in pre-modern exchange.[5] It would seem obvious that a materialist definition should help establish how certain objects come to be used as money, and also the kinds of functions those objects are capable of serving. Jevons, for example, has argued that a monetary object must ideally possess five physical properties, namely, portability, indestructibility, homogeneity, divisibility and cognizability.[6] Jevons's criteria might be helpful for understanding the physical limitations on whether certain objects can usefully serve as money in pre-modern contexts. But they cannot provide a reliable guide to distinguishing between monetary and non-monetary objects in general.[7] After all, any object could in principle be used as money as long as it is designated as such. Even the limiting conditions outlined by Jevons cannot generate an exhaustive list of objects suitable for this role. His criteria seem useful only in a negative sense, suggesting conclusive reasons for arguing that the monetary use of certain objects is highly unlikely, but not that their use as money is likely or even probable. Even if probability could be established in this respect, it would not help distinguish barter from monetary exchange where an identical object is involved. No physical description of the object itself could fully explain how it comes to fulfil monetary functions. For example, shells and shell-necklaces have been used as money in the communities of New Caledonia, Yap, Kusaie and the Banks Islands, but the self-same objects are used as gifts in the Kula ritual of the Trobrianders.[8] This rules out a materialist definition of pre-modern money. There is no necessary connection between the physical and symbolic properties of monetary forms in pre-modern contexts. The absence of such a connection renders objects used for monetary purposes virtually indistinguishable from objects that may be bartered or offered as gifts.[9]

A materialist definition of money can only lead to confusion. There is a need, rather, to focus on the social relationships that monetary transaction involves, not the objects which mediate those relationships. Einzig has conducted one of the most wide-ranging surveys of pre-modern monetary objects. Despite this devotion to physical detail he nevertheless defines money as a social institution rather than a 'mere lifeless object'. Uses and perceptions of particular objects, more than their physical properties, underpin their monetary role.[10] Such a consideration is hardly insightful, unquestioningly dependent as it is on the definition of money conventionally used in economics. This comprises a list of three basic monetary functions, namely, medium of exchange, store of value and unit of account.[11] The test for this definition of money is less straightforward than for its materialist counterpart. Pre-modern monetary forms are conventionally regarded as having fewer functions than modern money. For example, the stone money used by Yap islanders is simply too heavy to use as a medium of exchange, serving mostly as a store of value.[12] To regard the stones as non-money because of such limitations, however, would lead to the laughable conclusion that virtually no pre-modern monetary form should be defined as money at all. Indeed, such an approach may even suggest that money does not exist, whatever the historical period in question. Alternatively, the Yap stones could be defined as specialist money, reflecting their limited functions.[13] If this approach is taken, however, the simple test of the economic definition becomes to distinguish not between money and non-money but between modern and pre-modern money, holding *a priori* that only modern money fulfils all the economic functions.

The functional distinction between modern and pre-modern money is certainly compatible with the study of money's physical properties, but with conclusions only slightly less puzzling than those suggested by the materialist definition alone. At its simplest, the combination lends itself to common sense. Limitations on the use of Yap money obviously arise from the physical properties of the objects in question, their lack of portability being a limiting condition which restricts and even prevents their use as a medium of exchange. Polanyi's application of functional criteria to the distinction between pre-modern and modern money is more comprehensive but less acceptable. He defines pre-modern and modern monetary forms as, respectively, limited- and general-purpose money, denoting the range of functions each form is capable of fulfilling. Polanyi's definition is not based simply on the physical limitations of pre-modern money in relation to its potential functions, but draws in the relationship between money and its economic, political and cultural setting. Indeed, he is concerned less with the physical than the symbolic properties of pre-modern money. Polanyi's distinction between pre-modern and modern money is informed by a critique of economics. He rejects the idea that all economic action consists of the rational pursuit of maximum satisfaction, arguing that this applies only to modern conditions where economic life has been clearly differentiated from other dimensions of society. In pre-modern contexts, on the other hand, economic concerns are embedded within other forms of social, political and cultural integration such as kinship and religious ties. Under these circumstances, the modern definition of economic action is untenable, for aims other than maximization, from which economic behaviour cannot be divorced, are consequential. To account for the distinction, Polanyi formulates two definitions of economic life.[14] His formal definition is compatible with contemporary economics, and refers to the pursuit of maximum satisfaction wherever there are scarce means and alternative goals. His substantive definition refers to the process of interaction between the natural and social environment in specific contexts. This process conditions how maximizing behaviour is manifested, with the consequence that self-interest may not be pursued in its purest sense but will instead be embedded within and thereby constrained by non-economic patterns of integration. In cases such as these, the formal analysis of economic behaviour is inappropriate. Polanyi's distinction between types of economic action corresponds exactly to his distinction between types of money.[15] It is because pre-modern economic life is embedded within specific forms of social, political and cultural integration that pre-modern money is limited in its functions. For example, the capacity of money to function as a generalized medium of exchange will obviously be limited if economic relationships are restricted by kinship and tribal groupings which prohibit mutual exchange. Only in a modern context it would seem, where exchange is unencumbered by such restrictions, can the mediating role of money be fully generalized.

It is in a modern context, however, that Polanyi's analysis is at its weakest. The caution of his approach to pre-modern economic life is compromised by a somewhat inexact analysis of modern society. The distinction between formal and substantive economic action, once applied respectively to modern and pre-modern societies, entails assumptions about contemporary economic life which cannot withstand closer scrutiny. In effect, Polanyi implies that there is a core or essence to all economic action consisting of maximizing behaviour. This is stifled in pre-modern societies and only fully unleashed once the economy, in its modern form, has been fully differentiated from other dimensions of society as a series of interconnected markets. This occurs not because patterns of integration specific to pre-modern and modern societies generate corresponding types of behaviour, but rather because the drive to maximize is constricted by pre-modern patterns as if from the outside. In other words, Polanyi implies that maximizing behaviour is not absent from pre-modern societies but merely latent. This seems obtuse, for it suggests that formal economic action in its modern manifestation is 'natural' in a way that pre-modern economic behaviour is incapable of being. As a result, Polanyi implicitly reproduces the questionable equation of rational economic action, operating on its own terms and according to its own laws, with political freedom. In a disciplinary context, the upshot of this is clear: modern economic life lies outside sociological study. The inadequacy of Polanyi's analysis when applied to a modern context is readily demonstrated in relation to money. The idea that modern money is general-purpose, fulfilling all the possible monetary functions, is simply incorrect. There exists no form of money which serves all such functions simultaneously. Legal-tender notes are rarely used to store value in practice. Notes and coins represent standard units of value without literally embodying them; indeed, if they did so they would be worth considerably more than their legal-tender equivalents. Cheques, credit cards and bank drafts serve only as means of payment. It is absurd to regard these monetary forms as general-purpose.[16]

The functional definition therefore fails the simple test of distinguishing between pre-modern and modern money. This is possibly because the distinction itself is unworkable. Limitations may of course be placed on the functions of modern money for different reasons than their pre-modern counterparts. Restrictions on the use of cheques and credit cards, for example, derive from institutional regulations concerning security and administration rather than from tribal or kinship associations. But this cannot be discerned by reference to monetary functions alone, for they reveal little about the sociological framework in which money is transacted. This is a major shortcoming of the functional definition of money even when applied solely to modern money, and explains why economic theories of money enjoy considerable notoriety among policy-makers for consistently failing even the simple test of distinguishing between money and non-money. Once it is conceded that no modern monetary form is able to fulfil all potential monetary functions, the task of defining money in this context must focus on two specific functions, namely medium of exchange and store of value; all financial and monetary instruments, after all, are denominated in an abstract unit of account. The relationship between these two functions, or rather between the efficiency with which a particular monetary or financial instrument fulfils them, tends to be inversely proportional.[17] For example, legal-tender notes and coins tend to lose value over time as a result of inflation, and so are best used chiefly for exchange and payment purposes. Assets which store value stably over time or even appreciate in value, on the other hand, are linked to securities or other investments which make them difficult to convert into a form suitable for payment or exchange, perhaps losing value on conversion or carrying a time constraint delaying conversion. In terms of monetary policy, these considerations define the liquidity of a particular asset. They have crucial implications for any attempt to control the money supply. In this context, the supply of money refers to the quantity of money in circulation for payment and exchange purposes. Where this quantity is taken to determine the level of prices as in monetarist theory, control over the quantity of money has a vital role to play in restricting price inflation. The liquidity of an asset refers to the ease with which it can be converted for payment or exchange and thereby become an effective part of the money supply in circulation. This is obviously important to defining which assets to treat as money for purposes of control. If control of inflation is deemed to rely on controlling the money supply, it is vital to know what money is.[18] This depends on understanding the relationship between money and liquidity.

The Liquidity of Money

The dictionary definition of liquidity refers to 'the state of being liquid'.[19] This is not entirely appropriate to money, which does not flow when in circulation but undergoes a series of emissions from one transactor to another.[20] Indeed, the time period governing the relationship between payment and receipt is logically instantaneous. In this sense, money does not circulate through time at all, unless this is characterized as quantum time.[21] These considerations are essential to economic theory, where the measure of liquidity refers not to a rate of flow but to the efficiency with which a monetary instrument or financial asset can be interchanged with another instrument or asset, in other words, the ease of its emission. But the concept of liquidity has a range of applications in monetary theory and policy. For example, liquidity can refer specifically to different measures of the money supply, with legal-tender notes and coins, designated M0, having greatest liquidity. Here, liquidity denotes the efficiency of the monetary form as a means of payment and exchange. This application can also be used to distinguish between money and other assets, particularly instruments defined as near-money. Significantly in this case, monetary instruments and financial assets are not ranked continuously as if possessing varying degrees of liquidity. Their relationship is regarded as discontinuous. Instruments categorized as money have perfect liquidity. Other assets have degrees of imperfect liquidity.[22] The concept of liquidity can also have a more general application. This refers to the ease with which the contents of a portfolio of assets can be converted for payment or exchange, metaphorically into liquid form. This version of liquidity is applicable to the economy as a whole, usually referring to the availability of credit. But attempts to incorporate this definition directly in government economic policy have persistently failed.[23]

The concept of liquidity has been problematic for monetary policy for two main reasons. First, imprecise and inconsistent application of the concept to various monetary instruments and financial assets has been unhelpful for attempts to use the notion to identify what money is. There is indeed an absence of clarity in the minds of theorists and policy-makers as to what liquidity actually is. It is not at all clear, in any case, that monetary instruments and financial assets possess specific degrees of liquidity with any constancy over time. Efforts to define money in this way hardly seem worthwhile, for the results of such efforts are almost always unreliable. Second, the very characteristic of money and other financial instruments and assets which generates liquidity in the first place has tended systematically to undermine attempts to identify and control the money supply. This problem is expressed in what has come to be known as Goodhart's law. This states that as soon as a particular instrument or asset is publicly defined as money in order to be controlled, that asset ceases to be used as money because substitutes will be produced for purposes of evasion.[24] When controls are introduced to restrict the supply of certain monetary and financial instruments, alternatives are produced to which the controls do not apply. These alternatives then take the place of those instruments in need of targeting for control. This problem disrupts monetary policy almost irrespective of which method of control is in vogue at a particular time. It applies as much to direct credit controls as to efforts to target levels of increase in specific measures of the money supply. Direct monetary and credit controls implemented in Britain during the 1960s were hindered in exactly this way. The measures focused principally on hire purchase agreements and bank lending, but inevitable gaps and loopholes allowed effective substitutes to be produced. This resulted in a lop-sided regulatory framework, with certain fringe institutions escaping control altogether, distorting rather than reducing the difficulties of monetary control.[25] Similar problems were experienced in the United States with the implementation of Regulation Q during the late 1960s. This was designed to reduce holdings of dollars, restricting the interest rate offered by domestic banks to domestic and foreign holders. But the policy allowed foreign banks to offer competitively higher rates of interest to holders of dollars. A range of alternative instruments denominated in dollars were produced which stimulated the development of offshore markets.[26] More recently, the process of substitution referred to by Goodhart's law has disrupted attempts, informed by monetarism, to identify and control specific measures of the money supply. The movement of funds between different monetary instruments and financial assets generates continual shifts in the definition of money.[27] This difficulty has been exacerbated by the process of deregulation within key international financial centres during the 1970s and 1980s. The range of financial institutions offering payments' services has been broadened. Consequently, the number of instruments which can serve as means of payment or exchange has increased.[28]

The problems of pursuit and evasion expressed in Goodhart's law result from precisely that quality, loosely called liquidity, which makes money so difficult to define. Clarity is vital to understand the exact nature of this difficulty. To attempt to define something which can be readily identified is one thing. Seeking to identify something which meets the criteria of a pre-existing definition is another. The difference is epistemological. It embraces the contrast between the empirical and analytical approaches to defining money discussed in this Introduction. In anthropological studies of pre-modern money, the definitional problem involves understanding what is distinctive about the material and symbolic properties of objects whose usage within a particular society or group has already been identified as monetary. The analysis of modern monetary forms for purposes of control does not proceed in exactly the same way. Here, 'money' consists of an analytical category defined with reference to liquidity. The task for policy-makers is to establish which instruments and assets fit into this category at any one time. In other words, they are trying to identify what qualifies as money according to their own pre-established analytical definition. The difficulty for policy-makers arises because instruments and assets move in and out of this pre-existing category, systematically if Goodhart's law is to be believed. As a consequence, the identification of money lacks constancy over time, but not the definition. The distinction between the empirical and analytical approaches to money is probably rarely as straightforward as this in practice. This is partly because the definitional problem in each case is complicated, but more importantly it also stems from a lack of epistemological clarity as to what exactly is being attempted. As an outline of what essentially is involved in each approach, however, the contrast should be clear: in one case the problem is definitional, in the other an issue of identification.

The contrast between the empirical and analytical approaches to defining money raises a number of issues which are of central importance to the arguments I shall be pursuing in this book. The empirical study of pre-modern money has been misled by a preoccupation with the physical and symbolic properties of monetary objects. This precludes examination of the social and cultural conditions which enable monetary transaction, using any object whatsoever, to take place. To focus on the features of monetary objects can obviously be informative. But it is also too specific, providing no exhaustive guide to understanding the preconditions for establishing money as a social institution within a particular society or social group, however limited its use and functions might be. This prevents comparison of uses and perceptions of money across cultures and between societies and social groups. The analytical approach seems on the face of it to share this failing but for the opposite reason, because it is too abstract. Certainly, once it is acknowledged that no single monetary form fulfils all the potential monetary functions or possesses anything like perfect liquidity, the simple task of distinguishing between money and non-money seems impossible. This can lead to the absurdity of defining particular financial assets as near-money, not as money in the strict sense but as assets which behave like money. But the difficulty which generates this confusion is not one of abstractness but of generality. To argue that the functional definition of money is inadequate because it covers too wide a range of instruments, some of which should not be identified as money at all, is to suggest that it is too general. To contend that a definition falls down because it applies to monetary forms in different societies without enabling them to be properly distinguished and compared is to say that the definition is too abstract. The difficulty which arises from the functional definition of money, particularly the concept of liquidity, is one of generality. It is at this level that the analytical approach to money warrants reappraisal.

Monetary Networks

To overcome the problem of generality in defining money requires establishing criteria which distinguish money from non-money in different societies. The difficulty of over-abstraction arises when these criteria prevent various monetary forms from being distinguished from each other. Comparison between monetary exchange and barter provides the best starting-point for tackling the problem of generality and establishing what is distinctive about monetary exchange. This is merely an extended version of the simple test of distinguishing money from non-money. Monetary exchange is more convenient than barter. It saves on the time and effort needed to search for potential co-transactors and to compromise or extend the relationship when the requirements of each transactor do not match.[29] In barter, the key requirement of transactors is for information. This mostly concerns the location and trustworthiness of potential co-transactors. Money dispenses with this. Where a standardized monetary form is used, there is no need to search for potential co-transactors. Money paid or received can be handed on elsewhere at a later date. Once money is received as payment for something, the relationship between transactors can be concluded rather than extended into the future by promises or other obligations. The process of search and compromise necessary in barter is effectively performed by money rather than by transactors themselves. Crucially, money does not carry or transmit the information required in barter but replaces it with information of its own: that it can be re-used in the future, that it will be accepted by other members of a society or social group, and that it truly represents its face-value and will continue to do so over time. These issues govern the form and content of the information that transactors require when deciding whether to trust money.

Consideration of the advantages of monetary transaction compared with barter does not necessarily explain how or why money evolves in particular societies or social groups.[30] But this is not the issue at hand. The information implicit in monetary transaction provides the most fundamental point of distinction between monetary exchange and barter. Significantly, this distinction arises not from comparison of monetary and non-monetary forms but from examination of the network of social relationships integral to each as a type of exchange. Characteristics of the network itself, rather than the instrument exchanged or even the social relationship established through the exchange, underpin this comparison. It follows that to understand what is distinctive about money requires reference to the network of social relationships which makes its transaction possible, not to the object exchanged or the exchange relationship itself. This view does not necessarily contradict the functional definition of money. Each function relies on an extended network of social relationships. Such a view does, however, resolve some of the confusions which arise from the functional definition, particularly the problem of generality. For example, the capacity of money to store value depends on the existence of a monetary network no less than its function as a medium of exchange. It is not difficult to imagine that different monetary instruments within the same network will be developed which specialize in specific functions without fulfilling them all. Comparison between pre-modern and modern money or of monetary exchange within different societies and cultures must proceed not with reference to the functional capacities of specific monetary instruments, but by examining differences between the networks on which the transaction of such instruments depends. The analysis of monetary networks provides a basis for detailed empirical study of specific monetary forms without ruling out comparison between them or presupposing which types of social action monetary transaction principally involves.

The utility of the monetary network for empirical and analytical purposes obviously depends on the accuracy and precision with which its basic properties are conceptualized. As I have suggested, the network depends on the presence of certain kinds of information. This distinguishes monetary transaction from other forms of exchange. It seems reasonable to examine such information to establish what the minimum properties of such a network might be. This chiefly concerns the spatial and temporal properties of the network, for example its extensiveness in relation to a geographical or geopolitical area. More specifically, the information transmitted through monetary transaction reflects the sociological conditions in which the network is established, for example the political means employed to validate money or prevent counterfeiting, and the institutional mechanisms for operating a payments system. This information is implicit in the decision to place trust in money. It refers to the possibility of money's re-use in future, its likely acceptance by other members of a society or group, and the validity and stability of its face-value. All these conditions are necessary if monetary transaction, as distinct from any other form of exchange, is to consist of a fleeting or instantaneous emission requiring no prior search for information regarding the co-transactor, at least not where the monetary form itself is concerned. They are also essential if the transaction is to be conclusive, enabling the relationship between transactors to end there and then. These, then, are minimum requirements regarding the information which must be present in order for monetary transaction to proceed, even among the smallest of groups. Monetary networks are in this sense networks of information.

The requirements referred to above can be translated into five abstract properties characteristic of even the most minimally extensive monetary network. First, the network will contain a standardized accounting system into which each monetary form within the network is divisible, enabling its exchange with anything priced in terms of that system. Second, the network will rely on information from which expectations regarding the future, or more accurately money's relationship with the continuity of time, can be derived: money is accepted as payment almost solely on the assumption that it can be re-used later on. Third, the network will depend on information regarding its spatial characteristics: limits placed on the territory in which specific monetary forms may be used will probably derive initially from measures designed to prevent counterfeiting, although they will eventually refer to the institutional framework governing the operation of a payments system. Fourth, the network will be based on legalistic information, usually in the form of rules, concerning the status of contractual relationships which are fleeting and conclusive: to pay with money is literally to pay up. Finally, the operation of the network presupposes knowledge of the behaviour and expectations of others. This is usually derived from experience, but can also be sought out and even paid for. Such information is vital in generating trust in money's abstract properties. Anyone in possession of money must be able to anticipate, as a matter of routine, its re-use with other transactors within a specific social group or across a pre-defined territory.

These observations refer to the basic spatial and temporal properties of the monetary network. They are deliberately abstract. As I suggested earlier, the functional definition of money falls down not because of its abstractness but because of its generality. Information binds the network together. More detailed analysis of the content of this information should lead to closer understanding of the specific sociological conditions in which monetary transaction takes place. These are a matter for empirical study. The importance of information for the operation of money can be more precisely explained by returning to the simple test of examining the differences between monetary exchange and barter. As I have already discussed, the information implicit in and specific to monetary transaction enables exchanges to take place which are more fleeting, conclusive and, as far as the network of exchanges is concerned, more extensive than is possible with barter. This information is not lacking in barter exchange, but is of a qualitatively different order: different things need to be known or assumed in order to undertake barter as opposed to monetary transaction. In principle, the information is no less compli-cated, perhaps even more so, than in the case of barter. But where a monetary network is well established, these issues need not be articulated or pondered at length. The uncertainties transactors actually face under these circumstances are of a different magnitude altogether. Issues fundamental to the existence of the network, on the other hand, can usually be assumed. This is rarely the case with barter, and probably never so once a network of barter exchange expands beyond a certain scale. With money, the reverse is possibly true: the expansion of a monetary network is usually an indication of its reliability and long standing, both good grounds for trust. To express this from the opposite point of view, while both monetary exchange and barter take place in conditions of inherent uncertainty, the object of uncertainty in each case is quite different.

Uncertainty refers to a lack of information: information which forms the basis of decision-making and should enable the transactor to proceed with greater confidence or perhaps suggest withdrawal from the exchange altogether. In barter, there will be uncertainty as to the trustworthiness of the co-transactor, the authenticity of the object offered in exchange, or the possibility of the re-exchange of that object in the future. Whatever the specific uncertainties involved, they will have in common an inherent association with the *modus operandi* of barter as a form of exchange: they

depends on size of community of bartereres

will dictate whether the barter transaction takes place at all. Significantly, these uncertainties, although they concern the operational characteristics of barter exchange, pose no real threat to the existence of barter as a system of exchange within a society or social group. They are part and parcel of its everyday occurrence. This is not the case with money. There are of course uncertainties which do arise whenever money is used, and which are, as in barter, part of its everyday transaction. But these are questions concerning specific aspects of the information conveyed through monetary transaction rather than the abstract properties of monetary networks: uncertainty, for example, about the future path of inflation, rates of exchange between currencies and rates of interest on borrowing. These substantive concerns are not entirely distinct from abstract questions. Alarmingly unstable rates of inflation or rapidly falling rates of exchange may discourage transactors from using a particular monetary form altogether, thereby threatening the continuing operation of the network itself; the limits uncertainty must reach in order to have this effect will depend on particular cases. In general, however, uncertainty in relation to money will concern questions of substance which do not determine whether a monetary network operates at all but the character of its operation under specific conditions. Because this operation will be directly affected by how transactors respond to such uncertainty, by the information they obtain and the decisions they take, the information conveyed by monetary transaction is reflexive. This has important implications for monetary analysis, which I explore later in the book.

Monetary transaction is not merely a form of barter in the presence of more or higher quality information. It is altogether distinctive. It requires the pre-existence of minimum forms of information, extended through time and across space, in order to proceed. If uncertainty prevailed at this level over any length of time, the monetary network would begin to disintegrate altogether. With barter, the most basic information must be sought out, articulated and negotiated. Even where a bartering relationship is of long standing, the information which supports the relationship remains specific to it, and can be applied elsewhere only in limited ways. For this reason, barter exchange cannot possibly be anonymous in the way that monetary transaction invariably is. Crucially, then, it is the type of information involved in each of these forms of exchange, not the relative quantity of information, which makes barter a personal, and monetary transaction an impersonal, form of exchange. The anonymity of monetary transaction derives not from the characteristics of particular monetary objects, nor from their range of functions, but from basic information concerning the abstract properties of monetary networks.

These properties must, as a condition of existence of the network, be subject to routine expectation derived from ongoing trust.

Clarity in respect of the epistemological status of these observations is vital. My argument is designed to overcome the problems of specificity and generality which, respectively, characterize empirical and functional definitions of money. The variety of uses and perceptions of money within and between different societies is of substantive importance to the way money actually works in such contexts. It is therefore essential to formulate a definition of money sufficiently abstract to enable such cases to be compared without generalizing to such an extent that important variations cannot in fact be accounted for or explained. I have sought to do this by introducing the concept of the monetary network and outlining its abstract properties. These properties determine the existence of the network, its constitution in relation to space and time. They are, I have suggested, requisite for even the most minimally extensive network to be established. Given the nature of the properties outlined, however, it is important to recognize that they cannot exhaustively describe the characteristics of actual monetary networks. They merely provide a framework for empirical study and substantive analysis. The framework is not, it should be emphasized, an ideal type in the sense employed by Weber. The ideal type represents characteristic features of a particular form of social organization. But these features are largely descriptive, and may even be absent from specific cases.[31] If the components of the Weberian framework are typical, then, the properties of the monetary network outlined in this introduction should be regarded as necessary: they must be present in order for the network to operate at all. But nor are the properties intended to refer to functional prerequisites in the sense employed by Talcott Parsons.[32] Such a view implies a causal explanation of the origins of money which I reject in the arguments of this book: namely, that the sociological conditions underpinning the properties of monetary networks emerged historically as a result of their efficacy from the point of view of money. The development of money has on the contrary been considerably more uneven than such a view would allow, and is not characterized by the inevitability which a list of prerequisites would suggest. The properties outlined are intended to provide a basis for examining the sociological conditions which facilitated the emergence and development of money as a social institution under a range of historical circumstances. This approach is not meant to be overly schematic. It should, however, prevent our regarding historically and culturally specific examples of the use and operation of money as more than just examples, imputing to them an unwarranted naturalness and inevitability. This too readily leads to the construction of theoretical articles of faith and, in contemporary monetary theory, has served to justify errors of perception and organization in the implementation of monetary policy whose consequences are occasionally calamitous and almost always unintended. Throughout the monetary literature, social, political and cultural consequences tend to be ascribed to the use of money which, if not always inexact when applied to particular empirical circumstances, can be misleading for monetary theory if taken out of context. More bluntly, there is an acute need in contemporary monetary theory to stop confusing contingency with necessity in the operation of monetary and market systems.

I have tried to show that to focus on the abstract properties of monetary networks provides the best means of passing the first simple test of any definition of money, namely, to distinguish between money and non-money. The properties outlined here represent a preliminary approach to understanding what such networks are and how they work. In succeeding chapters, I shall attempt to substantiate and extend this approach within a more rigorous sociological and empirical framework. The existence of money within a society serves to alleviate the kinds of uncertainty inherent to a system of barter exchange. Such uncertainties as an imbalance between the supply and demand of particular goods, lack of information regarding future levels of supply and demand, insecurity as to the trustworthiness of others, the authenticity of the goods they bring to an exchange and the contracts they seek to establish are, from the point of view of economic reasoning, imperfections. The responses of different societies to such imperfections, for example their political and legal mechanisms and banking institutions, have been varied and, from the viewpoint of monetary efficiency at least, rarely completely successful. It is nevertheless important to realize that imperfection is not merely a consequence of fallible human efforts to establish and maintain money as a social institution. The social, political and cultural realities which generate economic uncertainty are no awkward intrusion into the world of monetary analysis. They are the condition for the very existence of monetary networks in the first instance. It is for this reason above all that money is the legitimate focus of sociological study. I shall attempt to vindicate such a view with the arguments of this book.

PART I

1

The Political Economy of Money

I argued in the Introduction that money's role and significance in society can only be fully understood in relation to conditions which from the point of view of economic reasoning would be regarded as imperfections. It is perhaps inevitable that money should occupy an ambiguous position in models derived from this form of reasoning. Indeed, the major bone of contention between economic theories of money has long concerned whether money plays a significant role in the workings of the economy in its own right. Two of the approaches to monetary analysis that I shall discuss here, derived from classical and neoclassical economics,[1] begin with a barter model of the economy which implies that money is neutral. There are two kinds of neutrality, logical and political, which need to be clearly separated. The notion of logical neutrality suggests that when the economy is in an equilibrium state, money simply mediates the production and exchange of goods, making no intrinsic difference to real economic variables. The concept of political neutrality suggests that money can express inequalities of wealth and power but can never generate them. Neither idea is tenable on closer examination. I shall discuss each of them in turn.

In the first section of this chapter, I examine the concept of logical neutrality which is central to classical and neoclassical theories of money. Although the conception of money's role in the economy in each approach is far from identical, the same basic difficulty undermines both approaches to monetary analysis. This derives from the confusions which arise from money's dual function as a medium of exchange and store of value.[2] A view of money confined to the medium of exchange function lends itself readily to a barter model of the economy. A view taking into account the complexities of the store of value function categorically does not.[3] Where money's function as a store of value is concerned, it is vital to develop a clear understanding of the sociological, psychological and cultural reasons why individuals express a demand for money as well as how they actually use it. In neither classical nor neoclassical theories of money is this question addressed in sufficient detail or with sufficient clarity. In the second section of the chapter, I shall criticize the concept of political neutrality, drawing on although not necessarily agreeing with Marx's theory of money to argue that an understanding of the structural relationship between money and the organization of power in society must be integral to any approach to monetary analysis, whatever its disciplinary context. It should be stated at the outset that no attempt will be made to provide an exhaustive summary of the three schools of thought under discussion. This is beyond the scope of a single chapter and is not my main objective. The focus of my argument will be on the difficulties all three approaches have in common, concerning the nature of the demand for money and the relationship between money and power.

The Logical Neutrality of Money

Money cannot seriously be regarded as neutral other than in the clinical world of economic logic. Within such terms, money's primary function is to enable the production and exchange of goods without the spatial and temporal constraints of a barter system. In classical and neoclassical economics, a barter model of exchange is employed to explain how commodities are produced and distributed between independent producers across an economic network consisting of a division of labour. Money plays a mediating role within this network. The difference between barter exchange and monetary exchange is addressed in quantitative rather than qualitative terms. Money helps the production and exchange of goods to proceed more efficiently and extensively. But nothing fundamental has changed. Economic life with money proceeds much as it did without. Money, in this logical sense, is neutral. In both classical and neoclassical economics, however, assumptions additional to the barter model of the economy tend to be made which directly inform prescriptive claims regarding how the economy itself, and the role of money within it, should be organized. These assumptions, without which neither theory would amount to very much, let alone a theory of money, undermine the basic supposition that money is neutral.

Monetary theories which focus on its economic functions and characteristics tend to start out, almost by definition, from a specific set of assumptions regarding human behaviour. It is important to understand, however, that the major differences between classical and neoclassical approaches to the political economy of money over the role of money in society are not reducible to a contest between different philosophies of human nature: contrasting conclusions regarding the social and political consequences of the use of money in society are derived from virtually identical accounts of how it is handled by individuals themselves. In particular, both approaches underestimate the importance of individuals' perceptions of money to how they actually use it. It is this area of monetary analysis which is in greatest need of development, for it is vital to the issue of neutrality. The classical theory of money rests on a view of rational human agency best understood in terms of the distinction between passions and interests. Albert Hirschman has argued that the work of Adam Smith marks the stage in economic and political thought when the human passions whose restraint had been a preoccupation of moral and political thinkers, defined by Vico as 'ferocity, avarice and ambition, the three vices which lead all mankind astray',[4] began to be assimilated with the idea of self-interest oriented to the rational pursuit of economic gain. Hirschman sees no real incompatibility between *The Theory of Moral Sentiments* and *The Wealth of Nations*. Smith's attention to the passions in the former work generates two important conclusions: first, that in accordance with a tradition of thought stretching through Hobbes and Machiavelli, to be consumed by the passions was a characteristic of aristocracy rather than 'the great mob of mankind' which is Smith's central concern; and second, that rather than conflicting with one another in their higher and lower forms, the passions could in fact be satisfied through the pursuit of economic improvement.[5] Smith's concentration on self-interested economic behaviour in the latter work is consistent with both conclusions. This having been said, Smith's was none the less a moral examination of the economic processes and political institutions of his time: if not exactly a moral justification of capitalism, then at least an exploration of the moral consequences of its modes of operation and organization. He addresses the rational pursuit of economic interest as a product of quite specific sociological developments, principally the eighteenth-century expansion of commercial life.[6] Neoclassical economists by contrast, with the exception of Friedrich Hayek,[7] are not noted for dwelling on moral facets of economic life, but begin instead with a straightforward account of economic action as comprising the rational pursuit of maximum gain. They address the *homo oeconomicus* in ahistorical terms, as integral to economic activity irrespective of place and time. Economic action is placed within an abstract framework, addressed not in terms of a set of natural human dispositions but as a founding methodological principle.

The differences of approach between these schools of thought consequently depend on how the institutional arrangements around which economic life is organized are understood. This, more than anything else, seems to have influenced the conceptualization of money in each case. Reference to the relationship between money and rational economic action is none the less vital to explaining money's origins, and this underpins the barter model employed in both approaches. For reasons discussed in the Introduction which need not be reiterated here, monetary exchange is superior to barter in mediating an extensive network of exchange relationships. In both classical and neoclassical economics, the historical emergence of money is explained by its practical utility, its technical superiority over barter. Smith, for example, notes that the inconvenience of matching requirements through barter generates the rational step of utilizing a commodity 'few people would be likely to refuse in exchange for the produce of their industry'.[8] Similarly for Menger, writing from a neoclassical perspective, money emerges because individuals consistently seek to maximize their own economic interests, taking into account the interests of others only in so far as they affect their own success or failure. Money originates as 'the unpremeditated resultant, of particular, individual efforts of the members of society, who have little by little worked their way to a determination of the different degrees of saleableness in commodities'.[9] The order and coherence of monetary networks are an unintended consequence of a disparate series of maximizing actions. For the neoclassical economists, then, monetary order is generated by the curious phenomenon of inevitable spontaneity: inevitable, given the assumption that maximization is foundational to economic behaviour;[10] spontaneous, because monetary networks are held together not intentionally but as a consequence of the sum of actions undertaken by individual economic agents for disparate purposes.

To derive an explanation of money's nature and functions from an account of its origins as a medium of exchange is not, however, a secure strategy. It is one thing to compare barter and monetary exchange in these terms, but quite another to regard the technical superiority of the latter over the former as the sole explanation for its emergence. It is far from clear that all or even most instances of the emergence of money within a society fit the transitional thesis whereby money originates as a special commodity mediating awkward exchanges.[11] There is considerable disagreement among theorists of money as to which monetary function is most common whenever money first originates within a society or community.[12] Moreover, as Einzig points out, there are conceivable cases where money's emergence from barter at all is not inevitable, despite its unarguable technical superiority: where, for example, there may already exist an advanced system of non-commercial payments in which there would be little use for money, where there exists a lack of intellectual faculty in arithmetic within a community, or where there is a lack of confidence in money resulting from its previous abuse or poor handling.[13] There is in any case an important difference between examining the origins of something and explaining its functions later on: the identification of origins provides a useful but rarely exhaustive guide to later functions.[14]

Smith's approach to the political economy of money is based on a model of the economy as a network of independent producers. Interrelations between these producers are mediated by 'the propensity to truck, barter, and exchange one thing for another'.[15] Smith refers to this network as the social division of labour. It is made possible when individuals specialize in productive tasks, and also relies on the capacity and desire amongst these individuals to exchange the products of their labour with one another. Need and desire go hand-in-hand. As productive tasks become more specialized, most of the needs of each person within the network can only be satisfied by exchanging the surplus of their own labour for products of the labour of others. The extensiveness of the division of labour is in this sense defined by the extensiveness of the market. Producers will allow themselves to become dependent on others only if the network of exchange is sufficiently extensive and efficient to ensure that their own needs will be satisfied. The desire to enter into exchanges has in this sense not only economic importance for the way things are produced but moral significance for the growing interdependence of individuals for the satisfaction of their needs. But it is individual self-interest, the desire for satisfaction through exchange, which generates and secures the network of social relationships, enabling the needs of all participants to be met. Smith's conception of the logical neutrality of money derives from this account of the emergence of a complex division of labour. He is unambiguous in asserting that 'it is not for its own sake that men desire money, but for the sake of what they can purchase with it'.[16] The link between this contention and the idea of neutrality is demonstrated in Smith's critique of the Mercantilists, a term he applies to seventeenth- and eighteenth-century pamphleteers rather more disparate than their retrospective identification as a group suggests. They argued that money has a crucial role to play in stimulating trade, and therefore should bolster a positive national balance of trade in the form of a permanent inflow of specie.[17] Smith condemns the idea that money's presence within the economic system makes such a difference to the social product. This is important, however unjust it might be as a representation of the views of the writers he criticizes. There is no compelling reason, according to Smith, to assume that increasing the quantity of money will expand the volume of trade, which in his terms must begin with an increase in production. An influx of specie will most probably result not in a stimulation of trade but in the purchase of more foreign goods. This not only tends to redress the imbalance of trade but 'promotes prodigality, increases expense and consumption without increasing production ... and is in every respect hurtful to the society'.[18]

This is as close as Smith seems to move towards a discussion of the specie-flow mechanism in *The Wealth of Nations*, although he examines this issue explicitly in his earlier *Lectures on Jurisprudence*. There, Smith follows Locke's argument that an influx of specie into a country will not only encourage the purchase of imported goods but will increase the level of domestic prices. Two points arising from Smith's treatment of the specie-flow mechanism are significant. First, he suggests that real changes in levels of production and trade are generated through real economic activity, not monetary fluctuations. Second, and as a corollary of the first point, Smith views the role of money within the economy as nothing but a mediator of the production and exchange of goods and services: when real economic activity proceeds efficiently, there is no need in principle to incorporate money within a model of how the economy works. According to this reasoning, money is neutral. This view is reiterated by other classical economists, particularly John Stuart Mill,[19] and is summarized in the law of markets formulated by Jean-Baptiste Say. At its simplest, Say's law states that excesses in the supply of goods or the demand for money will tend to balance themselves out through prices and interest rates.[20] For example, if the supply of goods outstrips demand at a given price, this amounts to an excess demand for money which can be corrected through falling prices. In short, the market for money will always tend towards equilibrium, towards a condition where the operation of the economy could be represented by a barter model. These views have an important relationship to what has come to be known as the Quantity Theorem. Here, the reasoning underlying Smith's arguments is taken to an extreme, transposed into a logically coherent but fatally impractical set of methodological principles. There are illuminating differences between the application of central assumptions behind the theorem in classical and neoclassical theories of money. These can initially be understood by clarifying the main point of distinction between the basic principles of political economy which define each approach.

Smith's depiction of economic interdependence is not static in the sense that a model of barter exchange might suggest. His primary concern is with the pursuit of economic expansion through production and trade. It is in this respect that his view of money as neutral in relation to real economic activity is most difficult to sustain, even though this consistently follows a line of reasoning stemming from his initial characterization of money as a medium of exchange. Smith's emphasis on the importance of competition between producers must be understood in terms of the dynamic process through which wealth is accumulated. In this context, the concept is different from the end-state implicit in the neoclassical idea of perfect competition, for it is more of an economic process.[21] If classical approaches to the political economy of money deriving from the work of Smith are principally concerned with the dynamics of production and wealth creation, neoclassical theory is essentially static, concerned above all with economic equilibrium. The condition of economic equilibrium is defined by Walras as 'a normal state towards which things spontaneously tend under a regime of free competition'.[22] Walras contends that money can and should be abstracted from the formulation of equilibrium conditions, where 'land-owners, labourers and capitalists receive from the entrepreneurs a certain quantity of products in the form of rent, wages and interest in exchange for a certain quantity of productive services in the form of land-services, labour and capital services'.[23] Indeed, he did not incorporate money fully into his general equilibrium model until the publication of the fourth edition of *Elements of Pure Economics* in 1900.[24] The quantity of money in this model is divided between savings and money in circulation: the rate of interest, which should in this context be understood to mean the price of money, tends towards equilibrium in much the same way as any other commodity. To demonstrate how its equilibrium price is achieved, Walras employs the marginalist principle, arguing that 'the price of the commodity varies *directly with its utility and inversely with its quantity*'.[25] These basic differences between classical and neoclassical approaches to money are reflected in the application of ideas contained in the Quantity Theorem in each case.

Before examining what the Quantity Theorem is, it would help to clarify what it is not. The Quantity Theorem is not, taken by itself, a full-blown theory of money. Specific assumptions need to be added for it to be more than a truism. That principles underlying the theorem are present in both classical and neoclassical economics provides no grounds for concluding that these approaches to money are identical.[26] The important differences lie in additional assumptions. Taken by itself, the Quantity Theorem is to all intents and purposes uninteresting. In basic terms, the theorem states that money and prices will always be directly proportional to each other. Prices rise and fall in accordance with changes in the quantity of money and the velocity of its circulation. With more money in circulation, or alternatively with a higher velocity of circulation, prices will rise. With less money in circulation, or with a slower velocity of circulation, prices will fall. This idea is expressed by the simple equation, $MV = PT$. M denotes the quantity of money in circulation, V the velocity of its circulation, P the price level and T the volume of transactions. In so far as money serves solely as a medium of exchange, there is little which is contentious or surprising about the theorem itself. If there is a definite quantity of money and a definite quantity of goods to be sold, the prices at which those goods will be sold is an elementary question of arithmetic, at least once values for the velocity of money's circulation and the volume of transactions are known.

Problems arise, however, as soon as the question of cause and effect is introduced. The economic logic behind the Quantity Theorem cannot exhaustively account for how and why individuals handle money; or more technically, why the demand for money is at a certain level at a particular point in time. This issue will always be subject to empirical supposition, which in practice means that there will tend to be a gap between the tidy logic of the analytical imagination and how money actually works. This is exemplified by Smith's arguments on saving. Smith regards saving as the mainspring of economic growth. Espousing the principle that '[c]apitals are increased by parsimony, and diminished by prodigality and misconduct',[27] he dismisses the belief, populist in his time, that saving is unhelpful for economic growth because it directs money away from its function as a medium of exchange, thereby detracting from its effects in stimulating trade. For Smith, on the contrary, '[w]hat is annually saved is as regularly consumed as what is annually spent, and nearly in the same time too; but it is consumed by a different set of people'.[28] In other words, what is saved is immediately invested, being subsequently consumed not by the saver as luxury spending but, in the form of income, 'by labourers, manufacturers, and artificers, who reproduce with a profit the value of their annual consumption'.[29] Saving is to be urged, not discouraged, for it is the root of productive activity and therefore economic growth. But this argument is undermined by a painfully constricted view of the reasons why people hold money. The logic made explicit by the Quantity Theorem lies behind Smith's contention that hoarding, a non-productive form of saving, should be regarded as an exceptional occurrence unworthy of extended consideration.[30] His account of the relationship between saving and investment is direct and mechanistic: what is saved is automatically and immediately turned into investment. But this proposition relies on moral, cultural and institutional conditions of which Smith seems completely aware but unable or unwilling to build into his theory. There is a clear moral dimension to his analysis of parsimony. His contention that 'every prodigal appears to be a public enemy, and every frugal man a public benefactor'[31] is boldly prescriptive. But this over-extends his central theme regarding the relationship between individual economic activity and its consequences for the social product, its potential contribution to the good of all. There is a world of difference between advocating a specific course of individual economic action because of a conviction that such action must have collective benefits, and working through a theory of economic development on the assumption that such action will in fact take place. To say that a state of affairs should prevail is of virtually no relevance to establishing that it will. Because Smith confuses these questions, empirical loose ends are introduced which disrupt the tight logical framework on which his argument depends.

Smith's advocacy of saving stems not only from moral urging but from the supposition that saving is rational from both individual and collective points of view. But the nature of the demand for money, particularly as a store of value, has been persistently puzzling for monetary theorists who base most of their assumptions about money on the idea that it serves primarily as a medium of exchange. Although this is not simply a question of whether or why people might hoard money, Simmel's investigation of cultural aspects of individual attitudes towards money as a desirable medium in itself, which I discuss in chapter 3, provides an illuminating contrast to Smith's view of acquiring money with the sole purpose of re-exchanging it for something else. To be sure, Smith introduces into his theory questions concerning why individuals accept or even yearn for money, and how they use it once they have it. But on closer examination, the reasons are less straightforward, consistent or even rational than his own logic would allow. There are good grounds for not assuming that the passions can so easily be subsumed by the interests where the handling of money is concerned. However compelling Smith's reasoning might be in strictly logical terms, it is considerably less so once there are firm doubts as to whether his arguments are empirically tenable. And unlike the later neoclassicists, he would almost certainly not have countenanced an approach to the analysis of economic life which continues to assert the primacy of economic reasoning even in the face of contradictory evidence.

Problems of a different magnitude have arisen with the application of the Quantity Theorem in neoclassical theory, but similar to classical approaches, these also suggest that the conception of money as logically neutral cannot be sustained beyond its statement as a truism. Where the Quantity Theorem has been treated as a theory in neoclassical economics, the main causal assumption made is that changes in MV cause changes in PT; in other words, the direction of causality in the equation is from left to right. Two further assumptions tend to be made: first, that changes in V and T are due not to changes in M but to non-monetary factors such as rates of productivity or new banking regulations; and second, that changes in M are due not to changes in people's demand for money but to external factors such as the production of precious metals or the issuing policy of the central bank.[32] These assumptions having been made, it should be clear why it is so important in neoclassical theory, which is chiefly concerned with short-run monetary disequilibrium, to regard money's role within the economy as confined to that of medium of exchange. Setting aside assumptions concerning V and T for a moment, if variations in the price level match fluctuations in the quantity of money, it has to be presumed that individuals use money almost exclusively to exchange it for something else, for buying things. The relationship between the quantity of money and the price level will be disrupted as soon as other reasons for holding money have to be accounted for. More importantly, even if there is a causal relationship between the quantity of money and price levels, the apparently logical nature of its depiction in the Quantity Theorem disguises a range of further propositions and assumptions which depend on quite specific empirical conditions. As Blaug notes, the theoretical principles stemming from the Quantity Theorem are that 'secular changes in the price level are *principally* due to changes in the stock of money or that any instability of prices stems *fundamentally* from monetary rather than non-monetary causes'. These arguments are irreducible even to additional assumptions regarding the nature of changes in M or the stability of V, for they rest on 'a whole series of empirical hypotheses about the nature of monetary injections, the speed of adjustment processes, the identities of debtors and creditors, the saving and investing propensities of different income recipients, etcetera'.[33] For example, it needs to be established not merely how money is injected into the economy but what ensures its effects on prices. A rise in prices may be generated by consumption practices because people have, in nominal terms at least, more money.[34] But this can only be fully understood with reference to who such people are and what kind of spending they engage in. These questions demand investigation of the economic practices and outlook of different sectors of society.

Decisions concerning what to do with money are a function of sociological, psychological and cultural factors. Even by making additional assumptions, however, the principles underlying the Quantity Theorem, which are needed to turn it into a theory, are of a substantive nature impossible to formalize in terms of the theorem itself. It is far from clear that enough is known about how and why people hold money to render the Quantity Theorem workable in practice, even as a guide to what economists call long-run equilibrium. Money is not simply a neutral, transparent token mediating the exchange of goods and services as classical and neoclassical theories suggest, but has cultural and symbolic associations generated by its use as a form of wealth and as a foundation of power, its conceptualization in relation to freedom, happiness and morality, and its retention as a basis for confidence or simply for its own sake. It seems incurably naive to suggest that such a range of attitudes towards the acquisition and use of money should be depicted on the basis of a logical relationship between the quantity of money and the level of prices.

The Political Neutrality of Money

Money's disruptive role in respect of economic logic stems not only from confusions over the demand for money but, in practice, from the organization of power in economic life. Money is politically consequential in ways which must be fully grasped in monetary theory.[35] Indeed, understanding the connections between money and the structural conditions of its transaction plays a vital role in the formulation of any economic theory of money, however disinterested the proclamations of its author might be in this regard. Significantly, the three approaches to the political economy of money discussed in this chapter veer apart from each other most markedly where the argument moves furthest away from the analysis of the relationship between money and the individual, even if, as in neoclassical economics, large-scale economic institutions or firms are regarded as reducible to this basic model. There are, indeed, parallels between Marx's approach to money and classical and neoclassical theories where the analysis of individual economic action is concerned. Marx, in common with these other schools of thought, regards money's exchange function as primary. He contrasts barter and monetary exchange by depicting them respectively as C–C, where one commodity is exchanged directly for another, and C–M–C, where the exchange of commodities is mediated by money.[36] He thereby draws out the sense in which money enables commodities to be exchanged without the eventual recipients needing to be present in one place at the same time, nor even to know each other. This formulation is exactly the same as that of Smith: where the requirements of two individuals to purchase the product of another's labour do not match, money saves them the time and effort of searching for other potential co-transactors. A further parallel between Marx's approach and classical and neoclassical theory is suggested in so far as Marx characterizes economic action in terms of the rational disposition to maximize.[37] But despite these similarities, the central theme in Marx's work stands in stark contrast to that of his classical and neoclassical counterparts. This concerns the structural relationship between money, wealth and capital and the distribution of power in capitalist society. Neither of the other approaches addresses this theme in such explicit terms.

Marx, like Smith, regards production as the driving-force of economic life. He also characterizes production in terms of a series of historically specific economic circuits. But this represents only half the story for Marx. As soon as he locks exchange into the production process, money becomes an expression not of exchange relationships as such but of the structural conditions which underpin capitalist relations of production. Smith's independent producers are replaced by Marx's exploited labourers as the mainspring of economic development. Accordingly, money ceases to provide the instrument by which the activities of independent producers can be co-ordinated within a social division of labour. It becomes instead a vital means by which labour power can be commodified in abstract form, bought and sold on the labour market and squeezed for the accumulation of profit. Money's role within the economy thereby ceases to be neutral. For Smith, as I have pointed out, money is logically neutral because it enables relationships of exchange to go on as they would have done in its absence, only more efficiently and extensively. In Marx's terms, this view of money is sustainable only as long as the focus remains solely on the process of exchange. To be sure, Marx regards money as an expression of the economic contradictions and political tensions characteristic of capitalism, not as their direct cause. He criticizes the Proudhonists for example for suggesting that money's abolition would alleviate the structural contradictions inherent in capitalism. Money objectifies these contradictions but does not intrinsically generate them; hence removing money would lead only to its re-emergence in another form.[38] But there is an important difference between this counterfactual argument and the historical thesis at the heart of Marx's analysis of the role of money in capitalist society. As soon as his specific, capitalistic characterization of money as a commodity is placed in the context of his analysis of production, money quite clearly does make a substantive difference to economic life. Without money, by which abstract labour power can be not only quantified but loosened from the spatial and temporal constraints of feudal production and rewarded in the form of money-wages, the relations of production that Marx examines could not have developed as to his eyes they did. Money is therefore vital not merely to the everyday operation of those relations but to their historical emergence. This is not to suggest that money itself generated the asymmetrical property relationship on which Marx's analysis of capitalism is focused, merely that its role in facilitating the historical process by which that relationship came into being is at the heart of his approach to the political economy of money.

I am not saying that differences between the conclusions of Smith and Marx regarding the role of money within the economy derive from their accounts of the nature of money. These are broadly similar. Nor do the differences stem from their understanding of the ways in which money is handled by individuals themselves. Again, there is virtual identity in their approaches. Rather, the distinctive conclusions drawn by Smith and Marx in the political economy of money are based on distinctive theories of the property relationship on which the productive activity under-pinning economic development is founded. Money itself cannot be divorced from these theories and sealed inside the vacuum of economic logic, for it is tied to the social relationships, in all spheres of economic activity, which enable exchange to take place at all: tied both in historical terms and in relation to the everyday operation of the economic system itself. To be sure, both Smith and Marx realized this. But Marx was able to examine the historically specific form which money enabled relations of production to take under capitalism, namely its commodification as abstract labour power. There is no need for wholesale adoption of Marx's economic theory to understand the sociological significance of this insight.

Marx's explanation of the formation of monetary value is closely linked to his theory of the organization of power in capitalist society. Like the classical writers, he is dealing of course with forms of money which either consist of or are linked to precious metal, principally gold. It follows from this that the central explanatory question concerns whether money's value is derived from the costs entailed in the production of precious metals, from the value or price of those metals at the point of exchange, or from some combination of the two. Whichever route is taken, money tends to be characterized first and foremost as a commodity, produced and sold like any other. Complications arise, however, as soon as it is conceded that money is at least a special type of commodity, attained not to be consumed but either to be re-exchanged with something else or hoarded. For both Marx and the classical economists, this dual quality of money, its character as both a mere commodity and a special commodity, is at the root of most of the problems entailed in seeking to understand the formation of its value. Conclusions drawn at this level tend to shape what can be said about money's significance in the context of the economy as a whole, particularly its connection to relations of power in society.

Marx's theory of value is different in important ways from that of Smith. In general terms, it is possible to draw from Smith's work three quite distinctive theories of value: a labour theory, a cost-of-production theory, and an exchange theory linking value with price.[39] It seems unlikely, given his consideration of other factors of production in relation to the question of value, that Smith's is a straightforward labour theory of value, and more likely that his arguments imply a cost-of-production theory; although given his lack of clarity on this issue also, it is perhaps most likely that he has no systematic theory of value at all.[40] Marx's analysis of value is superficially similar to that of Smith, particularly in emphasizing the origins of money as a medium of exchange. Both Smith and Marx characterize money as a commodity, and do so by focusing on the close historical association between money and precious metals. But beyond this, their theories of money are quite different, particularly in identifying the common element between values which allows them to be quantitatively compared when exchanging the products of labour. In so far as it seems unlikely from Smith's arguments that his is a labour theory of value, this suggests that money is the only common denominator between values. This would be consistent with his views on the role of money within the economy as a whole. For Marx, by contrast, labour itself provides the only valid measure of value.[41] This contention is not entirely plausible, for it implies that exchange is only possible if the values exchanged are linked to the production process. As Elster has argued, it is not difficult to envisage an economic system which is fully automated so that 'goods would be transferred between firms and from firms to consumers, according to well-defined notional prices, yet no labour would enter into the production of goods'.[42] A more plausible candidate for the function of the common element between values is utility, but this property is not exhausted by Marx's concept of exchange even when broadened out to refer to useful products of human labour.[43] Although Marx's formulation is not completely tenable in empirical terms, it is at least consistent with his characterization of money as a crystallization of capitalist relations of production. Money's expression of price is also an expression of the unequal relationships generated by the commodification of labour power. This derives not from market relationships but from the exploitation of labour.

Problems arise in Marx's account when he addresses the relationship between monetary value and the commodity which serves as money, specifically gold. It is crucial to understand that Marx's references to the origins of money focus first and foremost on money's status as a commodity, with all that this entails given his theory of capitalist political economy. From here, Marx extrapolates an approach to money's mediating role within the economy which is harshly critical of the arguments of Smith. Marx's preoccupation with money as gold is in this sense something of a red herring: it is with money's status as a commodity that he is chiefly concerned. His reference to the origins of money as a basis for explaining the formation of its value is misleading for exactly this reason. Indeed, it is difficult to establish whether the evolution of money actually matters in his terms: depending on whether one's interpretation is based on *Capital* or *Grundrisse*, the issue of origins may or may not be peripheral to Marx's theory of monetary value. In *Capital*, for example, there is little doubt that Marx identifies the commodity, usually gold, as the source of money's value, even where money is represented by a token. It is not money's special role in the exchange relationship which underpins its value but the other way around. Money's value derives from its status as a commodity: the adoption of a specific commodity as money within a community gives that commodity 'not its value but its specific value-form'.[44] In *Grundrisse*, on the other hand, Marx provides more scope for the analytical separation of money from its status as a commodity. He recalls the position of the Cartalists, for example, who argued that money's function as the generalized equivalent, as 'a *particular* commodity alongside the others', acts as the source of its utility, and thus value, as money. Henceforth, the monetary object 'will be exchanged not for the purpose of satisfying a need, not for consumption, but in order to be re-exchanged for other commodities'.[45] This suggests that money's use-value derives from its exchange-value.[46] In this way, Marx seems to draw a distinction between the commodity and monetary source of money's value. Historically, money emerges as a solution to the practical inconveniences of barter, in which case it follows that money's commodity status is key. But Marx's argument can also be interpreted as a theory of monetary value focusing on the distinctive use-value of money. It is open to debate whether the two approaches to monetary value discussed here should be addressed separately, perhaps as opposing theories of monetary value, or should be regarded as consecutive stages in the development of money as a social institution. The details of Marx's formulation in *Grundrisse* suggest the latter course:

first of all, 'the commodity becomes money because of its particular use-value'; this relation is then inverted as the money-object 'acquires its particular use-value from its serviceability as money'.[47] This seems the most sensible interpretation of Marx's argument. It would in any case be insensitive to his overarching theory of capitalism to address the latter stage of this scenario as in any way a contradiction of the first. To address both stages together is wholly consistent with Marx's thesis that money objectifies the social and political relations inherent to capitalist production.

For Marx, money's primary role within capitalist society is to facilitate the crystallization of abstract labour power in the form of commodity exchange relationships, in which case it does not especially matter whether money itself is represented by gold or banana peel. Ultimately, the source of money's value cannot be explained without reference to the production and exchange relations which generate the circulation of commodities. It is principally as an expression of these relations that money is sociologically significant. Whether money is in practice represented by a token or a commodity possessing intrinsic value, it is its functional connection with capitalist relations of production which enables money to function as it does. Money's value is therefore derived not from the physical properties of the commodity which serves as money but from the capitalist labour process by which goods are commodified. This, not the technical debate between a labour as opposed to a cost-of-production theory of value, is the most important issue on which Marx differs from Smith. The question of money's origins as a commodity is important to Marx's theory only in so far as this serves as a reflection of the ongoing relationship between money and the capitalist political economy. The primary question then becomes not whether money breaks away from its commodity status and becomes a token, but rather how money continues to provide the abstract expression of capitalist relations of production. In this sense, his theory of monetary value is quintessentially sociological, irreducible either to the analysis of the physical properties of monetary objects or to abstract economic formulations.

Discussion of the relationship between money and the organization of power in society cannot, however, be confined to the process of production but raises important questions about the institutional structure of banking. This is as pertinent to theories of money derived from the logical principles underlying the Quantity Theorem as it is to Marx's analysis of money and capital. If Smith's advocacy of saving suggests good grounds for more closely exploring social and cultural practices associated with the acquisition and use of money, his

conception of the mechanistic relationship between saving and investment begs more thorough investigation into banking practices,
particularly the networks of influence and power on which such
practices are based. Smith is clearly sensitive to the idea that banks do
not simply mediate the passage of funds from saving to investment but
have a crucial role to play in determining both the level and destination of
both. He is critical, after all, of the practice of over-issue.[48] His criticisms
of banking practices are designed to maximize the efficiency with which
money fulfils its mediating role. But there are other means besides the
process of issuing money by which banks can influence and disrupt such a
role which he fails to address. To this extent, Smith moves no further
than Cantillon, who regards banks merely as facilitators of the
circulation of money as a medium of exchange, injecting into circulation
money, in the form of loans, which would otherwise lie dormant, in the
form of deposits.[49] Smith does not, for example, take into account the
relationship between levels of saving and the rate of interest, addressing
saving instead as a matter of frugality which, where the wealth of a
country is concerned, will be determined by 'the general character of the
inhabitants as to industry or idleness'.[50] But saving, however much it
might depend on attitudes towards money which have an important
social and cultural dimension, cannot accurately be addressed outside the
context of specific institutional circumstances which help condition not
only comparative levels of expenditure and non-expenditure of income
but also rates of return on the latter. Cultural factors closely interrelate
with rather than override these circumstances in a way which cannot be
reduced to inherited predilection. Banks, after all, are engaged not merely
in passing funds on from savers to investors, but in multiplying deposits
in the form of loans, in credit creation.[51] This is one, though not the only,
important area in which interest rates can be utilized not merely as a basis
for the commercial activities of banks but as a vital instrument of
government economic policy, which raises significant questions not only
about the organizational structure governing the operation and
administration of banking networks but about regulations and supervisory practices installed by governments and state agencies. It remains to
be asked whether these institutional and political conditions undermine
the concept of money as merely a mediator; and if so, whether this
warrants scrapping or simply reformulating the barter model of economic
activity suggested in Smith's approach to the political economy of
money. The discussion here is not meant to be parachronistic, accusing
Smith of failure to take into account issues which characterize the
present-day organization and transaction of money. My argument,
rather, concerns the reasoning behind Smith's conception of the

mediating role of money within the economy as a whole, reasoning which, after all, has persisted in modified form in approaches to the political economy of money up to the present day.[52]

But Marx's approach too is undermined by the self-imposed rigidity of a form of reasoning derived from a substantive economic theory. His analysis of money's role in investment is based on a characterization of money as productive capital. In contrast to Smith, Marx regards investment not as the transfer of money from saving to investment and thereby into income, but as the process by which exchange-value is increased.[53] It is impossible, in Marx's view, to exclude production from the analysis of the process by which this expansion occurs: exchange-value is increased only through productive activity, never through exchange alone. That surplus-value is realized through exchange should not detract from the fact that this is only a manifestation of the operation of the industrial circuit of capital.[54] To assume otherwise is to veil the real social relationships through which the circuit is reproduced. It is in this aspect of his theory of money, however, that Marx's emphasis on the relationship between money, value and productive activity is placed under most strain, particularly with reference to the present-day institutional arrangements of monetary and financial markets. Marx resists the idea that exchange relations might develop independently of the sphere of production and act as a source of the expansion of exchange-value, although he does seem to envisage the possibility that exchange relations alone might be a source of disturbance within the production process. In a marginal note added to his own copy of the first volume of *Capital* and included by Engels as a footnote to the third German edition, Marx suggests that a monetary crisis can arise independently of the real economy which 'affects industry and commerce by its backwash',[55] whereas, by and large, monetary crisis occurs 'as a particular phase of every general industrial and commercial crisis'.[56] In itself, this need have no bearing on Marx's characterization of the industrial circuit of capital: the circuit explains the expansion of capital, while Marx's comments on crisis are an anticipation of the implications of international monetary exchange for the stability of the real economy. It is none the less possible to argue that these developments undermine any claim that Marx's analysis of capital is exhaustive. To characterize money-capital as self-expanding[57] is, in Marx's terms, to confuse processes of the capitalist system of production which are expressed by money with properties of money itself. Money-dealers, for example, simply mediate the industrial circuit of capital: they 'can do no more than shorten the technical operations that go with buying and selling, and thus reduce the amount of cash money required to turn over the commodities'.[58] Likewise with commercial capital transactions, the profit derived from exchange is merely a portion of the surplus-value generated when commodities enter and leave the production process. Commercial trading of capital may contribute towards the attainment of a larger surplus - either by 'shortening the time of circulation' or by making available a larger portion of 'social capital' for production[59] - but cannot itself generate that surplus. It is not necessary to concur with the labour theory of value in order to accept these arguments on historical grounds. While there may be analytical reasons for rejecting the labour theory of value,[60] this does not necessarily mean that Marx's characterization of the industrial circuit of capital is inadequate as a descriptive account of 'how an industrialist proceeds'.[61] As an explanation of the expansion of capital in every case, however, Marx's approach is seriously deficient.

There are indeed several respects in which Marx's arguments about the nature of money in general are difficult to incorporate within an analysis of money's role in contemporary society. First, the relationship between the real and financial sectors of the economy in contemporary Western societies cannot be accounted for in terms of the economic model, centred around production, formulated by Marx. Within present-day international currency and capital markets profit can be generated, and so money-capital expanded, even though their connection to the productive sphere is more oblique than he suggests. There is an inflexibility in Marx's theory of money stemming from his preoccupation with the relationship between money and industrial circuits of capital. This undermines any contemporary application of his theory, because exchange is locked into the productive circuit. Commercial capital transactions form part of profit-generating circuits which, while not excluding production altogether, display characteristics which suggest that to include production as an *integral element* of these circuits in the manner suggested by Marx would require tortuous stretching of the analytical imagination. As I shall discuss in later chapters, this break between circuits of capital and production is highly significant for understanding the volatility and instability of present-day international monetary networks, and their often disruptive effects on the real economy.

A further limitation of Marx's theory on contemporary analysis concerns his neglect, in accounting for how individuals actually handle money, of the ways in which their interpretations of their own and others' actions inform what they actually do. The connections between capital circuits and the productive sphere have an interpretative dimension which cannot be characterized functionally in the way he maintains. As I shall argue in later chapters, money's role in the transmission of information plays a substantive role in the operation of international markets. This has a significant impact on the relationship between the real and financial sectors of the economy which cannot always be characterized in functional terms because, as I shall show, such information can have a profound and consequential significance irrespective of whether it is objectively accurate. Marx does not provide a secure basis for a complete grasp of this area of monetary analysis. In founding his analytical framework on the process of production, and demoting monetary transactors to the functional status of mere 'personifications of economic relations',[62] he can provide no substantive basis on which to examine the implications of the expansion of exchange spheres across geopolitical boundaries. In so far as this concerns the reasons underlying the demand for money, it is a failing he shares with classical and neoclassical theorists alike.

Marx is no more helpful as a guide to understanding the contemporary pre-eminence of consumerism. The role of individuals in economic life has increasingly been centred around their role as consumers no less, and perhaps even more, than as producers. This is fundamental to the very real sense in which individuals are empowered by money. There is no need to buy into some of the more celebratory accounts of consumerism to acknowledge the cultural significance of this aspect of contemporary monetary relations. To be sure, Marx acknowledges money's capacity to empower transactors. But he tends to regard this as nothing other than a reflection of socio-economic relations specific to capitalism. For Marx, the freedom given over by the possession of money is not freedom at all, but simply a means by which individuals are embroiled in and thereby become reproducers of the capitalist mode of production. As I shall move on to argue in later chapters, very little is gained in analytical terms by addressing monetary transactors largely as economic automata. The historical developments briefly referred to here cannot be incorporated even within a modified form of Marx's analytical framework. On the contrary, they raise conceptual issues which place that framework under severe strain.

Indeed, all three approaches to the political economy of money under discussion in this chapter are inexhaustive and ultimately misleading for the analysis of money's role in contemporary society. The form of reasoning underlying monetary theories in classical and neoclassical economics, expressed by the central idea that money is logically neutral, obscures the importance of the demand for money, of the reasons people hold on to money and their perceptions of how they use it. This problem also arises in Marx's work, albeit for different reasons and with different results. Marx convincingly undermines the idea, implicit in classical and neoclassical reasoning, that money is politically neutral. But in doing so, he binds monetary analysis to assumptions which cannot be sustained on closer scrutiny: not merely, it should be emphasized, because they have become outdated, but because they are questionable in themselves. Theoretical rigidity in Marxist economics means that, similar to the classical approach, the historical importance of production in the capitalist economy is treated as a foundational rather than a substantive question, providing only a restrictive basis for examining the institutional structure of banking. Banking practices condition the role of money in the economy in ways which cannot be explained within the terms of a theoretical framework in which functional primacy must always be ascribed to production. The relationship between production and exchange is historically complex, and cannot be conceptualized in the form of a clear, binary opposition. This is not to suggest that such difficulties can be solved by resorting to the ahistorical framework of neoclassical economics, for this would be to gloss over important issues concerning the relationship between money and the organization of power in society. Neoclassical economists also rely on a form of reasoning which is inflexible, deriving theoretical foundations from a limited series of empirical observations. Indeed, it is because of the rigidity of the reasoning underlying each of these approaches to the political economy of money that a further set of questions essential to understanding the organization of money in the present day has hardly been touched upon, for none of the theories I have examined provide a basis on which to do so. In all three approaches, the role of the modern state in underpinning both the validity of money itself and the legal and institutional framework of monetary relations in society tends to be sidelined if not altogether ignored. The role of the state in relation to money is regarded either as reducible to, or as an irritant for, allegedly more fundamental economic imperatives. This is a serious misconception, for historical and theoretical reasons I move on to explore in the next chapter.

2

Money and the State

The political economists discussed in the preceding chapter ascribe social and political consequences to monetary transaction which cannot be understood by reference to a list of standard economic functions alone. They nevertheless provide an economic explanation of the origins of money's value, linked to its status as a commodity, its crystallization of capitalist relations of production or its utility for purposes of exchange, not fully applicable to modern monetary forms which are not commodities but tokens without intrinsic value. In contemporary society, monetary tokens are only likely to be accepted as payment when backed by legal guarantees regarding their face-value. It is the state which promises either to convert monetary tokens into commodities such as gold or silver on demand, or to produce and validate money in such a way that its value will remain stable over time. In most present-day countries, only the second of these promises still applies. But reference to high or unstable rates of inflation in many such countries suggests that the state's role in issuing and validating money may not be essential but damaging. State promises which refer not to conversion but to monetary stability rely on trust rather than legal enforcement. It is far from clear, however, that governments or other state agencies are best equipped to keep their promises in this respect. The relationship between money and the state is of paramount importance in contemporary debates concerning the independence of central banks, the feasibility of monetary union between states, and the denationalization of money. In this chapter, I shall explore legal, economic and sociological accounts of the relationship between money and the state so as to flesh out what I consider to be the confusion underlying arguments on one side of the major present-day division of opinion over state monetary policy. Opponents of monetary union in Europe seem to be contending that the state, in its role as the rule-formulating and sanction-wielding political authority, has an indispensable part to play in the issue and validation of money without which monetary stability would be difficult and perhaps impossible to maintain. Yet their arguments regarding the symbolic and political significance of the role of individual states as opposed to a union of states in producing and validating money lend themselves to the view that, although the relationship between money and the state is essential to understanding how money has evolved towards its present form, this does not rule out envisaging in principle a monetary system in which the role of the state in issuing and validating money has been reduced or even severed altogether.

Considered reflection on the continuing debate over European Monetary Union (EMU) suggests that its terms of reference are at best mistaken and at worst systematically misleading. Yet the emotiveness with which opposing sides of the debate have been presented does at least provide unquestionable confirmation that the historical association between money and nation-states, whether perceived as a question of nationalist symbolism or administrative requirement, has been and will continue to be politically compelling. This is especially so when addressing the most vexed question emerging from the Maastricht Treaty of 1992, namely, the programme of steps towards establishing a single currency valid across European Community member states and administered by a European Central Bank. I do not intend to enter into this debate directly in this chapter. Because many of the arguments within the debate are essentially reactive in the face of political and economic contingencies, its terms of reference cannot be pinned down in a way sufficiently robust to draw lasting conclusions. But more than this, fundamental questions raised by the debate over EMU have been misconceived, ignoring significant conceptual and historical facets of the relationship between money and the nation-state. The central focus of this chapter is the concept of monetary sovereignty. My aim is to establish whether the relationship between money and the nation-state can be regarded as an issue of functional and administrative necessity, or whether the relationship owes more to historical contingency. These positions need not be regarded as mutually exclusive, but examination of the differences between them should at least help clarify contrasting approaches to conceptualizing the political dimension of monetary relations. The first position, that the relationship between money and the state is definitive, suggests that, because of the intrinsically value-less nature of modern monetary forms, any departure from this relationship should be greeted with caution. The second position, that the relationship is mostly due to historical contingency and may therefore be dispensed with if circumstances allow, need not encourage a stance towards monetary union which is any less cautious, but might at least help us to understand the reasons behind and implications of some of the more panic-stricken, perhaps even mythologizing, reactions to such union.

But as I intend to show, even if it could be established that monetary sovereignty owes much to historical contingency, the importance of this to the fiduciary character of modern monetary networks is far from clear: the precise implications of monetary union would remain obscure. There clearly does exist a functional relationship between money and the nation-state whereby the modern state, as the legitimate political authority within geopolitical boundaries, acts as the rule-formulating and sanction-wielding monetary administrator. But it is in precisely this respect, rather than with regard to the historical relationship between money and the nation-state, that the contribution of sociologists and social theorists to monetary analysis has been least convincing. I shall explore how this weakness might be remedied in later chapters. My argument in this chapter proceeds in three stages. First of all, I discuss the work of two theorists, Georg Knapp and Max Weber, who argue that there is a definitive relationship between money and the state which derives both from money's legal status and from the fiscal duties of the state itself. There are serious weaknesses in this argument, however, the implications of which I shall draw out in the second section through an examination of historical links between money and the state, asking whether the relationship is more a consequence of contingencies of statehood than of intrinsic necessities concerning the administration and validation of money. In the third section, I extend this enquiry by assessing Hayek's argument, characteristic of an approach to economic liberalism derived from neoclassical economics, that the relationship between money and the state, even monetary sovereignty itself, is not only dispensable in principle but should be dispensed with, for it undermines monetary stability.

The Legal Status of Paper

As I argued in the Introduction, money's circulation depends on the coherence of a transacting network. This is composed of a series of relationships between transactors which persist over and above the simple fact that they enter into transactions with each other. Sociologically, these relationships take three basic forms: rational, fiduciary and political. They are at the heart of the interconnection between money and the modern state. Trust in money's abstract properties is, by extension, trust in those agencies responsible for monetary administration. Trust in this sense partly depends on the political legitimacy of the state in question. But it must also depend on the technical proficiency of the monetary administrators themselves, such as the Treasury and central bank. This combination of conditions suggests to Knapp and Weber that the circulation of paper money is not feasible without state backing. They argue that money depends for its value and stability on issuing and regulating agencies backed by the state. State control and regulation of money amounts to a monopoly[1] over the production, supply and validation of legal-tender, these days classified and measured as M0. For purposes of this discussion, the nation-state should initially be distinguished from the state in general and the state apparatus in particular, and also from society. The nation-state is defined by geopolitical borders, but as Giddens notes, while this is characteristic of modern nation-states, 'it is very often not the case with other types of society, whether these are 'states' or small localised groups'.[2] A further, technical ambiguity exists in definitions of the state. On the one hand, the state seems to encompass the social system. On the other, the state comprises a set of institutions, a state apparatus.[3] This is a vitally important distinction for discussion of the relationship between money and the state here and in later chapters. Bearing these points in mind, it might be helpful to set out a working definition of the modern state, which I take from Weber and Mann,[4] as a differentiated set of institutions and personnel; constituting an administrative and legal order subject to change by legislation; being largely centralized in so far as political relations radiate outwards from here; and encompassing a territorial jurisdiction throughout which is exercised binding authority over rule-making, supported by the legitimate (i.e. monopolized) use of physical violence.[5]

Knapp argues that a monetary system comprising tokens depends on state backing. Moreover, he contends that the political framework in which money is transacted is essential to its character as money in the first instance. For this reason, money's status as a commodity has little to do with how it actually works, and provides no real guide to the nature of money itself.[6] Money is on the contrary a creature of law, and depends on legal ordinances for its validity. But Knapp does not specify the precise status of such ordinances, which would be essential for an exact assessment of the relationship between the administrative and fiduciary components of the state's role in validating and issuing money. This problem shows up in the two systems Knapp employs for classifying money, the genetic and functional schema, which emphasize distinctive and not necessarily compatible aspects of the role of the state.

Knapp's genetic schema is based on the straightforward proposition that the unit of account, the numéraire,[7] must persist through time if a stable system of payments, incorporating credit, is to be sustained. As long as this arrangement is in place, the identity of the object which serves as money may change any number of times, for debts can still be calculated and paid in so far as the relation between each new monetary form and the existing numéraire is defined.[8] As I argued in the Introduction, a standardized accounting system is one of the basic properties of any monetary network. For Knapp, this system must be fixed under law. As the best illustration of this, Knapp cites paper money, since 'on close consideration it appears that in this dubious form of 'degenerate' money lies the clue to the nature of money'.[9] For Knapp, the circulation of paper money proves that transactors accept and hold money not because of its intrinsic value as a commodity but because of guarantees regarding its future re-exchangeability: the 'satisfaction ... of the holder does not depend on possession *per se*, but on possession with a view to future use for payment'.[10] These guarantees must be provided by the state. Knapp maintains, further, that the value of money is derived from its connections with the state, for they reassure transactors that the money-object in question is re-exchangeable at face-value.

In his functional schema, however, Knapp suggests that transactors' trust in the re-exchangeability of a particular currency can be derived merely from the expectation of its continuing circulation. Transactors will want to ensure they possess the correct money with which to meet their largest, most regular financial obligations, and these will usually involve the state. Because of this, even those transactions which do not directly involve the state will be carried through in the monetary form that the state agrees to accept. But this has more to do with the economic status of the state than with its political authority. These are by no means self-evidently inseparable. Knapp's two schemes cause confusion because he tries to answer two questions at once which are not necessarily reducible to each other. As Frederick Mann observes in a legal textbook on money, the question of what can be treated as money under law has 'nothing to do with a quite different problem; what is money in an abstract sense, what is its essence, its intrinsic attribute, its inherent quality?'[11] By claiming that '[t]he soul of currency is not in the material of the pieces, but in the legal ordinances which regulate their use',[12] Knapp clearly tries to fuse these questions together. Yet his arguments provide no substantive basis on which to suggest that this is a feasible approach to take. Were Knapp to suggest that the validating role of the state is symbolically important and not just a technical question in the legal sense, his two schemes might have been compatible. As it is, they appear only to contradict each other. In so far as it is conceivable that state acceptance is important for the identity of money only as a result of the size of the state as a transactor, as Knapp's functional schema suggests, this might just as readily apply to a non-political institution such as a large firm. If the significance of the declaration by an institution that it will accept only a particular monetary form as payment is proportional to the scale of monetary obligations to that institution, this is an economic rather than political consideration. While it is true that the state's fiscal operations provide the reason for its dominance within the payments network, this nevertheless means that the relationship between money and the state need no longer be defined exclusively as a political or even a legal question. The state's importance with regard to the identity of money would cease to be a question of trust or administrative competence and become instead an issue of economic obligation.

The different views implied by Knapp's two schemes are also taken up by Weber. Weber's discussion of the relationship between money and the state must be understood in the light of his account of the role of the state in the emergence of modern capitalism. He focuses on the fiscal dimension of the interrelationship between state and economy, on the function of the state as leveller and collector of taxes. In Weber's view, while money is essential to any form of capitalism, it is only in respect of the continuous productive and financial processes of modern capitalism that a truly extensive monetary system emerges. But the importance of the fiscal demands of the state to this development need not mean that the relationship between money and the state is inevitable or indispensable. Weber implicitly recognizes this by acknowledging the distinction between the political and economic role of the state in relation to the monetary system. While noting the significance of the fact that '[t]he modern state has universally assumed the monopoly of regulating the monetary system by statute', he concedes that '[q]uite apart from the monopoly of monetary regulation and issue, because of the tremendous importance of the financial transactions of the state the behaviour of the state treasurers in their monetary transactions is of crucial significance for the monetary system'.[13] Here, Weber suggests that the economic status of the state, its relationships with private economic agents, is of at least equal importance to its political functions where money is concerned. This distinction corresponds respectively, in Weber's terms, to money's function as a means of payment, its formal validity, and as a means of exchange, its substantive validity. The latter function, which derives from the economic operations of the state, is given primacy by

Weber, for 'the state needs money to a large degree, sometimes even entirely, as a means of exchange to cover future purchases of goods and supplies in the market'.[14] This is to some extent merely a logical distinction: money's formal and substantive characteristics will usually be assimilated as long as the state dominates the payments system, which it does by raising taxes.[15] The distinction is nevertheless significant because it suggests that it might be possible to establish a private monetary network without state backing. This also seems to have occurred to Knapp, for he notes that pay groups separate from the state have the capacity to create their own unit of value, adding that '[t]he State is only the most familiar, the oldest society of payers; it is not the only one'.[16] There can be little doubt, given Knapp's functional schema, that the state is in some respects an economic agent. Its constituent institutions must remunerate those in their employ, and obviously require some command over monetary resources to do so. Yet this need have no special significance as far as monetary administration is concerned other than to indicate that the state constitutes a large firm.[17] This provides virtually no guidance as to whether a definitive link exists between money and the state. It would therefore be erroneous to conclude, at least on the basis of the arguments of Knapp and Weber, that a monetary network could not exist on a territorially extensive scale without the backing of the state.

Money and Contingencies of Statehood

By characterizing the relationship between money and the state as a combination of legal authority and economic power, neither Knapp nor Weber provides a clear basis on which to establish what actually distinguishes the role of the modern state with regard to money, particularly in respect of the fiduciary relationships underpinning monetary transaction. Perhaps it is impossible to separate the political function of the state in issuing currency from its economic position as a major transactor resulting from its fiscal demands: both, after all, are political operations with economic consequences. But it would be sensible at least to examine the historical role of the state in the establishment of monetary systems in the light of this distinction. This should help clarify whether the administration of money does indeed contain an irreducibly political dimension.

Weber contends that the tightening of the fiscal organization of the modern state, which involved the institution of a system of exclusively money-based taxation, was an essential historical condition for the establishment of rational capitalist enterprise.[18] The confinement of the state's relationship with the economy to this fiscal role created 'an optimal environment for a rational market-oriented capitalism'.[19] Under these conditions, capital and labour could be freed from all political obligations other than those deriving from their engagement in rational, profit-oriented capitalist activity, the most prominent of these being taxation. The state's role in generating an environment favourable to rational capitalist enterprise was furthered, according to Weber, by the spur provided by fiscal accounting to the development of double-entry bookkeeping.[20] This theme is also taken up by Giddens, who argues that the rational administration of the state's fiscal accounts is bound up historically with the development of its surveillance activities. For example, assessment of the means and activities of individuals is both a necessary condition for and consequence of territorially extensive taxation. The production and validation of modern, spatially extensive monetary systems comprising tokens is closely connected with this.[21] For these reasons, reference to the fiscal state does at least suggest that the modern state has been a distinctive *political* agency with regard to the administration of money, for the state's fiscal duties are of a political nature which cannot be reduced to the objectives of a large firm. These duties are based on the link between the institutions making up the state apparatus and the territorial borders of the nation. They are defined in political terms by the assertion of and claim to universal statehood. As Mann notes, '[t]he state and the interests it serves have always sought to uphold its authority by a claim to 'universalism' over its territories, a detachment from all particularistic, specialised ties to kin, locality, class, church, etc.'[22] More specifically, he characterizes state control of the monetary system as one of four 'logistical techniques' bound up with the 'long-term historical growth in the infrastructural power of the state'.[23] Mann's analysis of the state owes much to Skocpol, who characterizes the state as a distinctive and autonomous institution which cannot be reduced to the push and pull of economic forces. For Skocpol, the state 'is no mere arena in which socioeconomic struggles are fought out' but rather 'a set of administrative, policing, and military organisations headed, and more or less well coordinated by, an executive authority'.[24]

If the relationship between money and the state is addressed from a historical perspective, it can be demonstrated that monetary administration has been no less important a resource for the nation-state, given its fiscal requirements, than has been the state's political authority for the validation of money. Indeed, it is quite likely that the state's utilization of its privileges over the issue and validation of money has often been exercised at the expense of monetary stability. That the state's role in monetary administration has been functional from the point of view of the contingencies of statehood can be demonstrated in more detail by examining the pivotal role of monetary administration in the transition from absolutism to the nation-states system in Europe. During this period, monetary administration was chronically implicated in the domestic consequences of war, principally in the fiscal pressures generated by its industrialization, as well as with efforts to foster an international environment conducive to free trade.

The absolutist system of states persisted in Europe throughout the sixteenth, seventeenth and eighteenth centuries. Historically, absolutism marked the period of transition between traditional state forms and the contemporary nation-state, and was characterized by the gradual institutionalization of a bureaucratic state apparatus in place of a hierarchical social structure dominated by hereditary succession.[25] This process paved the way for the emergence of the nation-state, and helped generate the infrastructural changes integral to the development of territorially extensive monetary networks. Changes in the legal framework administered under state jurisdiction - namely, its assumption of an impersonal structure, the establishment of the private character of property, and the adoption of state-administered sanctions - were integral to this process.[26] Under absolutism, despotic state power began to be supplanted by state power co-ordinated between centre and regions: power previously disseminated throughout a system of estates but now conjoined with and subject to a centralized state apparatus. In this respect, the absolutist state directly anticipated the nation-state. Although the system of estates characteristic of traditional state forms began to undergo a process of transition under absolutism, the transition was by no means clear cut.[27] The somewhat messy, transitional character of absolutist states was due principally to the fact that absolutist structures did not exactly replace but tended to be superimposed on existing institutions. The constitutional monarchies of England and the Netherlands contained more efficient fiscal structures which were consequently more conducive to the emergence of capitalist enterprise. Within constitutional monarchies the landed-rich and trading-rich were, by and large, taxed evenly and consensually. Indeed, the nobility, gentry, yeomanry or merchants may be referred to loosely as capitalists insofar as they were 'more uniform in their political orientations, and less amenable to monarchical divide-and-rule strategies'.[28] By contrast, the landed-rich under absolutism continued to enjoy tax exemption, making up a distinctive layer in the fiscal structure.[29] Absolutist states were in this respect infrastructurally weaker than constitutional monarchies.[30] The enduring presence of an estates system comprising a relatively autonomous nobility preoccupied with maintaining their privileges meant that varieties of coinage rather than a unitary monetary network were subject to uneven production, validation and supply within absolutist states. The difficulties entailed in prising open such self-perpetuating arrangements were viciously circular: the funds extracted through taxation were precisely what were needed in order to build up the bureaucratic structure necessary for extensive taxation.[31] This was only ever achieved with dubious success under absolutism. For this reason, state monopoly over the production and validation of money was never fully achieved by absolutist states. This was chronically fiscally problematic.

In certain respects, however, processes set under way within absolutist states were crucial precursors of the modern nation-state. They were correspondingly conducive to establishing a state monopoly over the validation, production and supply of money. Principal among these was the process of formalizing state boundaries, the transition from diffuse frontiers to definitive borders.[32] Infrastructural strength was obviously important in the context of the highly competitive, rather unstable system of absolutist states.[33] Absolutism marked the beginning of a process of consolidating state boundaries, as the state came to refer to a distinctive geopolitical area coterminous with linguistically and culturally homogeneous subject populations.[34] While the operations of a central administrative apparatus were at the heart of this development, they also served to undermine absolutism itself. The drive to establish and control a state-wide monetary system was crucial in this respect, deepening the fiscal penetration of the state apparatus to the extent of actually cutting into absolutist institutions. This was largely a consequence of external pressures, most significantly the industrialization of war,[35] which generated socio-economic forces sufficient to undermine the over-hangs from traditional state forms.[36] Increasing and increasingly technological military power required both administrative efficiency and political legitimacy. An efficient tax system could not be organized or sustained by coercion, necessitating the clear separation of standing armies oriented outwards and civil police oriented inwards. Internal pacification was a condition for the state's capacity to withstand fiscal pressures generated by the industrialization of war.[37]

It would none the less be mistaken to imagine that the industrialization of war exhaustively explains the infrastructural changes undertaken within absolutist states. The requirement of military integrity, of professionalizing an efficient army, cannot seriously be regarded as an end in itself, however intimately connected to the survival of absolutist states themselves. The military and fiscal policies pursued were more positive and more ideologically embroiled, less politically plain, than this.

The military and infrastructural consolidation of states as distinctive geopolitical entities with clearly demarcated territorial boundaries was closely related to the emergence of such states as commercial agents in their own right, replacing 'a close and complementary relation between territorial states and small but specialized commercial polities (most of them republics or city-states)'.[38] To some extent, the pressures to enhance international trading relations were the self-same pressures for military survival as those underpinning fiscal reorganization. The latter process was in itself a vital spur to new and widening trade relations which both generated and were further enhanced by states being 'increasingly drawn into the regulation of more precise, technical, yet more universal property rights'.[39] The novel alliance between military strength and international trade which emerged during the absolutist period also relied on a shift in the conceptualization of the relationship between politics and markets.[40] As the process of internal pacification prised the idea of the citizen apart from its association with the warrior-citizen possessing the inalienable right to bear arms,[41] so the idea of national strength was redefined: 'Survival for a state now required not only wealth and power, but also the ability to keep wage costs firmly under control'.[42] But this process of redefinition cannot be characterized as a straightforward separation of politics and markets as domains of social action. On the contrary, the interrelationship of military, commercial and fiscal measures underlying the territorial consolidation of absolutist states rested on the spatial identity of states and markets within the geopolitical boundaries undergoing consolidation. As Pocock suggests, 'modern politics and economics arose and flourished together'.[43]

At the root of the administrative demands placed on absolutist states were straightforward problems of cost related to military expenditure. Mann, for example, discerns a cycle during the absolutist period in which expenditure and borrowing increased sharply during war, followed closely by debt repayment in the immediate postwar period.[44] He contends that the pattern and magnitude of military expenditure was a 'precipitating factor' in the 'secular trend' towards the extension of the infrastructural penetration of the central state apparatus, and thus an important step towards the formation of the nation-state. These developments went hand-in-hand with a clear structural shift in class relations, a 'transition from broadly 'feudal' to capitalist economies'.[45] Significantly, this is indicated by the identity of state creditors. As Giddens notes, the nature and extent of state borrowing for military ends was such that 'princely rulers of post-feudal Europe all became dependent on loans from bankers, who in conjunction with entrepreneurial mercenary commanders, were the makers and breakers of monarchs'.[46] Not only absolutist states but an expanding capitalist class comprising elements of the landowning aristocracy and an entrepreneurial and mercantile bourgeoisie depended on military organization and infrastructural integrity for their survival.[47] This combination of administrative and infrastructural reorganization underpinned the process whereby states gradually monopolized and centralized the production, validation and supply of money and credit.[48] For example, the establishment of the Bank of England in 1695 provided a significant advantage for England over France in garnering financial resources for military ends, the Bank of France being set up nearly a century later, in 1791.

The institutionalization of monetary and credit systems centrally administered by state agencies therefore stemmed from a series of trends and pressures of considerable historical complexity, comprising territorial centralization of the nation-state, the expansion of capitalist enterprise, the enlargement of states' military strength, and the intensification of their fiscal administration. To this extent, the historical importance of the transition from absolutism to the nation-states system for the development of monetary systems can be readily established. Significantly, however, it is difficult to characterize this process in political or economic terms alone. This observation is borne out by Mann's analysis of the geopolitical developments under discussion here. The state's role in monetary administration can be interpreted in terms of two 'opposite causal patterns' entailing, first, a flow of power upwards from civil society towards the state, and second, a reverse tendency extending from the state downwards into civil society.[49] The seizure and utilization by absolutist states and subsequently nation-states of the privileges of issuing and validating money in response to military-related fiscal pressures would seem to fall under the second of these patterns. But the state's seizure of control over the production and validation of money can be addressed just as convincingly in terms of the depoliticization of economic relations which, in Mann's view at least, characterized even absolutism.[50] Depoliticization in this context refers to the fact that the institutionalization of a stable and politically neutral monetary system provided critical infrastructural support for capitalist enterprise. For this reason, the state's monopoly over the money supply was no straightforward political innovation. It none the less seems clear from this discussion that there is a significant geopolitical dimension in the operation of money. It is rather less clear whether the relationship between money and the modern state is one of functional necessity as well as obvious historical importance. The arguments examined here provide no grounds for regarding the fiduciary assurances provided by a politically legitimate state as indispensable for the operation of money. The geopolitical dimension in the historical development of money rests on the state's fiscal duties arising from the need to secure territorial integrity around a centralized administrative authority. Political legitimacy is undeniably an issue here, but is by no means straightfor- wardly connected to the fiduciary character of money-tokens. There remains no compelling reason to conclude that the state plays an essential role in the validation and administration of money. It remains open to question, then, whether money could be denationalized.

The Denationalization of Money

In order to understand Hayek's recommendations for denationalizing money, it is essential to grasp the economic reasoning behind them. For Hayek, the organization of economic relations within a market structure, with money operating as a kind of universal joint, is not more efficient in any straightforward sense than alternative modes of economic organiza- tion such as central planning. Markets are not exactly technically superior, a notion which would imply that they are some sort of invention, but evolve in so far as they help overcome basic shortcomings in the capacity of any society rationally to co-ordinate the complex range of factors, relationships and decisions which characterize any large-scale economic structure. Human beings are, in short, too ignorant to achieve such co-ordination themselves, in the sense both that they lack sufficient information and that they are not clever enough. It is for this reason that Hayek advocates the abandonment of any notion of common human purpose in both economic theory and economic action. Only by narrowly pursuing our own interests as individuals, he suggests, will a form of social order emerge - the market - which is capable of co-ordinating economic relations right across society. For this reason, market order is the unintended consequence of the rational actions of individuals, having nothing to do with grand human design.[51] Before moving on to explore the implications of this thesis, it is worth noting how his abstract conception of market order can be directly applied to institutions as well as individuals. Economic actors are in Hayek's view no more than decision-making units, even though his more qualified approach to the economic behaviour of individuals complicates this somewhat. When addressing decision-making units in this way, it is immaterial whether one is discussing individuals or firms: both are economic actors, both are deemed to be seeking to maximize gain, and both have the status of individual transactors where monetary analysis is concerned. This compression of individuals and firms is essential to Hayek's argument that money should be denationalized.

In Hayek's view, the role of the state as both political authority and monetary administrator involves a fundamental conflict of interests. He is particularly critical of the practice of central banking. By providing lender-of-last-resort facilities to the banking system, central banks reduce the incentive to private banks to exercise restraint in their lending policies and other decisions. Moreover, a central bank monopoly over issue of the legal-tender currency provides the government, in instances where it controls the central bank, with an easy but damaging means of resolving political problems over the short term.[52] For Hayek, 'governments will of course occasionally be forced to borrow from the public to meet unforeseen requirements,' yet 'it is highly undesirable in any circumstances that these funds should be provided by the creation of additional money'.[53] The monopoly over money can too easily provide a shield for inept government. But the relationship between money and the state is unnecessary, having nothing to do with the objective of monetary stability. Indeed, the concept of monetary sovereignty itself is based on flawed reasoning: the 'superstition that it is necessary for government ... to declare what is to be money' stems from the common conviction that the state or sovereign has always been engaged in the minting of coins, which springs ultimately from the 'naïve belief that such a tool as money must have been 'invented' and given to us by some original inventor'.[54]

Hayek argues that monetary stability cannot be maintained over the long term unless governments abrogate their monopoly over money. He advocates a system of private note issue in which currencies are not confined to a country or region of issue. Not only the stability but the survival of particular forms of money, under such circumstances, would depend on sustaining the confidence of transactors themselves because alternatives would always be available to them. Issuing banks would therefore be compelled in their own interests as private firms to exercise caution in their issuing and lending policies. The failure of one bank need not lead to the failure of the entire system. Freedom of issue suggests on the contrary an evolutionary pattern, with fluctuations in the value of notes leading not to damaging price inflation but rather to their eventual withdrawal from circulation. Hayek's denationalization thesis is informed by his approach to economic behaviour in markets. He asserts that if institutions maximize on their own behalf, this will ensure that monetary order is sustained without having to resort to the monopoly power of the state.

Although a free banking system does not necessarily entail the institution of a transnational system of competing currencies but relates principally to the cheapness of credit, White's study of free banking helps to illuminate some of the institutional processes on which the arrangements envisaged by Hayek would depend. White proposes the establishment of a banking system in which competing banks issue their own notes, a system he likens to Scottish banking prior to the Scottish Banking Act of 1845.[55] His argument, like that of Hayek, is based on the assumption that it is in the interests of profit-seeking banks to co-operate through the clearing mechanism, for the saleability of a bank-note increases in proportion to the number of banks with which it is redeemable.[56] For this reason, he contends, state agencies need have no major role in the regulation of banks. Should a problem of over-issue arise within the system, it would be checked automatically within the clearing system: other banks redeeming the notes of the over-issuing bank would enjoy positive clearings against the offending bank, while the latter would experience a proportionate loss of reserves.[57] It would therefore be in the interests of the individual bank not to over-issue, subject as this is 'to an unacceptably high risk of exhausting its liquid reserve and consequently defaulting its note obligations'.[58] Even where all banks over-issue, White contends, the clearing system could cope as long as something like a gold standard is reintroduced. In the case of simultaneous over-issue within a particular banking region, for example the nation-state, there would be a drain of reserves out of the system due to the subsequent cheapness of specie there. Where over-issue occurs on a worldwide basis, involving all banking systems, there will be a drain inwards 'to meet the public's desired specie holdings'.[59]

Both Hayek and White seek to undercut some of the more cherished assumptions on which the monetary policies of all Western governments are now based. Their own and similar arguments have nevertheless had some political impact, and could even be described as populist.[60] The reasons for this are numerous, but principally concern the cyclical and sometimes not so cyclical demonstration that Western governments seem unable to control inflation. Conceptually, the persuasiveness of the arguments of Hayek and White owes much to their internal consistency, based as this is upon a narrow set of assumptions about a single decision-making unit. Yet this is also the main analytical weakness of their approach. Even for firms, the idea that to maximize constitutes a straightforward way to make decisions regarding specific economic actions is difficult to sustain. The proposition has even less credibility in respect of individuals; indeed, it must either be watered down and broadened out to the point of becoming a truism (i.e. we all want what is best), or else showered with exceptions to the point of having only minor analytical significance, more trouble than it is worth. In other words, it is the form of reasoning behind the proposals of Hayek and White, less than their arguments about the practices of specific institutions, which is in greatest need of clarification and critique. I shall be attempting to provide precisely this in subsequent chapters.

Hayek may well be correct to suggest that the denationalization of money should be interpreted as a threat more to the political machinations of modern governments than to the stability of money itself. Discussion of the historical process by which the modern state came to assume a monopoly over the issue and control of money and credit certainly bears this out. It is somewhat less clear, however, that Hayek's own proposals suggest a valid alternative either in practice or in principle. First, the political and economic assumptions behind the proposals are questionable in themselves. Whether concerning the independence of central banks or the prudence of private banks, the polemical force of Hayek's argument derives from his adherence to an economic logic which, as I argued in chapter 1, cannot be made to work without the addition of some highly debatable empirical suppositions. I shall examine and criticize some of these in later chapters. Second, even if Hayek's proposals could be implemented within the institutional structure of banking as it operates in the present day, this provides no grounds on which to assume that the majority of individuals who actually handle money would respond with quite the hard-headed rationality on which the proposals so unquestioningly depend. There is a significant fiduciary dimension to the transaction of money of which economists and sociologists alike seem to have only a minimum of understanding. The relationship between money and trust, if this is what the fiduciary dimension amounts to, has no conceptual foundation in monetary theory, although the social theorists I move on to discuss in the next two chapters at least provide some indication of how this problem might be overcome. Knapp and Weber reveal an intuitive grasp of this question but ultimately confuse the issue by fudging what are, as they see it, separate political and economic aspects of the operation of monetary networks. Hayek certainly acknowledges the significance of the fiduciary dimension of monetary transaction, but lingers no further on the issue, dismissing the sense of trust implicit in the handling of money as an irritating (because irrational) superstition. Historical discussion of the connections between money and the modern state, finally, establishes very clearly that this relationship is significant from an administrative and fiscal point of view, but provides only a preliminary guide to assessing its symbolic significance for how individuals perceive the money they routinely accept, use, store and yearn for. The question of monetary sovereignty simply cannot be reduced to a discussion of the validating role of modern states or to the practices of modern government. Money's symbolic importance in society raises a whole set of questions concerning its relationship with the entire fabric of modern culture. Until these are addressed, discussion of the relationship between money and the modern state can proceed no further.

3

Cultural Aspects of the Mature Money Economy

The role of the modern state in producing and validating money depends not on technically efficient policy-making alone but on trust. For this reason, legal theories of money raise questions about the sociological conditions of monetary transaction which cannot be answered by reference to the state alone. As I argued in chapter 2, there is a fiduciary dimension to the transaction of money which has yet to be fully grasped in monetary theory. To overcome this weakness would require discussion not only of the nature of economic action and of the relationship between money and the state, but of the social relationships which bind monetary networks together. This raises important questions about the cultural framework in which monetary transaction takes place. In particular, there is a need to establish whether the expansion and universalization of monetary exchange in modern society has depended not simply on particular economic and political conditions, but on a set of human dispositions and relationships peculiar to modern culture. Nowhere is this issue more extensively examined than in the work of Georg Simmel. Although he denies seeking to contribute directly to monetary theory, Simmel's study of cultural aspects of the mature money economy contains many insights which other social theorists, even those working after Simmel, have failed to grasp or extend.

The originality of Simmel's work on money derives less from the historical felicity of his analysis, which has frequently been a source of criticism, than from its breadth of focus. He subjects money to a range of associations, many of them analogical, considerably beyond the scope of conventional monetary theory. Where the analysis of modern culture is concerned, Simmel's work is less restrictive than many social theories of modernity, such as those of Tönnies and Weber, for he does not assume that all social relationships involving money have a rational and calculating character. Simmel's work is also important in epistemological terms. Money is rarely addressed by social theorists as intrinsically interesting, and tends to be treated instead as a convenient exemplar for discussion of broader issues and debates in which economic theories of money are largely taken at face-value. Although Simmel's treatment of money appears on a superficial level to fall into this category, the methodological principles underlying his study, particularly his definition of money, are instructive for monetary theory in general.[1] They enable him to treat money as a symbol which expresses varied and sometimes contradictory aspects of modern culture in a unique way. For this reason, Simmel's arguments provide an important indication of how a systematic approach to the study of money in sociology might proceed. In this chapter, I shall explore three main areas of his work: first, his account of the relationship between human agency and monetary transaction, which serves as a basis for his theory of value; second, his analysis of the pivotal role of money within modern culture, especially in prising apart what he calls subjective and objective culture; and third, the epistemological principles behind Simmel's 'philosophy' of money, particularly their implications for the analysis of money in sociology.

God and the Theory of Value

For Simmel, money's value does not derive simply from its status as a commodity. By definition, money's distinctive features are not those it shares with other commodities but those it does not. The most prominent of these features is the scope of its exchangeability with other objects. In economic terms, money enables goods to be valued relative to each other. While goods may fluctuate in their relationship with each other, money provides a constant standard by which they can be valued, and an abstract intermediary through which they can be exchanged. In this sense, money is a 'stable pole' which 'contrasts with the eternal movements, fluctuations and equations of the objects its represents in exchange'.[2] But money's abstract qualities, its constancy and stability relative to other values, stem paradoxically from its character as the *actus parus*,[3] as a medium which, through exchange, seems to remain in continual motion. This dual quality of constancy and flux has a philosophical analogy in Simmel's work whereby money, which in economic terms expresses 'nothing but the relativity of things that constitute value',[4] embodies the principle of relativism. It is for this reason that he regards money as having cultural significance as well as economic importance. Money's omnipotence relative to other values excites feelings psychologically analogous to the worship of God. Just as 'the essence of the notion of God is that all diversities and contradictions in the world achieve a unity in him',[5] so with money, 'the relativity of things is the only absolute, and in this respect money is indeed the strongest and most immediate symbol'.[6] In epistemological terms, these self-same qualities of money lend to it a unique capacity to serve as a philosophical exemplar. This is why Simmel warns against addressing his analysis only in the literal terms of economic theory. He provides a historical account of how money achieves this abstract and timeless status. This can only be fully understood in terms of his theory of value.

Although Simmel does not really formulate a systematic theory of anything, he at least comes close to this when attempting to explain the constitution of economic value. He rejects the labour theory of value, and bases his own theory on the analysis of social forms which is central to his approach to sociology more generally. One might say that forms of interaction are foundational to Simmel's work in the same way that systems of action underpin the work of Parsons.[7] Simmel characterizes value, like money, in philosophical as well as economic terms. Value is 'in a sense the counterpart to being ... comparable to being as a comprehensive form and category of the world view'.[8] The process by which human beings ascribe value to things is part of a mental process by which they compartmentalize and make sense of the social and natural world around them. By nature, we employ a series of formal categories into which the contents of the world can be organized in the mind. Value is one such formal category. For Simmel, value is intimately connected to desire. But the value we place on things is not simply a function of how much we desire them. The things which have greatest value tend to be those which are most difficult to acquire. In other words, we value things which seem beyond our reach, which resist our desire to possess them.[9] Simmel's analysis of value is in this sense derived from a particular view of the relationship between human beings and the world they inhabit; or in his terms, the relationship between subjects and objects.

In explaining the nature and significance of value in these terms, Simmel draws a contrast between the orientation of human beings towards their surroundings when they are in a conscious as opposed to a pre-conscious state. In a state of pre-consciousness when the individual has an infantile view of the world, need and desire tend to be aimless. No distinction is established in the mind between subject and object, or self and other: 'consciousness is exclusively concerned with satisfaction and pays no attention to its bearer on one side or its object on the other'.[10] Simmel equates this mode of experience with aesthetic pleasure.[11] But the seamlessness is disrupted as soon as desire begins to be frustrated. A distance is gradually imposed between the subject and object which creates potential for friction between them. Without such friction, the concept of value would be meaningless, for our desires would meet with no resistance. It would also be impossible to distinguish one thing from another, for this only becomes possible for us when our desires go unfulfilled. For economics, this process explains the formation of the category of value. Philosophically, it accounts for the origins of the dualism between subjects and objects. It is because humans think in terms of this dualism that they need to place formal categories on the world around them and organize its content. This process therefore marks, for Simmel, the 'birth in experience' of form.

It is perhaps inevitable that Simmel's theory of value has often been interpreted in psychological terms, even as non-sociological. The concepts of distance and resistance at the heart of the theory certainly bear comparison with the marginal utility theorem in neoclassical economics. Reflecting this, Smelt has argued that Simmel's theory of value simply means that 'the value of an object is what an individual will sacrifice for it'.[12] But to reduce Simmel's arguments to this basic principle requires some effort at misreading them.[13] Indeed, Simmel himself categorically rejects the idea that value is subjective, merely a product of desire. To ascribe value to an object is not simply to desire it. This much is clear from his contention that, by definition, things are valued which are difficult to acquire. When an object is valued, its distance from the subject is not simply confirmed but becomes an integral part of how that object is defined: its value is one of its features. When we value an object we place 'the content of our desire outside ourselves'.[14] For this reason, value should be regarded neither as an intrinsic property of objects nor as reducible to the desire of subjects, but as a 'third category'.[15] There are two further respects in which a psychological interpretation of Simmel's theory of value is unsustainable. First, Simmel makes clear in his analysis of the relationship between subjects and objects that valuation is not simply the product of mental processes but is bound up with the way individuals interact with the world around them. This is as true of the category of value as it is of the other forms of interaction in Simmel's sociology: as Levine notes, these 'inform not only the cognitive realm, but any and all dimensions of human experience'.[16] Second, Simmel's discussion of value is very clearly located in the context of his examination of the social institution of exchange. Possession is the objective of desire, after all, and 'a value has to be offered in order to acquire a value'.[17] But this does not mean that the social act of exchange is based solely on desire or on the drive to optimize utility, as in neoclassical economics.[18] In Simmel's view, exchange is the fundamental condition of social life, for 'interaction between individuals is the starting point of all social formations'.[19] The sociological status of the category of value must be interpreted in terms of what Coser refers to as Simmel's dialectical method, where 'the socialized individual always remains in a dual relation toward society: he is incorporated within it and yet stands against it'.[20] On the one hand, the individual transactor is bound to the sphere of exchange, subject to its objective mechanisms of operation.[21] Value is intrinsically connected to a network of transactions organized around a price mechanism.[22] Anyone seeking to acquire a commodity can participate in exchange only 'as a representative or executor of these determinants [of value] which lie outside' the actions of individuals themselves.[23] Here, Simmel refers to what appears to be, in all but name, a market. On the other hand, individuals are never completely powerless, for their own actions and decisions are essential to the reproduction of the network over time. Significantly, the idea that individuals have volition, that they can and do make choices which inform their actions, is at the heart of Simmel's approach, even though he regards such actions as socially mediated: 'man is both social link and being for himself, both product of society and life from an autonomous centre'.[24]

Simmel's approach to money follows on directly from his theory of value. He argues that money's emergence in society is the end-point of an evolutionary process driven by the goal-directed activities of individuals. As the discussion of value suggests, he regards human beings as purposive by nature, pursuing goals with a conscious intent which distinguishes them from all other beings.[25] Human inventiveness is such that, through history, we will develop tools in pursuit of increasingly complex goals, each helping to further eradicate the distance between ourselves and the world around us. As the abstract expression of the interrelationship of all values, money is the ultimate such tool, the 'purest reification of means, a concrete instrument which is absolutely identical with its abstract concept; it is a pure instrument'.[26] To this extent, there are clear parallels between Simmel's analysis and the economic accounts of the transition from barter to monetary exchange examined in chapter 1. The idea of purposive action seems broadly similar to the concept of rationality. Moreover, the terms used by Simmel to define money as a pure instrument suggest that money emerges in society solely as a consequence of its technical superiority as a tool of economic exchange. But any inference of links with neoclassical theories of money must again be treated with caution. There is a clear fiduciary dimension to Simmel's analysis of money which has no place in neoclassical accounts. It is as a 'claim upon society' that money can serve as a pure instrument of exchange,[27] expressing the abstract creditor–debtor relationship which spans the network of actual and potential transactors. This relationship ultimately derives from the status of exchange itself as the 'original form' of social life. This suggests that the emergence of money in society, particularly its universalization in modern societies, cannot be fully explained by reference to goal-directed activities alone; or, in other words, to a process of rationalization. By far the more significant part of Simmel's study of money is provided by his exploration of the relationship between the mature money economy and modern culture.

Mammon and the Objectification of Culture

As a contribution to the analysis of modernity, Simmel's study of money has a twofold significance: first, as a description of contemporary life in Berlin whose 'seismographic accuracy' was celebrated by Gadamer;[28] and second, as an account of the divergence of objective and subjective culture whose application reaches beyond the temporal and spatial parameters of Berlin during the 1890s to embrace distinctive features of modernity. It is important not to be misled into regarding Simmel's focus on minutiae of social life as a fanciful obsession with trivia. The substantive historical theme running through his study concerns the social and cultural preconditions and consequences of the emergence of the mature money economy. He argues that modern life is distinguished above all by its disconnected character. Money is the most powerful, all-pervasive expression of this. Simmel's preoccupation with apparently minor details of social life, with fleeting relationships, is entirely consistent with the analytical primacy given to forms of interaction in his social theory. He does not suggest that social theory should be confined to the examination of such details, but explicitly acknowledges the importance of 'structures of a higher order': for example, institutions such as states and trade unions, and the structural properties of society as manifested in social class and the division of labour.[29] He is no less explicit, however, in contending that the analysis of social structures cannot provide a penetrating route into the study of modern society. He makes this point in a systematic way in the essay 'Sociology of the senses', where he characterizes modern society as a web whose 'delicate, invisible threads ... are woven between one person and another'.[30] But Simmel's approach can only be fully understood in the context of his argument that the fragmentation of social life has increased and intensified in modern society. This substantive argument lies behind his preoccupation with fortuitous, momentary and apparently less consequential aspects of social and economic life, for it is in precisely these that the essence of modern life consists.

The central theme in Simmel's characterization of modern society concerns, as I have just said, the fragmentation of subjective culture in the face of the increasing solidity and predominance, but also the increasing detachment, of objective culture.[31] This is what he means when referring to the 'tragedy' of modern culture. The most distinctive features of the objectification of culture are expressed, in Simmel's view, by the emergence of the mature money economy. In economic terms, his explanation for this process is neither startling nor original. He argues that an increasingly complex division of labour is one of the principal causes of the standardization of monetary exchange and the development of markets centred around the price mechanism. But he is more concerned with the consequences of these developments from the point of view of individuals, for they are at the root of the fragmentation of subjective life in modern society. The emergence of the mature money economy has generated new forms of human association, 'uniting people while excluding everything personal and specific'.[32] The division of labour alienates individuals both as workers and consumers. Echoes of Marx are unmistakable in Simmel's contention that 'exchange relations become increasingly complicated and mediated with the result that the economy necessarily establishes more and more relationships and obligations *that are not directly reciprocal*'.[33] The reference to reciprocity here is indicative of the priority given to forms of interaction in Simmel's social theory. His analysis of alienation differs from that of Marx in so far as Simmel focuses above all on interaction, on the relationship between subject and subject, while Marx's approach is rooted in a philosophical anthropology chiefly concerned with the interaction between humans and nature, the relationship between subject and object. To contend that transacting relationships and obligations are established within the mature money economy which are 'not directly reciprocal' is to imply that relations between subjects have been distorted. More specifically, the reciprocal relationship at the heart of the monetary exchange relationship has been compromised. The significance of this can be understood by recalling Simmel's characterization of money as a pure instrument. He argues that money's abstract quality enables it, in principle at least, to be freely manipulated according to the will of its holder: 'money alone, unlike one-sidedly determined objects, does not determine its future use and fructification'.[34] When Simmel argues that exchange relationships within the mature money economy are 'not directly reciprocal', this suggests that the exercise of the human will through money, the empowerment of individuals by money, has been restrained. It remains to be established, then, exactly how the process of restraint occurs.

It can be inferred from Simmel's arguments that the inherent reciprocity of exchange relationships involving money in modern society is compromised in three ways: by conditions stemming from outside the transacting relationship; by an asymmetry arising within the relationship itself; and, to adopt Simmel's own terminology, because the 'inner life' of individuals has been diminished, distorted and fragmented. Simmel discusses all three conditions, although the third is most significant for purposes of my argument here. The first condition arises by virtue of the institutional framework in which money is transacted. Individuals are restrained in their use of money by regulations governing its use, many of them enforced by legal sanctions. From the point of view of monetary theory, it is vital to understand the nature of these regulations, particularly the extent to which they shape uses and perceptions of money in different societies. They are largely a function of the role of state agencies and banks in the administration of money. The second condition is characterized by Simmel in terms of the risks which confront us whenever we use money. As I argued in the Introduction, the liquidity of money can be most accurately addressed not in terms of a flow but as a series of emissions. This is a vitally important distinction from the point of view of transactors. Money empowers its holder by virtue of its purchasing-power. But to use that power is also to dispense with it. The perceived level of risk undertaken in dispensing with money's purchasing-power will obviously vary according to wealth and income. But it will also be a function of the propensity to consume. As I suggested in chapter 1, this, under the guise of the demand for money, has been a source of considerable puzzlement to economists. Whenever money is not being used for the purchase of absolute necessities, the decision to use it depends on a range of psychological factors which, in studies of the behaviour of consumers and investors, tend to be subsumed by concepts such as rational expectation, confidence and optimism. Simmel's study of the relationship between money and modern culture does not exactly resolve some of the more problematic features of monetary analysis in this context, but he does at least widen and deepen the scope of an enquiry which is of considerable need of development. To understand this point more fully, the third source of the distortion of modern exchange relations must be examined in greater detail.

Significantly, Simmel rejects any idea that the asymmetry which often characterizes the transaction of money as a result of differential risk arises from features of money itself. Money has in principle no intrinsic connection with asymmetries of wealth and power in society. In practice, the connection derives from forces and conditions which shape the exchange relationships involving money.[35] To this extent, Simmel moves no further than the political economists discussed in chapter 1. Yet in focusing on the consequences of the objectification of modern culture for the inner life of individuals, he serves as a constructive guide to understanding how the attitudes, perceptions and dispositions which inform how individuals actually handle money are shaped. Indeed, this is to go to the heart of his study of money. I have already pointed out that Simmel, by defining money as a pure instrument, emphasizes the freedom of choice which the possession of money can provide. This freedom has important psychological consequences. In modern society, paradoxically, it has diminished rather than nourished human creativity. Simmel does not suggest, as might have been expected, that the mature money economy places constraints around the freedom of individuals to take economic decisions for themselves. While this may be true with regard to many aspects of modern economic life, it could not be further from the truth where money is concerned. By virtue of its abstract nature, irrespective of the context in which it is used, money empowers its holder. This can have positive as well as negative consequences. It is not a question of freedom as such, but rather how that freedom is used. Simmel sets out this argument by juxtaposing 'freedom *from* something' with the 'liberty *to do* something'.[36] The freedom of choice provided by the possession of money is, in modern society, closest to the former, and 'may be compared with the fate of the insecure person who has forsworn his Gods and whose newly acquired 'freedom' only provides the opportunity for making an idol out of any fleeting value'.[37] Here, then, Simmel switches attention from the fact that money empowers its holder in principle to the actual substance of the relationship between money and human volition within modern society. He asks exactly what purposes are being expressed when we use money. For Simmel, the unique capacity of money to empower its holder has been the main source of the fragmentation of subjective life. In the mature money economy, money's empowering features have compromised that very freedom which money itself promises to embrace. Monetary freedom has in this sense been alienating. It is a freedom which is empty of content, having only negative connotations linked to the removal of constraint: 'In itself, freedom is an empty form which becomes effective, alive and valuable only through the development of other life-contents'.[38] These life-contents will be stunted whenever money is treated as an end in itself. This is exactly what has happened in modern society. Money, as the ultimate economic instrument, has been turned into the ultimate economic goal. It has imploded in on itself as mammon.

Simmel encapsulates more powerfully than Marx the ambivalence of monetary transaction within modern society. Money empowers its holder by virtue of its anonymity as a pure instrument. Money is able to serve as an extension of the human will within transaction, adjusting 'with equal ease to every form and every purpose that the will wishes to imprint it with'.[39] The possession of money is in this sense liberating, giving 'to consciousness that free scope, that ominous self-extension through an unresistant medium, that self-absorption of all possibilities without doing violence or denying reality, all of which are part of any aesthetic enjoyment'.[40] But in a succinct expression of the double-edged character of modern cultural life, Simmel identifies precisely this freedom as the source of alienation within the mature money economy. The empowering features of money, rather than simply being an instrument of desire, are the very basis of its status as an object of desire.[41] This is why, in Simmel's view, the expansion of the money economy has been accompanied by a greater tendency among owners of property to sell, to turn assets into money.[42] As a consequence of this, the tempo of economic life, specifically the rate at which property changes hands through monetary exchange, inevitably rises. But there is a further, qualitative development within this scenario which has fundamental significance for Simmel's analysis of modern culture. Objects are sold and resold 'which are not meant to be sold'.[43] These objects, such as 'businesses and factories, works of art and collections, landed property, rights and positions of all kinds', have a quality as possessions which is anathema to the impersonality and anonymity of money. They 'have the character of permanent possessions and seem to be destined to be tied to the personality rather than to break loose from it in a rash exchange'.[44] The satisfaction which can be derived from such possessions has been overpowered by the intoxicating freedom provided by the possession of money. But because that freedom is entirely lacking in content or direction, our fascination with it can lead only to profound dissatisfaction which, for Simmel, 'explains why our age, which, on the whole, certainly possesses more freedom than any previous one, is unable to enjoy it properly ... why the freedom of liberalism has brought about so much instability disorder and dissatisfaction'.[45]

It is important to realize that Simmel does not formulate this thesis in so one-sided a manner as to let go of the ambivalence which runs through his characterization of modernity. He resists depicting forces bound up with the development of the money economy which are so powerful and all-encompassing as to render the individual helpless beneath them. His characterization of money itself as a pure instrument is crucial here, suggesting that the fragmentation of the will is neither inevitable nor intrinsically connected to money *per se*. There always exists a possibility, however remote, that transactors will be able to realize the potential for self-expression given to them by the possession of money.[46] Simmel allows for the fact that we can and do express choices through money, however limited or ill-informed those choices might be. Unlike Marx, he refuses to predispose individuals to actions and decisions which are merely a reflection of social and economic forces over which they have virtually no control and of which they have even less understanding. He more subtly suggests that monetary freedom cannot be fully exploited if the inner lives of the parties to an exchange relationship have been distorted and fragmented, leaving them unable constructively to fill the vacuum money provides. Constraint of the will is in this sense an act of self-constraint.[47] This is not simply a question of one party or class exercising power and privilege over another. Simmel's idea of alienation has a more pervading, inclusive character than this. The sense of distortion and fragmentation in modern culture is most powerfully expressed, at all levels of society, by a craving for the very freedom and absence of constraint which is subsequently squandered, for the 'lack of something definite at the centre of the soul impels us to search for momentary satisfaction in ever-new stimulations, sensations and external activities'.[48] The increasingly empty, meaningless and transitional character of exchange relationships within the mature monetary economy has had fundamental consequences for the entire fabric of modern culture. Yet even here, ambivalence is at the core of Simmel's analysis. On the one hand, the proliferation of monetary exchange results in growing impersonal dependence between individuals: 'we are remarkably independent of every *specific* member of this society, because his significance for us has been transferred to the one-sided objectivity of his contribution, which can be just as easily produced by any number of other people with different personalities with whom we are connected only by an interest that can be completely expressed in money terms'.[49] On the other hand, it is precisely this condition which, in principle at least, 'is the most favourable situation for bringing about inner independence, the feeling of individual self-sufficiency', although 'mere isolation from others does not yet imply such a positive attitude'.[50]

Simmel does not confine his analysis of the alienating consequences of the money economy to exchange relationships. He also contends that the proliferation of monetary exchange has radically altered the relationship between human beings and nature, between subject and object. Simmel approaches this theme in terms of the division of labour, making the familiar point that production by several individuals prises the product away from the identity of the specific individual: 'Whenever our energies do not produce something which is a reflection of the total personality, then the proper relationship between subject and object is missing'.[51] He nevertheless characterizes the consequences of this in terms of exchange, reasserting the primacy of reciprocity in his social theory. There is, Simmel suggests, a direct logical relationship between the complex division of labour and the production of commodities for mass consumption, not merely because of factors of scale and quantity but also as a result of the impersonality of the production process and its inherent suitability for commodities widely exchanged: 'The broadening of consumption ... is dependent upon the growth of *objective* culture, since the more objective and impersonal an object is the better it is suited to more people'.[52] Simmel thereby implies that consumption has become the central economic activity within modern society. This raises the question, which I shall turn to in chapter 6, whether the so-called 'consumer society' often associated with the period after modernity is a particularly novel phenomenon, let alone, as many commentators have argued, a distinguishing feature of postmodernity.

A 'Philosophy' of Money?

Simmel's arguments have important epistemological implications for the approach to monetary analysis that I am seeking to develop in this book. His study suggests the need for a closer and more detailed interpretative analysis of the meanings imputed by transactors into the transactions in which they engage. Indeed, it is on this issue that his conceptualization of money is most constructive and insightful for the analysis of money in sociology. There are two reasons for this. First, his characterization of money as a pure instrument is abstract enough to ensure that this interpretative dimension is not foreclosed by presuppositions, arising from a theoretical understanding of the structural conditions under which money is transacted, about how individuals actually use money. This is precisely what happens in Marx's characterization of money in terms of capitalist relations of production: the freedom which money gives to its holder can only ever be illusory when addressed in Marx's terms, whereas Simmel enables such freedom to be addressed as real if not as absolute, at least in the context of actual transactions. Second, Simmel's examination of the consequences of the development of the money economy in terms of the objectification of culture, particularly the distanciation of subjective and objective culture, provides a theoretical framework with which such an interpretative analysis could at least begin.

Simmel places the act of exchange at the centre of his study of the ephemeral social relationships which define modern, and particularly urban, life. Perhaps this prevents him from undertaking a fuller analysis of the structural framework in which money is transacted in modern societies. But the epistemology behind his approach suggests that this is a charge he would have resisted. By no stretch of the imagination is Simmel's work reductivist. Such a contention would be credible only on the basis of lazy acceptance of the association of his sociology with symbolic interactionism. This is a distorted reading of his work which has remained virtually unchallenged for too long. Simmel's observations on the small scale make little sense without reference to what he calls the social totality. His analysis of the ambivalence of monetary freedom cannot be understood outside the context of his examination of the overarching cultural consequences of the development of the mature money economy. Indeed, the way he switches his analysis between localized, seemingly unique exchange relationships on the one hand and the social totality on the other suggests a means of reconciling detailed study of monetary transaction, of the role of human agency within monetary relations, with a theoretical understanding of the structural and systemic forces at play in the emission and regulation of money right across society. A reading of Simmel's work along these lines cannot of course ignore his apparent indifference towards money itself as an object of substantive sociological study. He claims to have embarked on the analysis of money only by virtue of its special suitability as an exemplar for a philosophical exploration of the objectification of culture.[53] Despite this, and without necessarily casting doubt on Simmel's analytical aims, it is possible to draw from his work a substantive analysis of the role of money in modern society. In particular, his characterization of the double-edged quality of money's empowerment of its holder reflects both the constraints and the opportunities generated by monetary transaction in modern society. Simmel's study is informed by his claim to be advancing a universalistic philosophy of money. His work none the less provides the basis for a thoroughgoing assessment of the links between money and modernity.

The first significant epistemological issue arising from Simmel's work concerns the relationship between production and exchange. To regard Simmel's work on money as constrained by the centrality he ascribes to exchange is to risk confining oneself to terms of reference which Simmel actually rejects. His approach to money can be readily distinguished from that of Marx given their respective characterization of exchange and production as the mainspring of economic activity. In contrast to Marx, Simmel views production as a form of exchange, specifically an exchange with nature. Moreover, he implies that exchange alone can generate value in so far as it leads to 'a surplus of satisfaction as compared to the situation before the action', seemingly irrespective of whether the act of exchange itself involves actual production.[54] In one sense, this is merely a shift of emphasis in Simmel's work which reflects his concern with the mature money economy rather than capitalism in the sense intended by Marx.[55] But more fundamental issues are at stake. While Marx regards production and exchange as separate points within a series of historically specific economic circuits centred around modes of production, Simmel addresses every act of exchange as a manifestation of the forms of interaction he regards as fundamental to social life itself. For Simmel, as I have suggested, the minimum condition for social life is not the relationship between subject and object but that between subject and subject, a relationship based on reciprocity.[56] For Marx, monetary transaction expresses relations of power because the institution of monetary exchange is built on the asymmetrical economic relations specific to capitalism. For Simmel, by contrast, monetary transaction involves power first and foremost because money itself empowers its holder, although it should be emphasized that he does not completely ignore the historical importance of the socio-economic relations in which transaction takes place. Indeed, in a number of ways Simmel's approach is more helpful as a guide to contemporary monetary analysis: for example, in the study of international monetary relations and the behaviour of individual consumers and investors. To be sure, Simmel's approach cannot be directly applied to the study of present-day monetary markets and financial institutions in the way that is obviously possible for an updated version of Marxist political economy, even though it seems reasonable to doubt whether the latter exercise could be seriously sustained. But in drawing out the sense in which money can empower individuals, Simmel provides a basis for a more precise interpretative approach than Marx to the perceptions transactors themselves hold of the nature and functions of money; and it is here, as I have already argued, that perhaps the greatest weakness of the contemporary political economy of money can be found. It is perhaps for this reason, in more general terms, that the monetary theories of Marx and Simmel might be regarded as complementary rather than as diametrically opposed. Frisby, for example, interprets Simmel's intention to 'construct a new storey beneath historical materialism' not as 'a *rejection* of historical materialism but ... a critical engagement with it ... preserving elements of its explanatory value'.[57] Frisby himself characterizes the relationship between Marx and Simmel by suggesting that the former focuses on objective, and the latter subjective, aspects of monetary transaction.[58]

This interpretation is certainly consistent with the derivation of each approach from a separate dimension of economic activity, but underestimates the potential importance of Simmel's work for supposedly objective features of monetary relations in the present day.

In analytical terms, Simmel's focus on exchange as the primary form of social and economic life, particularly his insistence on examining the consequences of alienation at this level, suggests the need to focus on the relationship between transactors in the process of monetary exchange, not merely on the properties of a broader-based monetary system. His work is not without its problems in this respect. He fails to provide a coherent analytical framework for assessing exactly how fleeting transacting relationships generate and sustain monetary networks, intersecting with financial institutions and state agencies. There is, in other words, a problem of scale in his work. It seems difficult, unless reference to some kind of transacting network is made, to align Simmel's historical thesis regarding the proliferation of the fleeting relationships of exchange within modern society - as generated by the expansion of the money economy - with the continuing requirement that, in order to operate at all, monetary networks must be bound up with institutions and social groups, in ways reinforced by various strategies, rules and sanctions, which enable such networks to be spatially and temporally extensive. A coherent and historically pertinent analysis of precisely how monetary networks are held together is essential. Simmel's study tends to lead away from, rather than help overcome, this difficulty, although, as I shall move on now to argue, his study is helpful for understanding the importance of the imaginative capacities of transactors as one aspect of the way in which monetary networks are generated and reproduced.

Simmel sets out the aims of his study by outlining objectives which 'lie on either side of the economic science of money'.[59] On the one hand, he seeks to formulate a philosophy of 'the conditions and connections of life in general' derived from a theory of cultural forms. On the other hand, he seeks to uncover 'the pre-conditions that, situated in mental states, in social relations and in the logical structure of reality and values, give money its meaning and its practical position',[60] which amounts to a substantive examination of the relationship between money and modern culture. Simmel's approach to money is in this sense twofold: 'The one part seeks to make the essence of money intelligible from the conditions and connections of life in general; conversely, the other part seeks to make the essence and organization of the latter intelligible from the effectiveness of money'.[61] The first of these aims plays a critical role in Simmel's theory of value. As for the second aim, his characterization of money must be understood in the light of his approach to the objectification of culture. There seems to be an uneasy alliance, in Simmel's study of money, between a universalistic theory of the objectification of culture and a historical analysis of the social and cultural consequences of the emergence of the money economy. The alliance is uneasy not because these projects are necessarily incompatible, but because Simmel seems reluctant to acknowledge the historical specificity of his analysis of the money economy. Consider, for example, his contention that the circulation of money is characterized by the 'fleeting relationships' of exchange. It is explicit within his portrayal of modern life that such relationships are the main distinguishing feature of the social fabric of modernity. Monetary transaction is addressed as their archetype. For this reason, it is difficult to accept that the links Simmel establishes between monetary transaction and the sociological characteristics of modern life are not causally significant, although exactly this is demanded by his philosophical aims. Simmel states that the objectification of value is integral to social life in any historical context whatsoever, arising from the fundamental fact that exchange is the condition of social life. It follows from this that the 'developed economy' is merely 'a special case of the general form of exchange'.[62] On closer examination, however, it is clear that Simmel does provide the basis for a systematic historical account of the roots and consequences of the money economy. Where his analysis takes the form of critique, for example in the discussion of style, historical references are quite explicit.[63]

That there is a tension between philosophical speculation and historical insight in Simmel's work can be demonstrated by reference to his characterization of money itself. He contends that money is capable of being completely manipulated by its holder, to the point of being coextensive with the will. Money presents to its holder, in principle at least, a pure instrument through which an almost limitless array of opportunities for its use is possible. On the face of it, to contend that money, as some kind of tool, has limitless possibilities for its use in principle is to say nothing at all. For example, a chess-piece does not, of itself, determine how it is to be used, but has the capacity to be moved in particular ways because of its subjection to a body of rules. Viewed in this way, money is not at all distinctive as an object of study. Perhaps this is the thinking behind Simmel's treatment of money as a philosophical exemplar, as a typical rather than distinctive phenomenon. Yet a different interpretation of his approach is possible. Unlike the chess-piece, the status of an abstract economic instrument is not an accidental feature[64] of money but its distinguishing characteristic. It is this which underpins the unique scope of its exchangeability. Money's status as a *pure* instrument does not derive from its character as an economic instrument but sets it apart from other objects of exchange. If money is yearned for and fetishized in the way Simmel suggests, this is precisely because of characteristics it does not share with other objects, because of an abstractness and utility which is definitive of money alone. Viewed in this way, money is not typical at all: it is inconceivable that Simmel could have written such an extensive study, so replete with philosophical analogies, about anything else.

The epistemological status of Simmel's arguments should none the less be clearly understood. His definition of money as a pure instrument is idealized: by which I mean not that his observations are imaginary but that he is more concerned with the idea of money than with the technical features of specific monetary forms. There can be little doubt that no monetary form exists or has ever existed which matches Simmel's definition. The scope of exchangeability of any monetary form is conditioned by specific institutional and geopolitical conditions. Empirically, there exist clear and specifiable limits to the spatial and temporal extensiveness of the circulation of any monetary instrument. The most which can be said about modern monetary forms is that they are 'a set of partial mediums of exchange with the appearance of generality'.[65] Moreover, in no society past or present has money been acceptable for any kind of exchange whatsoever: the proverb that there are some things money cannot buy has some truth. But given the aims of Simmel's study, his essentialist characterization of money as a pure instrument should be seen as a source of strength rather than weakness. The symbolic power of money as Simmel describes it stems not from detailed understanding of the technical features of specific monetary forms but from a series of associations based on the idea of money, of what it is and what it can do. It is not enough to dismiss these associations as irrational or insignificant. Simmel's whole point is that they have had a shattering impact on modern culture, generating a pattern of practices and dispositions within economic life which are real because they are consequential. In other words, our ideas about money are intrinsically connected to how we use it, to our propensity to spend, invest, save or hoard the money we have. These ideas, as I shall discuss in the second part of this book, are linked institutionally with the agencies responsible for the administration of money, to the question of trust. In this respect, it does not essentially matter for example whether the belief that the state should be responsible for validating money is technically correct: if the belief is sufficiently widespread, it is significant enough to disrupt manoeuvres to denationalize money or embark on monetary union, for it will affect how money is actually used. This is a feature peculiar to monetary networks, integral to their fiduciary character. It is a feature which will always overwhelm monetary theories based merely on the force of economic reasoning.

This is the significant epistemological conclusion which should be drawn from Simmel's study of money, more important perhaps than his historical insights. His preoccupation with our ideas about money, and his examination of their consequences for modern culture, powerfully make the case that the analysis of money must contain a set of interpretative techniques sensitive to how money is perceived, to the range of dispositions and expectations which inform how it is used. This contention goes to the heart of the sense in which, as I argued in the Introduction, monetary networks are networks of information. But information in the sense discussed here should not be regarded merely as a lubricant which dictates whether or not money circulates efficiently. Information is on the contrary integral to how money actually works, to the pattern of its use and emission in society, no less than the institutional framework in which it is administered, saved, invested and spent. It would be a mistake to assume that this issue is confined to everyday or non-professional uses of money. To be sure, dealers in financial markets and governments and central banks responsible for the formulation and implementation of monetary policy draw on theories and forecasting models in a more conscious and deliberate way than those who use money for everyday purposes. But if anything, this reinforces the case for interpretative analysis at these levels. As I shall argue in later chapters, information plays a pivotal role in policy formulation and professional speculation in a way which is chronically unrelated to its objective accuracy. In this context in particular, there is a reflexive relationship between monetary theory and monetary practice which must be accounted for in monetary analysis. But the argument that there is an intrinsic connection between money and information needs to be placed in a more formal and systematic framework than Simmel himself provides. In the following chapter, I shall assess the attempt by two contemporary social theorists to do just this.

4

Money and the Social System

The explanations of the development of monetary exchange discussed so far in this book have ranged from the argument that monetary transaction rests on rational economic action informed by self-interest, through the contention that money's validity depends on state backing, to the proposition that money relies on a series of fiduciary relationships and psychological dispositions with quite definite cultural preconditions. In social theory, the latter explanation has gained prominence not merely through Simmel but in the later work of Talcott Parsons and Jürgen Habermas. Both theorists characterize money in terms of its role in the social system as a whole. Like Simmel, they define money with reference to social relationships and cultural associations which cannot be explained by focusing on economic activities alone. They argue that money is significant not only in economic terms but for what it reveals about the normative fabric of modern society. Moreover, neither theorist is concerned specifically with money as an object of study in its own right. But unlike Simmel, they treat the symbolic attributes of money not as a medium for philosophical investigation but as an example of a technical process whereby distinctive parts of modern society are integrated through patterns of communication. Parsons utilizes money as an exemplar for his theory of social differentiation. For Habermas, money's mediation of the relationship between the system and lifeworld provides the sharpest illustration of his theory of the internal colonization of the lifeworld.

Although Parsons and Habermas draw different conclusions from approaching money in this way, the basic understanding of money which features in their work is virtually identical. For this reason, the strengths and weaknesses of their approach can be generalized. As I shall suggest in the first section of this chapter, the major strength lies in drawing out the role of money in transmitting information. The breadth of focus of systems-theory enables the richness of the information transmitted through monetary transaction to be appreciated to an extent which cannot be achieved in narrower economic accounts. Yet it is precisely such breadth which generates the main weakness of this approach. As I move on to argue in the second section, both theorists are constrained in their understanding of money by their own analytical principles regarding the entire social system. Their arguments about money therefore contain weaknesses conventionally associated with systems-theory: namely, its rigidity in the face of historical change and variation between societies; its tendency to ignore or gloss over fundamental conflicts of interest and structural tensions in society; and the difficulty of applying its conclusions empirically. Both theorists undertake a sociological examination of money which is complementary with, rather than a challenge to or even a dialogue with, existing economic theories of money. Their work has consequently discouraged any attempt to formulate a coherent and distinctive approach to monetary analysis within sociology. That such an attempt can and should be made is a central theme in the arguments of this book.

Language

Parsons's characterization of money is on the face of it feebly conventional. His definition of money includes the three standard monetary functions, namely medium of exchange, measure of value and store of value. He adds to these a further four properties: money is institutionalized within the banking system; money has a specific relationship to action, for it cannot be used in any interaction whatsoever; money is circulable, it changes hands; and monetary systems are not zero sum, for credit can be created.[1] Parsons also argues, like most economists, that money's primary function in the economy is to transmit information.[2] It is his understanding of the content and derivation of such information, however, which distinguishes his analysis of money from formal economic theory. Parsons characterizes money as a symbolic medium. As language is the prototypical symbolic medium, money is analogous with language in its properties and functions. More specifically, money is a specialized language in the context of the social system as a whole, a role it shares with other media such as power, influence and value commitment. Parsons defines a specialized language as 'a generalized medium of communication through the use of symbols given meaning within a code'.[3] The four specialized languages function as media of interchange binding together the four sub-systems which make up the social system. For this reason, the emergence of the four media of interchange in society is causally linked to the process whereby the corresponding parts of society are gradually separated from each other. For example, money's capacity to transmit a specific kind of information enables economic activities to be differentiated from other spheres of action. This is possible because the information transmitted by money is functionally connected to the social system, conditioned by the relationship between the economy and other areas of society.

Parsons's definition of modern society as a social system consisting of four sub-systems is critically important to the problems which arise in his approach to money, not least because he relies on a form of reasoning against which I am developing the arguments of this book. Each sub-system specializes in a form of activity which has been differentiated out from the rest of society. For this reason, the process of differentiation enables each sub-system to operate more efficiently, and is therefore linked intrinsically to the phenomenon of rationalization. In order to be differentiated from other parts of the social system, each sub-system needs to have its own means for reproducing itself over time. Mechanisms must also be in place which ensure that the operation of each sub-system is integrated with and contributes to the maintenance of the social system as a whole. Parsons characterizes these mechanisms of reproduction and integration in terms of the theory of cybernetics.[4] This theory is represented by the AGIL schema depicting the functions of adaptation, goal attainment, integration and latent pattern maintenance. Together, these functions contribute to the reproduction and integration of the social system as a whole. Separately, they characterize the operation of each of the four individual sub-systems: namely, the economy (A), the polity (G), the legal and integration system (I) and the family and tradition (L). Within each sub-system, a steering medium functions both to bind together the operations of the sub-system itself and to control its relationship with other sub-systems, which is why Parsons calls it a medium of interchange.

In employing cybernetic theory, Parsons's aim is simple: he seeks to demonstrate how the four steering media help cut out time-consuming and energy-sapping procedures in everyday life by encoding certain types of information. The operation of the steering media is explained in terms of a cybernetic hierarchy, by which is meant an arrangement of sub-systems whose functional interdependence is regulated and maintained according to the principles of cybernetics. The hierarchy runs upwards through AGIL, with A consuming most energy and carrying least information, and L vice versa. The sequence AGIL (upwards) denotes limiting conditions, while the sequence LIGA (downwards) denotes cybernetic control: 'each cell categorizes the necessary but not sufficient conditions for operation of the cell next above it in the column, and in the opposite direction, the categories of each cell control the process categorized in the one below it'.[5] Money, for example, encodes the assumption that every transactor will be oriented to getting the best deal in economic exchanges, concerned with price rather than with the personal characteristics of a fellow-transactor. The price mechanism means that money can quantify qualitatively different things, acting as both a medium of transaction and a store of value so that one is able to exchange a particular quantity of money for just about anything, bypassing energy-sapping procedures of barter. In this way, money enables the economy to operate as a specialized sub-system which is differentiated from other sub-systems while also interacting with them. For example, money crosses the boundary between A and L via the relationship between wage-labour and the private household.[6] However, money not only operates on the symbolic level as a specialized language, but is conditioned by things insofar as it represents real goods and services. In this sense, money has a dual character consisting of a base, relating to real goods and services, and code, relating to symbols.[7]

Money, for Parsons, transmits information which is richer and more complex than its characterization in terms of the price mechanism would allow. Hayek's analysis of money as a universal joint within the market illustrates the conventional approach to money's transmission of information through price, an approach which Parsons rejects. According to Hayek, money transmits price signals which enable economic actors to adjust to what each other is doing.[8] Crucially, money's capacity to function in this way relies on the rational predisposition of economic decision-making units: they must maximize in response to price signals for the mechanism to work. Money in this sense sends messages regarding key economic variables, affecting those variables only as an enabling device for patterns of economic behaviour already in existence. Parsons's approach is quite different. He characterizes the function of money in transmitting information in terms of the integration of society. Money helps bind together the normative fabric of society, fulfilling a substantive integrating role within the economy not envisaged in the approach typified by Hayek. For Parsons, money is a motivating force in its own right, not merely an abstract means for the transmission of signals stemming from economic activities motivated by self-interest. For this reason, he rejects utilitarianism as an analytical framework for understanding economic life, in which the depiction of rationality is confined to the selection of means in the face of a seemingly arbitrary or random set of ends, or else subsumed by a vague notion of a natural order of goals or needs.[9] With Smelser, Parsons attempts a systematic critique of formal economic theory; advocating, however, not the wholesale rejection of economics as a discipline of study but its integration with sociology as a special case of the general theory of social systems.[10] This is consistent with the substance of Parsons's approach to money, but stems from what I want to argue is one of its most problematic features.

Parsons and Smelser apply the AGIL schema to the economy itself as well as to each other sub-system. They maintain that the economy can be addressed as a system in its own right, structured around the interdependences indicated by AGIL. This is a major source of difficulty in their approach to money, as can be demonstrated by reference to their characterization of consumption in terms of the interchange between Ag and Lg: that is, the relationship between the goal-attainment sub-system of the economy (Ag) and the goal-attainment sub-system of the pattern-maintenance system (Lg); or concretely, between the firm and the household. To characterize consumption in this way amounts to a rejection of the idea that the rational pursuit of self-interest forms a pre-given core around which the economy is structured. For Parsons and Smelser, the expression of demand through consumption does not simply stem from economic rationality, but has a symbolic component. It is for this reason that the information transmitted by money is richer and more complex than could possibly be conveyed through price alone: 'On the one hand, money represents the *generalization* of purchasing power to *control decisions* to exchange goods; on the other hand it symbolizes attitudes'.[11] The contention that money encodes not merely prices but values and norms derived from the function of latent pattern maintenance relies on the proposition that the economy does not constitute the core or infrastructure of society but is interdependent with three other sub-systems of equal status making up the social system.[12] But Parsons and Smelser over-emphasize the role of value consensus in the social system, both in itself and in relation to consumption in particular. As Alexander suggests, to characterize the media of interchange as symbolic media, with the term 'symbolic' having connotations of value consensus, conflates the dualistic conceptualization of money as comprising both base and code, which is the primary strength of this approach in the first place. This is an error, Alexander contends, which derives from an elementary but flawed syllogism: they proceed from the idea that interaction entails symbolic media, through the contention that language is the most effective of such media, to the conclusion that 'media represent a symbolic language'.[13] According to this reasoning, it seems as if the media of interchange have no relationship to things but operate on the symbolic level alone. Where money is concerned, this makes it impossible to understand the relationship between money and wealth insofar as the latter involves access to real goods and property and underpins the connection between money and the distribution of power in society.[14] This issue has important consequences for the application of cybernetic theory to monetary transaction.

There is a need, as I have argued in earlier chapters, to understand the fiduciary, or normative, dimension of monetary networks. But this should not be at the expense of understanding also that the use of money in society tends to be structurally connected to asymmetries of wealth and power, to conflicts of interest. It must be possible to support these two propositions at the same time rather than treating them, as generally seems to be the case, as mutually exclusive. Parsons's application of cybernetic theory to monetary analysis does not meet this requirement. For example, it follows from his theory that a medium from which trust has been withdrawn may only be redeemed from above, by 'calling on ... various cybernetically higher forces'.[15] In other words, only a full recovery of trust by means of a renewed fulfilment of expectations can put things right.[16] This ignores the possibility that one medium might be used to bolster another, in which case redemption need not be from above at all. This, for instance, would make the interrelation of economic and political power - buying political influence - difficult to explain. Parsons's framework is lopsided as far as money is concerned.

This weakness in Parsons's approach is taken up by Habermas, who argues that language is a less suitable analogy for money than Parsons suggests. For Habermas, language possesses unique properties linked to the fact that linguistic communication has an inherent universal structure which presupposes the orientation of speakers to a constraint-free society. He contends that the encoding of linguistic communication on the basis of instrumental imperatives originating in the social system as Parsons conceives it cannot therefore present a smooth path to an efficient society in the way Parsons hopes. The key points of distinction between the approaches of Parsons and Habermas stem directly from the question whether and how money and language are analogous. For Parsons, money, alongside power, influence and value commitment, acts as a pivot within the cybernetic mechanism shaping social action. In so far as the symbolic media cut out aspects of linguistic communication, this is of considerable interest to Habermas, who organizes his project of modernity around the assertion of an intrinsic relationship between communicative action and political freedom. He doubts, however, that cutting out certain aspects of human communication for the sake of goals derived from the social system is politically feasible, let alone desirable. His scepticism is informed by the concept of communicative action which stems from his so-called linguistic turn - away from the philosophy of consciousness implied by postulating a relationship between knowledge and human interests and towards a theory of language and communication - anticipated in his 1965 Inaugural Lecture[17] and confirmed in the postscript to the second edition of *Knowledge and Human Interests*.[18] There, the connection between truth in linguistic statements on the one hand, and the 'good and true life'[19] on the other, is clarified: any linguistic utterance contains implicit truth claims which are intrinsically linked to 'an inevitably idealized (if only hypothetically ideal) community of language'. The cleavage between this ideal community and the real world of communication is thereby 'built not only into the process of argumentative reasoning but into the very life-praxis of social systems'.[20]

In his essay, 'What is universal pragmatics?',[21] Habermas spells out more clearly his approach to language. He engages in the task of reconstructing what he calls universal conditions of possible understanding, which amounts to a full-blown theory of communication. By understanding, Habermas refers not simply to knowing what we mean but to principles of truthfulness and persuasion and rules of discourse and argumentation: in other words, not just what we say but what we are doing by what we say. This leads eventually to the notion of communicative action. In considering existing philosophies of language and language-use, Habermas complains that the analysis of language's formal character - the rules of grammar, syntax and so on - is restrictive as far as our understanding of actual communication is concerned. He seeks to establish a rounder theory of communication based on three worlds implicit in speech: namely, the world of objects, the speaker's own world, and the intersubjective shared world of the speakers. Inside these parameters, speakers advance validity claims of comprehensibility, truth, truthfulness and normative rightness. Habermas incorporates this account of the inherent features of speech within an evolutionary reconstruction of the processes of social, psychological and societal development necessary for the competencies implicit in the features themselves to be achieved. Communicative rationality houses the potential for human beings to release themselves from conditions of domination and exploitation. In Habermas's view, Weber, the Frankfurt School and Parsons all suggest that the rise of instrumental reason not only defines modernity but is inevitable and irreversible. Habermas rejects this, and seeks to show how existing theories of modernity fail to grasp the potential for political freedom, defined in terms of communicative action, also present in the modern world.

Against this background, it is possible to understand more clearly the fact that, for Habermas, two of the media of interchange within Parsons's theory impinge directly on communicative action: namely, influence and value commitment. For Habermas, neither influence nor value commitment can encode language in the ways envisaged by Parsons. As media of interchange, they simplify speech but cannot replace it. Both influence and value commitment depend on processes which must be worked through linguistically: the possession of influence or moral authority no doubt reduces interpretive energy, but still relies on reaching understanding through speech.[22] These aspects of social life are closely related to communicative action, and so must be subject to rational argumentation according to principles of communicative rationality; unless, of course, such principles are compromised, in which case pathological consequences will ensue. For this reason, Parsons unwittingly identifies an area of considerable tension and crisis in modern society. More importantly for my argument here, Habermas expresses specific doubts about Parsons's characterization of money in relation to language. Habermas accepts that money cuts out aspects of time-consuming and energy-sapping communication. But the sociological consequences of this are impossible to understand unless the role of language in general and communicative action in particular within the social system is precisely defined. Parsons fails to do this. Simply to acknowledge the role of language as the primary medium of all social relationships is not enough: substantive structural relations between media of interchange are at stake.[23] Habermas contends that there are features of linguistic communication which set limits to the possibility of their being encoded by money. The analogy between language and money still holds, but only to a point. He concedes that money can replace linguistic communication in respect of the double contingency usually present in social interaction: first, whether or not a validity claim is raised; and second, whether such a claim, once raised, is accepted or rejected. With money, both contingencies are avoided, for validity is built into the medium itself. Nevertheless, Habermas characterizes money not as 'a functional specification of language'[24] but, rather, as 'a substitute for special functions of language'.[25] Parsons's initial formulation is only partially retained.

Habermas tightens up his approach to money when he moves on to contend that the comparison drawn by Parsons between money and power is problematic. He highlights five issues in particular.[26] First, power is not as easily manipulable as money, for it has no special enumerative sign. Second, power is more restricted than money in the scope of its circulation, for it is likely to be 'bound up symbiotically with the person of the powerful' or confined to a particular organizational setting rather than generalized. Third, power is less readily deposited than money: with regard to the analogy Parsons establishes between money and power when comparing banking with elections, for example, the power deposited by votes may quickly depreciate, and its value will always be unreliable. Fourth, there is no quantifiable means for assessing the consequences of the exercise of power relations, which tend to be reflected in a monetary sense by inflation and deflation. Finally, the reflexive dynamic tends to operate with distinctive consequences in the cases of money and power: whereas with money, reflexivity - expressed in the development of credit and money markets - will contribute to internal complexity, with power, conversely, the most likely expression of reflexivity will take the form of opposition; in which case differentiation outwards, rather than greater internal complexity, is the outcome.

Despite these criticisms, Habermas rather oddly retains the analogy between money and power. He does so, by his own reckoning, because both media are involved in a social relationship structured around claim and redemption. Because of this, both relationships save energy in the way cybernetic theory suggests. With money, what happens in a transaction is predetermined by the characteristics of money itself: the role of each participant is standardized and predictable, allowing certain assumptions to be left unsaid. Similarly with power, a 'preference for compliance is built into the code through the prospect ego holds out for sanctioning alter in case the latter fails to carry out orders'.[27] Habermas differs from Parsons over what underpins this preference structure. For Parsons, each medium of interchange has a formative role in relation to its environment. But the reproduction of the social system is also based on direct interchange between its constituent sub-systems. They act as environments for each other. For example, money penetrates the private household by means of the institution of wage-labour - an interchange between A and L. It is a logical corollary of this that there will be at least some interchange between money and value commitment, between A and I, irrespective of whether this is labelled as one of the principal boundary interchanges. Indeed, Parsons seems bound to assume that there is interchange between A and I via money because of the way in which his overall theory of the social system is constructed, particularly the proposition that sub-systems act as environments for, and so mutually shape, one another.[28] To cite another example, the issue as to whether the mediatization of money between A and G through the institution of wage-labour is adequately met by appropriate levels of value commitment cannot seriously be based on theoretical presupposition. As Habermas argues, the entire point of the critique of the political economy of capitalism has been to ask whether the commodification of labour power through money 'constituted an intrusion into living conditions and interaction systems that were not themselves integrated via media that could not be painlessly ... cut loose from structures of action oriented to mutual understanding'.[29]

The significant difference between the approaches of Parsons and Habermas for the approach to monetary analysis that I am developing in this book concerns the distinction between the fact that money transmits information and the content of the information transmitted. Parsons contends that the capacity of money to function at all rests on generalized codes.[30] But its everyday operation is based also on the content of the information transmitted in specific transactions. He does not, however, provide a solid foundation for distinguishing between these levels. Given the location of generalized dispositions within the AGIL schema, it seems reasonable to conclude that the content of the information transmitted by money is dictated by demands emanating from the social system. This begs the question as to whether the substantive characteristics of money as depicted by Parsons might actually express only the imperatives of a particular social system at a particular point in time, in which case he seems to have translated empirical observations into theoretical statements without justification. There is a danger when translating empirical insights relating to the utilization of specific monetary forms for consumption and investment into theoretical findings about the operation of money in general of precipitancy at best and complete misunderstanding at worst. This danger was highlighted in my Introduction, and is important to the argument I shall develop in the second part of this book. The distinction to which it refers, between money in general and specific monetary forms, is easily lost in Parsons's analysis. He seems vaguely aware of this problem when he notes that 'money itself is by no means a simple entity, and in particular the development of credit instruments, banking and the like, has many variations'.[31] But the confusion in his work stems from more fundamental problems with his theory, above all the functional status he ascribes to normative integration. Habermas correctly argues that Parsons constricts understanding of the normative sphere. Indeed, this is inevitable in the context of Parsons's theory of social differentiation. Parsons defines social differentiation as, in Habermas's words, 'a heightening of systemic complexity'.[32] Systemic complexity is function-ally linked to problems of normative integration, establishing an 'analytical connection between the growing steering capacity of the social system and increasing inclusion and value generalization'.[33] Habermas seeks to separate out these two processes. This entails rejecting outright the cybernetic principles foundational to Parsons's theory. Habermas agrees with Parsons that a link between each sub-system and mechanisms of social integration is functionally necessary, but he refuses to suppose that it will inevitably be established and maintained. Like Parsons, Habermas regards money as one of several steering media. However, he addresses the normative control of such media as an empirical question, the object of inquiry rather than one of its founding principles. This approach does not focus on harmony and integration but on conflict and disintegration, and is integral to Habermas's theory of the internal colonization of the lifeworld.

Modernity

Both Parsons and Habermas address money in the context of a historical examination of the differentiation of the economy from the rest of society. Although they advance radically different interpretations of the role of money within contemporary society and in the future, both theorists accord primacy to a form of reasoning which has been central to, but in my view problematic for, the predominant sociological understanding of the emergence of modern society. Habermas's position is that there is only a limited sense in which money can fulfil goals set by demands of the social system as Parsons conceives it; there will be a point at which this process cannot go on without generating pathological consequences. This conclusion is derived from a basic disagreement with Parsons over the nature of language and its relationship to monetary transaction. Habermas's argument can best be understood by contrasting his analytical framework comprising the system and lifeworld with Parsons's AGIL schema. It should then be possible to follow through Habermas's historical projections regarding the development of money: these are directly informed by a broader theory of the pathogenesis of modernity, a process Habermas calls the internal colonization of the lifeworld.

Habermas's analytical framework for the study of modern society consists of the social system and the lifeworld. The historical process of their uncoupling is at the heart of his account of the onset of modernity. He argues that modern societies have developed not merely on the basis of advances in social labour but, as a logically distinctive process of evolution, by means of the reproduction of the human species through interaction. In both respects, there is a process of rationalization, involving instrumental rationality in the domain of the system and communicative rationality in the domain of the lifeworld.[34] For Habermas, it is because Parsons provides no account of social differentiation within the lifeworld that his analysis of modern Western society is distorted, conflating efficiency, value consensus and rationality. Habermas concedes that the system operates more efficiently the greater is its capacity to adapt to internal and environmental complexities, and that this involves its differentiation into more specialized sub-systems. It is over the precise nature and consequences of this process that he disagrees with Parsons. The lifeworld secures the maintenance of individual and social identity. It consists of a background or storehouse of unquestioned assumptions, values and skills, initially rooted in tradition, which are essential to the conduct of everyday social life. But the lifeworld provides more than just a background to social life, fulfilling a vital co-ordinating role based on principles of communicative action. Habermas argues that while the communicative skills integral to communicative rationality are not to be found everywhere, they embody a form of rationality which in principle is integral to communication wherever and whenever it occurs. The realization of such skills is the end-product of a logic of development underlying the history of all societies.[35]

This twofold characterization of rationality forms the backbone of Habermas's analysis of the role of money in modern society. Changes in the legal framework, itself part of the social system, have underpinned the separation of economic life from values and activities associated with politics and tradition. Money has been at the heart of this process. It symbolizes capital and labour under the freedom, in bourgeois law, to enter into contracts for private gain. It is on this basis that processes of integration within the system and lifeworld have been uncoupled. But the process of uncoupling is neither smooth nor simple. Uncoupling proceeds through rationalization, and this entails risk from the point of view of both system and lifeworld. Where the lifeworld is concerned, the more particular social practices or institutions are opened up to criticism and debate according to principles of communicative action, the more vulnerable they become. Where system integration is concerned, this can be damaging because economic action and political decision-making must draw upon lifeworld knowledge and institutions for their legitimacy. The risks entailed in the process of uncoupling are not, however, confined to each dimension of modern society as separate entities but concern the relationship between them. What might appear to be a gain in efficiency from the point of the view of the system may be profoundly unsettling within the lifeworld. Exactly this will happen if the development of the lifeworld is stunted; or more specifically, if the lifeworld is colonized by the system. The internal colonization of the lifeworld refers to the process by which institutions and imperatives associated with the system expand and break into, or colonize, institutions and values associated with the lifeworld. This process is mediated by money and power, and profoundly conflicts with the form of reasoning on which the lifeworld is based. Internal colonization distorts lifeworld consciousness because instrumental rationality suffocates the lifeworld, where communicative rationality should predominate. For this reason, key aspects of the process of uncoupling have been pathological, leading to profound social and cultural tensions.

A conclusion of this scale and depth, with money at its heart, is at least mildly surprising given the somewhat insubstantial nature of Habermas's analysis of money. He argues that money codifies certain aspects of communicative action, but can never do so entirely. As the medium of communicative action, language cannot be completely uprooted from the lifeworld and codified in the form of a monetary medium circulating within the system with no reference to lifeworld principles. Habermas concedes that there is a fiduciary dimension to monetary exchange which connects it to the lifeworld, but denies that this can ever be codified to the extent that money is independent of the lifeworld. As a social institution, money must draw on the lifeworld for normative support. Recalling the arguments of legal theorists, Habermas suggests that this is largely achieved by legal regulations governing the issue and validation of money. But his discussion of this issue is confused and contradictory. He states clearly that money has not always required a legal framework in which to circulate, but merely that this is the typical arrangement in modern societies. There is nothing objectionable about this as a description of the historical relationship between money and the state. But Habermas translates this empirical observation into a theoretical argument regarding the relationship between money and the lifeworld. It is here that his reasoning becomes confused. He tries to clarify what he means by reference to the contrast between money and power. Money mediates between opposing interests in the exchange process: the transaction will not intrinsically disadvantage either party. Power, by contrast, is always exercised by one actor at the expense of another. So to have trust in a system which institutionalizes power[36] requires a higher level of support from the lifeworld than is needed by money.[37] In monetary transaction, the interests of the transactors need not be placed in question. No agreement is required there and then to establish what those interests are. With power, there will always be a connection 'with the authority behind commands in contrast to simple imperatives'. This suggests to Habermas that power is 'less suited for the role of a steering medium designed to relieve us of the burdens and risks of consensus formation in language than is money, which needs no legitimation'.[38] More specifically, he argues that unlike money, 'power is not 'by nature' a circulating medium'.[39]

Three sets of questions are raised by this argument. All concern the sense in which money relies on fiduciary relationships of one kind or another. First, Habermas asserts that money is 'by nature' a circulating medium, prior to becoming a creature of law. Did the institutionalization of money under the state constitute a fundamental shift in the basis of money's role within the social system, or simply an evolutionary development? Second, is the legality of money functionally necessary or only of historical significance? Third, what does Habermas mean by asserting that, by contrast with power, 'no agreement among the parties to an exchange is required for them to make a judgement of interests'? Are such interests unquestioned, unquestionable, or simply unimportant in monetary transaction? The first of these issues cannot be adequately addressed without reference to the other two, and so I shall begin with the question of interests and work my way back.

Habermas, like Parsons, argues that money transmits information which ensures that certain assumptions need not be articulated when money is used. When handling money, transactors are predisposed to giving straightforward positive and negative answers in respect of the transaction itself, thereby 'shifting the [consensual] burden from the validation of claims to the utilitarian calculation of costs and benefits'.[40] Money 'can largely spare us the costs of dissensus'[41] because it uncouples 'the coordination of action from consensus formation in language and neutralize[s] it against the alternatives of achieved versus failed agreement'.[42] It is to this mutual predisposition towards the transaction of money that Habermas refers when he writes of the 'judgement of interests'. So with regard to my third question, it is not that such interests are unquestionable or unimportant but that, within the context of the transaction, they are unquestioned. Money relieves energetic attempts to reach understanding. To be treated in this way, money must nevertheless be legitimated by institutions which are meaningful in the context of the lifeworld: only then can money be characterized as a delinguistified steering medium which has been differentiated from the lifeworld. The theory of communicative action demands this. There is, then, a nagging ambiguity in Habermas's argument. On the one hand, he contends that money 'needs no legitimation'.[43] Yet he also acknowledges that the state quite clearly is a major source of money's legitimation in modern society. In making both claims, Habermas is perhaps distinguishing between the legal status of money in general and the question of trust in the context of particular transactions. In other words, it is the monetary form which carries already-constituted legitimation, being 'connected back to the communicatively structured lifeworld via legal institutions'. This, in turn, enables assumptions to be left unsaid in the context of individual transactions. Power, by contrast, is 'still in need of legitimation' on each and every occasion it is exercised. In this sense, money 'is not made dependent on processes of consensus formation in language as is the medium of ... power'.[44] The ambiguity of Habermas's account of the relationship between money and the lifeworld can be at least partly reconciled, then, by distinguishing between the normative framework of monetary exchange as a social institution and the fiduciary relationship between individual transactors. But this is not a distinction he himself employs, simply referring to both in connection with 'money'.

Ingram tries to shed light on this issue by arguing that, whereas monetary exchange is essentially a free exchange in so far as transactors 'are free to accept or reject any offer', refusal where the exercise of power is concerned is possible 'only on pain of reprisal'.[45] This seems clear enough, but fails to settle the ambiguity. Must every exercise of power be secured by reference to collective goals? If so, it seems absurd to continue to address power as a steering medium with a built-in preference structure.[46] Ingram adds, correctly in my view, that no complete security attaches to money, either: 'its trustworthiness is also - albeit indirectly - related to considerations of legitimacy'.[47] But the expression 'albeit indirectly' exposes a hole in Ingram's interpretation. He associates disappointment relating to money's stability and validity with actual transactions - for example, cases of fraud, theft and breach of contract - rather than to the abstract properties of money itself. This allows him to introduce legal principles - 'mandating, among other things, equal representation and accountability in the legislative process'[48] - as a means of tightening Habermas's formulation. It follows from Ingram's interpretation that if a specific monetary form is designated as legal this is a sufficient basis for its legitimacy. If a particular pattern in the exercise of power is instituted as legal this is, by contrast, no basis for its legitimacy. Money, unlike power, is supposedly neutral in its consequences for the parties to transaction, unlikely to strain the extent of its credibility in everyday circulation. The possibility that the legitimacy of money as a social institution might be undermined is, in this interpretation, difficult to imagine. Moreover, Ingram's reading rules out conceptualizing the relationship between money and asymmetries of wealth and power, whether conceived in structural or in symbolic terms.

These difficulties stem from theoretical rigidity in Habermas's approach. They are fatal once money is directly related to the internal colonization thesis. For Habermas, monetary transactions are among the 'interchange relations' which occur at the interface between the system and lifeworld.[49] These relations are based on social roles which he divides into two types: first, the 'organization-dependent roles' of employee and welfare state client; and second, the roles of consumer and citizen, which emerge as part of a self-formative process 'in which preferences, value orientations, attitudes, and so forth have taken shape'.[50] In the form of welfare benefits, money serves as compensation for the 'external effects of a production process based on wage labour'.[51] As a means for sustaining social stability, however, this is ultimately self-undermining, because money must penetrate 'situations embedded in informal lifeworld contexts'[52] in order to function as compensation at all. This is detrimental because monetary transaction inherently involves principles of instrumental rationality: or more specifically, with echoes of Simmel, 'an accumulation process that has become an end in itself'.[53] Money is therefore in tension with a lifeworld not amenable to such principles. In this way, an analytical problem - the interconnection of system and lifeworld - gains its political teeth whereby 'the *semantic question* of how something can be translated from one language into the other[54] can be converted into the *empirical question* of when the growth of the monetary bureaucratic complex affects domains of action that cannot be transferred to system-integrative mechanisms without pathological side effects'.[55] This has been clarified by Habermas in an interview, where he warns that the penetration by money and power of areas of society 'held together by their very nature through the medium of communicative behaviour' is 'more than an attack on traditions' for 'the symbolic reproduction of the life-world itself' is at stake.[56] In this way, the system imperatives expressed by money increasingly assume a dynamic of their own to which the lifeworld is ever more vulnerable: 'the rationalization of the lifeworld makes possible a heightening of systemic complexity, which becomes so hypertrophied that it unleashes system imperatives that burst the capacity of the lifeworld they instrumentalize'.[57]

Habermas associates money with instrumental rationality in so far as it operates as a steering medium within the system. Only by being linked back to the lifeworld by means of its legality, however, can money's circulation be sustained. This step is vital to his argument, because he is then in a position to examine the tension between money and the lifeworld which is at the heart of his internal colonization thesis. But within the parameters of Habermas's theory, only by not including normative dispositions in a substantive characterization of money is it feasible to address money's role as ultimately disruptive for the lifeworld. This role rests on systemic forces, even though it is true that only on the basis of its legality does money assume the capacity to circulate autonomously as a steering medium at all. But because money's penetration of the lifeworld is driven by the system imperative of capitalist appropriation, it appears to have sheered off from the initial source of its legitimacy. It now expresses a capitalistic rationality which is altogether autonomous from the lifeworld. Habermas cannot explain how this process occurs. Money is dependent on a form of normative integration in order to work at all in society, while also being a focus of structural inequalities of wealth and power, a source and expression of major conflicts of interest. Habermas seems unable to reconcile these two facts. Or rather, he is able to do so only in diachronic terms. He suggests that money initially has legitimacy in terms of the lifeworld, but loses it when the logic of system integration goes too far. But unless this argument is accompanied by a theory of money's impending collapse as a social institution, it cannot be sustained. Money possesses contradictory qualities as both a medium which requires normative support throughout society in order to exist and an economic instrument which symbolizes and generates major asymmetries of wealth and power. These qualities must be understood in synchronic terms, for they persist side by side.

Habermas's theory does not work because he fails to examine the consequences of internal colonization for the status and constitution of money itself. Money's penetration into the lifeworld, driven by system imperatives, brings on crisis. Precisely what results from this as far as money is concerned, however, is unclear. Will money come to be rejected as a social institution altogether, deemed to express principles of an increasingly rationalized system fundamentally in conflict with an increasingly colonized lifeworld? Or will particular monetary forms, specifically legal-tender, come to be rejected in so far as they express the legality of the issuing state? In other words, will crisis embroil money in general - focusing on the principles which money in general symbolizes - or monetary forms specifically linked to those institutions whose legitimacy is under threat? Habermas's characterization of money seems too confused to sustain the thesis of internal colonization, insufficiently precise to be rigorously assessed; too weak even to be categorically wrong. Because of this, there seems to be nothing in his analysis which excludes the possibility that money's status as a social institution might be sustained at a general level, with only the validity of particular monetary forms placed in question. In such a case, money's recurring raids into the lifeworld need not be repellant as far as money in general is concerned. Then the internal colonization thesis would remain open ended, with money in general continuing to express the tension between system and lifeworld, perhaps even exacerbating it. But this need not, at least on the basis of anything Habermas writes, entail actually propelling the tension between system and lifeworld into some kind of crisis leading ultimately to resolution. The alternative scenario set out here seems quite feasible, perhaps more so than Habermas's own; the point, however, is that it is inadmissible within the parameters of Habermas's theory, reflecting the basic difficulty arising in his analysis concerning the relationship between the system and lifeworld in respect of the constitution of money in general.

Habermas's characterization of money in relation to the lifeworld is problematic not only because he fails to clarify the relationship between money and asymmetries of power, but because he employs an overly narrow perspective on the way it is handled by individuals themselves. Merely to utilize money, he argues, presupposes that its holder will be committed to the generalized value of utility, which thereby 'binds every actor taking part in monetary exchanges, everywhere and at all times, and in the same way'.[58] But by defining monetary codes solely in terms of utility, Habermas negates the depth of perspective integral to his analysis of the structure of validity claims more generally within the lifeworld. This runs contrary to the theory of communicative action, where Habermas contends that all social action, by its very nature, presupposes the lifeworld background.[59] Habermas conflates the entire interpretative substance of monetary transaction into what is, in practice, merely one of its aspects. This problem cannot be avoided merely by invoking the theme of the uncoupling of monetary transaction from the lifeworld; unless, of course, action must be confined to the lifeworld, as Habermas defines it, in order to be characterized as social - which seems incurably absurd, merely confirming the questionable nature of the distinction between lifeworld and system in the first place. Habermas's account of the codification of money is insufficiently substantial to contain the concentric layers of meaning which he views as integral to all communicative situations. When he addresses money, the communicative scope of monetary transaction is suddenly, irretrievably and unreasonably narrowed down; not simply in the sense of taking an overly legalistic approach but also, and no less importantly, because he conflates the extent to which the lifeworld background of individual transactors informs their consumption and investment behaviour in ways which must be understood if a coherent and credible sociological approach to monetary analysis is to be developed.

Habermas's approach is painfully thin as a guide to the interpretative dimension of monetary transaction. In binding money, or rather its analysis in social theory, to the process of internal colonization, he ignores the presence of lifeworld principles in the ongoing transaction of money. As Misgeld argues, the placement of money at the heart of the internal colonization thesis reflects a misunderstanding of what actually happens when individuals use money. He interprets Habermas's argument that, as a codified steering medium, money serves as a 'substitute for special functions of language'[60] as meaning that money 'can replace linguistic communication in specific situations and in specific respects', hence reducing 'the need to engage in interpretative efforts' whilst minimizing 'the risks involved in attempting to secure agreement'. The expression employed by Habermas to characterize this process is *Technisierung der Lebenswelt*, which Misgeld translates as 'the *technical* reorganization of the lifeworld',[61] implying the reorganization of the lifeworld according to rational principles deriving from the system. As a corollary of this, 'money, and together with it 'the economy' ... are set apart from and stand above the activities of ordinary life which we may properly (and on closer inspection) designate as 'economic'.[62] Misgeld contends that Habermas 'does not consider *money* in terms of the various meanings money may have to people acting in ordinary circumstances'.[63]

Misgeld's critique can be interpreted in terms best described as weak and strong. In the weak interpretation, it could be contended that, if there are conditions under which economic life operates according to self-regulating market mechanisms, this is only ever a consequence of a process of reification in which agents' perceptions reflexively shape the economic activities in which they engage, the clearest instance of this being capital and currency markets (my example). It would follow that, while economic life may 'in some circumstances' be exhaustively characterized by reference to the rational principles that Habermas identifies with the system, this is neither naturally nor essentially the case but stems from interpretative activities which, in so far as they are embedded in 'daily life', must be addressed from the perspective of the lifeworld. The strong interpretation of Misgeld's critique, on the other hand, would entail contending that no sphere of economic activity, however perceived, can or does operate according to the principles Habermas associates with the system: any such characterization has an ideological content which, however greatly it may inform economic activities, can never exhaustively describe them. This suggests that to regard economic life as set apart from the rest of society as some kind of essence whose nature can be truly realized only by stripping away social, cultural and political fetters is to misunderstand the chronic embroilment of 'economic' activities within all these other dimensions (and vice versa). It is not clear which of these interpretations of Misgeld's argument is most accurate. Both are compatible with his central contention regarding the relationship between money and the lifeworld, that Habermas is wrong to claim that money 'can do what it does because in the development of modern societies the market has become a self-regulating institution, a sub-system of society, which is *only accessible to systems-theoretical-functionalist analysis*'.[64] But the differences between them are critically important to my argument in this book. The weak interpretation would entail reversing the direction of causality in Habermas's analysis of the constitution of monetary codes; their association with instrumental rationality would now be addressed as having been generated from within the lifeworld rather than by system-driven impositions upon the lifeworld, emphasizing the 'internal' component of the thesis, and thus the pivotal role of human agency within the transaction of money, to a greater extent than Habermas does himself. The strong interpretation, on the other hand, implies a substantive departure from the internal colonization thesis, for it could no longer be maintained that money is wholly bound up with instrumental rationality. Indeed, to address monetary transaction merely in terms of the system would amount to a distortion of what actually happens when money changes hands. If money continues to be shaped by assumptions and interpretations derived from the lifeworld in transaction, the question must now concern how and why this is no longer perceived to be the case, whether by transactors themselves or professional analysts and theorists. Indeed, this argument places the distinction between the system and the lifeworld itself under serious strain, particularly where the narrow conceptualization of the economy is concerned.

It is unavoidable, given Habermas's overarching theoretical aims, that the narrow rationality bound up with monetary transaction must be externalized from the lifeworld in order for the depth and richness of the universalistic rationality which he associates with the lifeworld to be retained. But this is to deny the degree of inventiveness, unpredictability and even freedom which, as Simmel contends, the possession of money can and does entail.[65] Individual transacting strategies must be the subject of empirical enquiry for monetary analysis in sociology, not an upshot of schematically accommodating assumptions. A more penetrating analysis of the interpretative dimension of monetary transaction would rule out the inflexible conclusions drawn by Habermas himself. It is because he insists on characterizing the system and lifeworld as two separate domains in modern society, associating money almost exclusively with the former, that he is unable to grasp the profound ambivalence of money's status in modern society. Structurally and symbolically, money both relies on generalized normative support and plays an integral role in the reproduction of inequality. Habermas, no less than Parsons, characterizes money in a way which cannot account for this. In the case of Parsons, this problem is based on an inherent theoretical rigidity in his understanding of money according to cybernetic principles. Habermas tries to avoid the same problem, but fails because of a confusion in his account of the status and importance of money's relationship with the state, a failure to distinguish between money in general and specific monetary forms, and a shallow characterization of the relationship between money and the lifeworld in relation to the interpretative dimension of actual monetary transactions. These fundamental difficulties arise from the efforts of both theorists to incorporate a model of money's nature and functions as an exemplar within a further-reaching theory of society, leading to conclusions regarding money whose scale and pretension is not matched by thoroughgoing analysis. Both confuse an empirically specific understanding of monetary forms with an account of the nature and functions of money itself.

These shortcomings in the work of Parsons and Habermas not only lead to a set of empirical inadequacies, but exemplify the problems which arise when theoretical rigidity takes precedence over analytic rigour. It is precisely this difficulty which I have sought to draw out in the preceding four chapters. All the approaches to monetary analysis discussed so far have in common a fundamental lack of clarity regarding the exact epistemological status of monetary theory. This lack arises in the first instance from a failure to grasp the distinguishing features of the nature of money as opposed to other instruments of exchange. As I argued in the Introduction, the distinctive properties of money cannot be adequately defined by reference to a standard set of functions, the origins of money as a special type of commodity, or the relationship between money and the political economy of a historically specific society such as capitalism. Money possesses abstract properties which, as Simmel correctly grasps, cannot be characterized without addressing the intrinsic connection between our ideas of money and the ways it is actually used. It is for this reason, as I suggested in chapter 1, that the nature and basis of the demand for money has been obscured in economic theory for so long. There is a significant fiduciary dimension to monetary networks which is bound up in the ways money is perceived by those who use it. This is a cultural and political question no less than an issue of fundamental economic significance. As soon as this is clearly understood it is impossible to reduce the debate over the relationship between money and the state to a straightforward question of administrative necessity or the prudence of banking institutions. As I argued in chapter 3, it is profoundly irrelevant whether our beliefs about the state's role in issuing and validating money are fanciful in the light of hard economic evidence. The point, rather, is that beliefs, superstitions and myths are no less integral to the operation of money in society than the economic relationships and dispositions which have conventionally been the focus of monetary theory.

It is vital for the kind of monetary analysis I am advocating in this book to develop a range of interpretative techniques by which the ideas and expectations associated with the use of money can be clearly understood. It is not enough to reduce these ideas and expectations to a form of rationality which owes more to the strictures of economic reasoning than to any rigorous approach to what people think, and no less importantly do not think, whenever and wherever they use money. The rigidity of a monetary theory subservient to the logic of economic assumptions should not be replaced, either, with the kind of rigidity which characterizes the attempts of grand theorists to incorporate money within their own efforts to explain the normative integration of modern, differentiated societies. Both Parsons and Habermas fail in their approaches to money because their own wider theoretical objectives constrain their understanding of, indeed prevent them from addressing, the range of actions and dispositions with which the use of money has always been associated. Both theorists establish quite explicitly that money's circulation relies on normative support. But by addressing this issue within the parameters of an overarching theory of the functional interdependence of different parts of society with each other they fail to explain or even imagine how money can, at the same time, symbolize the fundamental conflicts of interest and asymmetries of wealth and power with which its circulation is structurally connected. While Simmel does not examine this issue systematically, he does at least formulate an approach to the nature of money which enables its profoundly ambivalent status in modern society to be grasped. In doing so, he provides important epistemological clues as to how the problem of theoretical rigidity in monetary analysis might be overcome. He achieves this not by placing money within a systematic theory of modernity but, on the contrary, by treating money as an abstract medium of philosophical investigation. Simmel's conceptualization of money as a transparent means for philosophical study precisely matches his account of the symbolic and motivating force generated by money's transparency as an economic instrument. He neither predisposes individuals to act and think in particular ways when they use money, nor suffocates his own inquiry by formulating a definition of money conditioned by substantive theoretical assumptions. He is able to do this only by approaching money in terms of what he regards as its essential characteristics, which paradoxically liberates him to explore the full array of contrasting, conflicting and contradictory uses and perceptions of money in modern society. It is because Simmel refuses to build these into a substantive theory of money, let alone a substantive theory of modern society, that he succeeds in this. His work therefore has vital significance for the inquiry into the epistemological problems inherent in monetary analysis which are central to the arguments of this book.

In so far as ideas and theories of money play an integral role in how it is used, the reflexive relationship between monetary theory and monetary practices must be understood and its implications explored. This cannot be done by subjugating monetary analysis to the rigid requirements of substantive theories of economic and social life. Money can and should be incorporated in such theories, but must not be made to embody their assumptions as part and parcel of its substantive characterization. This is what I mean by emphasizing the requirement for analytic rigour in monetary theory; not a form of logical felicity to the suppositions of theory but, on the contrary, a theoretical flexibility in the face of the unique requirements of monetary analysis. Money, as I argued in chapter 3, is distinctive as an object of study because, quite unlike anything else, indeterminacy is its most essential property. Monetary theorists can only obscure this property by trying to formulate a series of substantive, definitive, statements about the nature and functions of money in general. Such an inquiry must be confined to the empirical study of specific monetary forms, not clamped onto characterizations of the essence of money in the form of contingencies transposed as necessities. My aim in the first part of the book has not been merely to examine different monetary theories but, by positioning myself against those theories, to inquire into the nature and status of monetary theory itself. In the second part of the book, this inquiry will be deepened and extended by systematically applying the conception of monetary analysis that I have begun to develop here to a substantive examination of the role of money in contemporary society.

PART II

5

The Politics of International Monetary Integration

Substantive analysis of the role of money in contemporary society is not simply a question of addressing money from the perspective of prevailing concerns of sociology. Monetary analysis can on the contrary illuminate key issues in contemporary social theory. The development of a rigorous approach to monetary analysis should enable core thematic concerns in the study of contemporary societies to be more fully understood. Monetary analysis has an integral role to play in reappraising classical sociological accounts of the developmental trajectory of modern societies, both from the West outwards and from the past into the future. Investigation of the relationship between money and social action is fundamental to undertaking a more penetrating assessment of the form of knowledge, virtually indistinguishable from economic rationality, which has underpinned the economic, political and military hegemony of the West throughout the modern age. Developments in the international organization of money and finance have been critical to a set of geopolitical trends referred to in social theory as globalization or Westernization. Analysis of these trends has begun to suggest that the form of knowledge on which that hegemony is based has been deeply misconceived. There is no doubt that economic rationality has been consequential on a globally extensive scale. But there must be considerable doubt whether this form of knowledge provides an adequate basis for understanding the nature of economic and geopolitical causality.

Assumptions about how and why money is used have been at the heart of an explanatory approach to the phenomenon of globalization which leaves an untenable number of its key features unaccounted for: the persistent vulnerability of nation-state governments to international economic fluctuations, to which the operation of monetary and financial markets is central; the ambivalent consequences of the simultaneous compression and expansion of principles of spatial and temporal organization; the increasing penetration of economic processes not only into Western social and cultural life but into the relationship between the West and the lives and livelihoods of anonymous others some distance away - a distance defined both physically and culturally; and the political and economic constraints which continue to obstruct reappraisal of the interconnection between human societies and their environment. The substantive and empirical issues raised in the study of economic life, and in the analysis of the role of money in contemporary society in particular, are inextricably linked with these questions in a way which is not merely causal but thematic. Monetary analysis therefore has a twofold significance for contemporary sociology: empirically, monetary and financial relations are undeniably consequential in respect of the historical developments taking place in geopolitical relations; but at one remove, the treatment of money as an expression and manifestation of these developments should enable social theorists to focus more closely and with greater clarity on the phenomenon of globalization itself - not just one of its aspects but in its entirety. These claims are made not only in acknowledgement of the obvious significance of money throughout contemporary society. No less importantly, they are informed by my conviction that the inherent difficulties associated with monetary analysis expose fundamental epistemological problems in the enterprise of contemporary social theorizing. My concern in the first part of the book was not merely to examine substantive issues of direct concern to monetary theory but to investigate the implications of inherent difficulties of monetary analysis for understanding what a theory sets out to do or achieve. These issues are sharply focused in the analysis of money because of its inherent resistance to existing ideas about the construction and application of theories. The distinctiveness of money as an object of study has prevented its analysis from being subsumed by the preoccupations of theoreticians throughout the social sciences. The implications of this can only be fully understood by developing my ideas about the nature and applications of monetary analysis through an examination of different facets of the operation of money in contemporary society.

International monetary integration is one of the more politically provoking themes of contemporary monetary analysis. In the guise of both monetary union among states and increasing interdependence between monetary and financial markets across state boundaries, integration has exposed serious confusions in the existing monetary literature over the purpose of the relationship between money and the state. Monetary instability amongst the G7 countries has long encouraged doubts right across the political spectrum that governments are the best agencies to carry out prudent monetary policy. The alternative involves taking control over the production and supply of money out of government hands altogether, either by adopting the German model and instituting a separate agency such as an independent central bank or by allowing the circulation of private notes, literally denationalizing money. Monetary sovereignty is a richly, almost superstitiously cherished component of government in many Western countries: not merely among officials and politicians, but by individuals who find the use of money without state guarantees difficult to imagine. From this point of view, the phenomenon of international monetary integration constitutes a threat which, significantly, advocates of monetary union between states claim to be seeking to counter. Historical perspective, as well as a tighter conceptual grasp of the relationship between money and trust, is vital to constructive discussion of these issues. State agencies exercise monetary control not merely through regulation but by transacting and intervening within international markets. It is in the latter role that states have contributed significantly to the expansion of international markets. While this process has strained the capacity of states to exercise monetary control through regulation, their continued access to international markets as transactors has in some ways enhanced their supervisory function. In other words, as I seek to demonstrate in the first section of the chapter, state agencies are having to rely less on enforcement than on trust in their relations with international banks and financial markets. As I move on to contend in the second section, the deregulatory measures undertaken by states in relation to such markets during the 1970s and 1980s must not therefore be viewed simply as reactive. Such measures have on the contrary been designed partly to enhance the international status of the key international financial centres, thereby delivering macroeconomic benefits. To this extent, as I argue in the third section, the phenomenon of international monetary integration can be viewed as a consequence of deliberate state policies no less than of so-called market forces operating beyond the control of states. The ultimate success or failure of such policies should be addressed in this light, and any perceived threat to the sovereignty of nation-states posed by monetary union should be treated cautiously.

Politics, Markets and Monetary Administration

Scrutiny of the structure and organization of monetary administration in its contemporary form places in sharp focus the difficulty of distinguishing between political and economic imperatives in so far as these bear upon the aims of monetary sovereignty and the means of sustaining monetary stability. Moreover, close analysis of procedures undertaken by central banks in the present day suggests that the association of money with the state so vehemently defended in discussions of monetary union, in so far as this tends to presuppose the idea of a unitary state, is far from robust. Such conceptual difficulties are hardly incidental, for they pose very real problems in establishing, in empirical terms, precisely what it is that proponents of monetary sovereignty are actually seeking to defend. The primary function of any central bank is to maintain the substantive validity or exchange-value of its currency. In addition, and with varying degrees of autonomy, central banks play a vital role in implementing government economic and monetary policy.[1] Analysis of how central banks operate in practice cannot, however, be exhausted by reference to formal procedures alone. As reference to individual cases should demonstrate,[2] the relationship between the central bank, other state agencies, and financial and banking institutions is neither constant nor formalized but continuously defined and redefined according to international conditions, the domestic political climate and even relations between individual personalities.[3] This continual process of definition and redefinition does not simply mark a series of variations from a standardized central banking model. On the contrary, the way central banking practices change according to circumstances owes much to the plasticity which is integral to the *modus operandi* of monetary administration itself.

Non-formal practices tend to predominate in central banking even where the actual directives under which the central bank operates are legally enshrined or directly subject to the policies of the government of the day. This argument can be supported by reference to Germany. Although the statutory position of the Bundesbank[4] implies that the objective of monetary stability is somehow above day-to-day politics as a purely technical matter,[5] there have been numerous occasions when the political implications of Bundesbank policies have been worked through along non-formal lines and under quite specific political pressures.[6] That this should have been so is hardly surprising. The goal of monetary stability can inhibit the expenditure objectives of an elected government, and the specific policies implemented in pursuit of monetary stability invariably weigh in favour of particular sectional interests. The formation of Bundesbank policy, within the framework of the ERM, is inextricably and sometimes explicitly tied to and conditional upon the objectives not only of the German government but of other European Community governments as well. Intergovernmental negotiations over a general realignment of currencies within the system during August and September 1992 demonstrate precisely this. The Bundesbank Council indicated willingness to implement a cut in interest rates as a condition of realignment, placing its own independent policy towards monetary stability in direct linkage with the domestic political pressures confronted by European Community governments as a result of the international strength of the Deutschemark.[7] In this instance, it is simply impossible to distinguish neatly between technical and political facets of decision-making within the Bundesbank, not due to lack of clarity about the facts but because the goal of monetary stability has an international dimension which cannot be separated from relations between governments.[8] The responsibility of the Bundesbank to engage in open market operations to defend ERM currencies against international speculation is a consequence of a series of political commitments undertaken by the German government. This is nevertheless of material significance for the technical objectives of the Bundesbank itself, not merely as a constraint imposed upon its policies from the outside but as an integral part of the process by which those policies are formulated and worked through.

The characterization of the Bundesbank as independent of politics is perfectly sensible in constitutional terms but provides a misleading guide to its actions as a monetary administrator. The relationship between Bundesbank and government is difficult to characterize outside of specific cases, for the agencies do not possess consistent degrees of power over time. The possibility that a central bank might obstruct the implementation of government economic policy implies the existence of a check on powers within the state, somewhat similar to a fourth constitutional power. This is by no means inevitably politically objectionable, of course. Monetary stability is a major political issue in its own right in Germany, and so an obstructive Bundesbank committed to this goal may enjoy broad political support for its position at times of open dispute. Indeed, the status of the Bundesbank is itself an issue of political legitimacy in Germany, particularly in the light of previous experience of domestic monetary and financial crises.[9] Such experience is reinforced by the interests of the large number of savers in West Germany, for whom high inflation is directly undermining. Thus it is arguably the commitment to a stable currency rather than independence as such which legitimates the quasi-constitutional position of the

Bundesbank. Such, indeed, is the political entanglement of the orientation to monetary stability, however carefully and systematically this task has been removed from political interference or public scrutiny.

Unlike the Bundesbank, the Bank of England[10] has no statutory duty to safeguard sterling and is in principle more closely tied by the economic objectives and monetary policies of the government of the day. Yet here too, albeit for quite distinctive reasons from the German case, tensions and conflicts arise from time to time between and within the network of relationships linking the Bank of England to the Treasury, to cabinet, and ultimately to parliament. It is especially clear in this respect that the equation of monetary sovereignty with the control of money by a unitary state can be seen to break down under close scrutiny. Like practitioners of monetary administration in Germany, the Bank of England - at least as exemplified in a series of speeches by Leigh-Pemberton, the governor until summer 1993[11] - regards non-statutory supervision as essential to maintaining flexibility amidst the continuous development of financial instruments designed to evade existing regulations.[12] The approach is largely based on informal procedures, historically underpinned by the homogeneous social background of a reputed financial community within the City of London, especially its higher echelons.[13] Indeed, the persistence of this homogeneity amongst individuals across the institutional nexus of the City of London, Bank of England and Treasury suggests that the sense in which the Bank itself can be regarded as under political control is ambiguous. The policy objectives of the Treasury tend to coincide with those advocated within the City of London. These frequently conflict with policy objectives espoused by pressure groups such as the Confederation of British Industry.[14] Within the parameters of the 1946 Bank of England Act, the Bank defers to the government in general and the Chancellor of the Exchequer in particular over monetary policy. The Chancellor may issue formal directives to the Bank but none has ever done so. No such powers were granted to the Treasury, whose directions to clearing-banks are issued through recommendations via the Bank. In so far as policy differences emerge between the Bank and Treasury, the capacity of each to exercise its will depends on individual relationships and political circumstances.[15] The principle of political autonomy has nonetheless been significant throughout the Bank's history. It is doubtful whether nationalization altered much in this respect.[16]

In both cases discussed here, monetary administration is not carried out in a way which can be straightforwardly summarized by a set of formal operational principles. Non-formal arrangements, bolstered by their own longevity in addition to specific conditions relating to the political system and administrative culture in which banks and banking regulators operate, seem as important to the everyday process of monetary administration as formal laws and regulations. Whether these conditions actually render the administration of monetary policy and regulation in the centres concerned more or less effective is open to question. This issue can be better addressed by examining the nature and consequences of the process of deregulation which has allegedly occurred in all three centres since the 1970s. It is the process of deregulation, after all, which has commonly been cited as one of the domestic financial conditions historically conducive to monetary integration across geopolitical boundaries.

Deregulation or Reregulation?

Deregulation refers to the straightforward dismantling of a regulatory framework, and for this reason carries connotations of freeing the activity previously regulated. Conceptually, deregulation implies the increasing separation of politics and markets, the lifting of political directives away from market processes and relationships. Reregulation refers to the institution of a different form of regulation with distinctive aims and targets. Monetary and financial systems in Japan, Germany and Britain are commonly reputed to have undergone a significant and consequential process of deregulation since the 1970s. The Japanese case is complicated by the implication that deregulation also amounts to a process of Westernization. Debates over deregulation generally focus on its roots; in particular, whether the measures in question have been driven by competitive pressures, instigated by administrative policy, or both. But this question, posed in such a way, is narrow and misconceived. To address the developments under discussion as reregulation can lead to a better understanding of the historical importance of a combination of geopolitical and commercial pressures to the present-day operation of international monetary networks.

Deregulation in Japan is as much a cultural issue as an administrative process. Japan's banking and financial system has conventionally been distinguished from Western international financial centres by the relationship between business, politics and a series of practices loosely referred to as convention and closely linked to a distinctive Japanese institutional culture.[17] Monetary policy in Japan[18] is administered by the Bank of Japan and Ministry of Finance.[19] Banking supervision comprises a mix of direct control, moral suasion - or window guidance - and voluntary self-restraint. The relative prominence of each approach depends on the banking sector in question, but in general, formal control seems to be less significant than non-formal channels of communication. Window guidance is bolstered by the *amakudari* convention, where ex-officials of the Bank of Japan take places on boards of private banks, 'enhancing not only the authorities' influence within the private financial community but also the banks' ability to understand and communicate with the government'.[20] Indeed, political and historical association seems to be integral to the very structure of Japanese banking. Japanese banks are distinguished by function and hierarchized 'according to a deeply embedded public view of their status and power'.[21]

Japanese banking practices can be traced back to the constitutional principles known as *hoshu honryu* instituted by Prime Minister Yoshida during the late 1940s and early 1950s. These principles were essentially pragmatic, prioritizing economic aims rather than traditional practices while none the less holding on to support from traditional interests. They required 'close relations among interest groups (in this early period, primarily big business and agriculture), the bureaucracy, and the conservatives'.[22] *Hoshu honryu* gave rise to a form of patterned pluralism within the Japanese economy, where the government pursues its own interests by means of 'an institutionalized accommodation among élites, interacting with pluralist elements'.[23] Murakami defines this practice more loosely as an 'informal parapolitical nexus' with roots in 'a unique and crucial interface between the polity and culture in Japan'.[24] A similarly close, non-formalized association has persisted between Japanese banks and industry. This was initially fostered by low accumulation of financial assets during the 1950s and 1960s. The liquidity shortage generated heavy bank borrowing by corporate business, encouraging close long-term involvement between banks and corporate clients.[25] For example, a bank occupying a key role within industrial groups might place its own executives on the board of a corporate client, sometimes even utilizing this as a means of rewarding or retiring its own executives or of exercising influence over a problematic client.[26]

To conceptualize deregulation as having been generated by market imperatives suggests that Japanese banking and financial practices have become decreasingly unusual to Western eyes, increasingly free, open and rational.[27] Regulatory changes in Japan have mostly involved changes in the administration of interest rates and the lifting of restrictions governing international monetary transactions. The Tokyo offshore market opened on 1 December 1986. After one month, 15 per cent of the assets of banks in Japan were booked with the market,[28] and the international assets of the market rose to $372 billion after three years.[29]

Interest rates in domestic markets had previously been administered (via the *Tanshi Kyokai*) to hold them below market levels, thus allowing the Bank of Japan and Ministry of Finance a greater hand in the allocation of funds during postwar economic regeneration.[30] Competitive pressures were heavily implicated in ensuing changes. The most open of Japan's financial markets had been the *gensaki*, the market for repurchasable bonds. The differential between rates in the administered bill-discount and call-money markets on the one hand, and in the *gensaki* on the other, was important to the withdrawal, in the former two markets, of the consultative process with the *Tanshi* in the determination of interest rates. That this measure was partly market led is suggested by the higher rate of growth of the *gensaki* market, especially during periods of official monetary restraint.[31] On the other hand, several deregulatory measures in Japan were instigated directly by the requirements of government. For example, a secondary market in bonds was generated by the increase in flotations[32] to fund the social welfare programme of an election-wary Liberal-Democratic government.[33] This opened up the banking sector significantly.

It is in any case difficult to establish exactly how much regulatory changes actually blunted the penetration of Japanese state agencies into the financial and banking system. Arguably, the channels through which the Bank of Japan and Ministry of Finance spoil, delay or exploit commercial objectives for political and administrative ends can be little affected by regulatory changes alone. The political and administrative culture of Japan cuts into formal procedures in such a way as to soften the impact of regulatory changes on commercial banks and monetary administrators. Non-formal practices have been integral to Japan's postwar industrial development, and it seems doubtful that these could be stripped away merely by adjusting regulations. Interest groups and élites have penetrated the Japanese state to such an extent that they have become integral to its operation. Conflict or disagreement proceeds along established lines, between consistent alliances founded on consensus regarding not merely how the system operates but the identity of macroeconomic priorities. It is not at all clear that calls for Japan to reform by imitating Western practices - or arguments that this process has been under way with deregulation - can be sustained on the basis of some kind of free market thesis. Deregulation in its Western sense - the form advocated in contemporary discussions with Japan's trading partners, especially the United States, which involves movement towards a market framework as defined in the West - would, in Japan, entail not only lifting specified regulations but establishing new laws, a process of *re*regulation which disrupts and undermines procedures regarded abroad as anti-competitive. The 'freeing' of the financial system in Japan must, it appears, be contrived by means of an active legislative programme, not the straightforward removal of administrative obstacles.

The weakness of conceptualizing deregulation in terms of market forces is further suggested by reference to the relationship between the government and financial sector in Germany. The banking system in Germany is open in regulative terms to the extent that there are virtually no official obstacles to the type of business in which banks can engage, although financial power is heavily concentrated in the three largest commercial banks, the Deutsche Bank, Dresdner Bank and Commerz-bank. During the postwar period a consistently successful co-ordination of strategies by the state and the financial and industrial sectors has been based on a convergence of interests.[34] This need not suggest, however, that political imperatives have necessarily been accorded priority over financial concerns. Rather, commercial incentives in Germany are inextricably linked to political priorities. Indeed, government preference may in some cases constitute a commercial incentive. Formal discussions between state and banks in Germany are undertaken through banking associations and interministerial committees. By and large, personal contacts predominate; for example, bank officials regularly accompany ministers on official visits abroad. These kinds of communication are difficult to define analytically. They do, however, reflect a consensual basis to strategic decisions which penetrates monetary policy, enabling the potentially divisive legal framework connecting the Bundesbank and government to work to the advantage of both. To characterize the German financial system and the relationship between politics and monetary administration therein as broadly *laissez-faire* may be credible in formal terms. But this fails to address the importance of the high degree of concentration, strategic consensus and convergence of interests on which the role of finance in Germany's postwar development has been based. In this light, any attempt to distinguish between the political and market dimensions in Germany seems arbitrary. Neither dimension is of sufficient substance and integrity to allow such a sharp distinction.

Similar compression of specific political and commercial imperatives characterizes the relationship between certain sectors of government and the banking and financial sector in Britain. Important deregulatory changes have undoubtedly been undertaken in Britain, for example the 1979 and 1987 Banking Acts, the 1986 Financial Services Act and the 1986 Building Societies' Act. But it is by no means clear that they constitute any kind of separation of politics and markets in the manner implied by the concept of deregulation, accompanied as this has been in Britain by a polemical thesis advocating the government's role in fostering politically unfettered markets. The measures in question can more accurately be characterized in terms of the pressing need to accommodate international developments, as a defence of national monetary sovereignty which is ambiguous in its consequences. There are of course clear commercial imperatives entailed in the development of the City of London as a favourable environment for international banking. But these are imperatives which cannot be neatly aligned with an abstract capitalist class nor straightforwardly juxtaposed with the broader policy aims of a unitary and benign state. The financial system in Britain is distinguished by its large share of international business. Arguably, the international prominence of the City of London is closely linked to the non-interventionist supervisory approach in operation there. But it is important not to be carried away by this in the manner of Hall, for example, who seeks to place financial deregulation in Britain in the context of a seemingly irresistible 'worldwide trend towards a deregulated, global financial services market'.[35] Closer examination of specific measures indicates a process rather more ambiguous than Hall's sweep allows. There is certainly a case to be made that the abolition of exchange controls in 1979, the absence of credit controls, and the scrapping of minimum commissions in 1986 enhanced the City as a competitive environment by increasing commercial opportunities and the scope for innovation. There are several other factors, however, which have made the City of London attractive for international business: for example, the pool of suitably trained labour, recently declining levels of personal and corporate taxation, the supply of suitable premises within the City itself, the relative stability of the British political climate, and London's favourable location between the time-zones of other principal financial centres, chiefly Tokyo and New York.[36] In its details, deregulation in Britain seems to have been less a straightforward removal of regulation than a qualitative shift in the mix between regulation and supervision, with certain aspects of the former having been actually strengthened, in other words a process of reregulation. Many regulatory changes in Britain have been generated by the blurring of functional distinctions between financial institutions as they diversify amidst an international climate of integration. This has made supervision on the basis of categories of institution more difficult and less even-handed, with some institutions being covered twice and others not at all. Long-established practices passed on through banking personnel became increasingly difficult to sustain as entry to the system or activity in question eased. The supervisory aim was to maintain what Leigh-Pemberton idiomatically refers to as a 'level playing-field' for the different categories of institution who engage competitively in a broader range of activities.[37]

The relationship between politics and monetary administration is characterized above all by an intersection of commercial and political imperatives. The points of intersection pervade ongoing relations between government agencies and financial institutions, affecting the terms within which debates are held, according to which the various parties pursue their own objectives, and on the basis of which commercial and political strategies are formulated. In Japan, unambiguous intervention in financial markets by the Bank of Japan and Ministry of Finance is integral to the ongoing operation of the financial system. Political intervention is part and parcel of the everyday operations of the financial sector. Specific measures may be opposed sometimes, but rarely the right of officials to act at all. Moreover, the declaration of a specific project as national acts as a spur for commercial activity. Similarly in Germany, the use of incentives by government reflects an attempt to weight the commercial attractiveness of particular schemes. But the criteria by which banking strategies are formulated do not shift in nature when political objectives are accommodated: they are not purely commercial in the first instance. While its formal and practised powers enable the Bundesbank seriously to question and even directly undermine government policies, the absence of deeper conflicts reflects an under- lying consensus over monetary stability closely linked to the framework of coalition politics. In Britain, the intersection of political and financial spheres is based on a sociological nexus between the Treasury, Bank of England and City of London. This suggests that the kind of clear distinction between a unitary political (state apparatus) and financial (set of markets) dimension implicit in the debate over monetary sovereignty is no more than a conceptually convenient but empirically erroneous abstraction. In so far as there is a sectional divide between the City of London and industry,[38] this is linked to priorities arising from the City's international status. The international dimension in the cases discussed here is no less important than issues of political culture and administrative convention. Regulatory changes have been oriented both to attracting institutions into financial centres and insulating those centres from the potentially damaging consequences of integration: in other words, state agencies have sought, largely through reregulation, to foster an international financial system which is still controllable within the parameters of the nation-state system. To this extent, international markets have clear roots in the political and administrative structures on which they depend for their persistence, but upon which they threaten to encroach. It is to this issue that I shall now turn.

International Monetary Networks

It is worth clarifying why I have taken the development of offshore financial markets as the basis for a discussion of international monetary integration, whereas I could have focused directly on recent and current developments in relation to EMU or on the period of the gold standard. Both the latter instances of monetary integration are defined by a blurring of political and commercial imperatives. My aim in this chapter, on the contrary, is to flesh out the sense in which the distinction between them is presupposed by the concept of monetary sovereignty itself. Offshore transactions, according to more alarmist analyses, have developed on the basis of a historical separation of commercial and political dimensions. This is implicit in the very concept of an 'offshore' transaction. More significantly, a consistent theme in much of the literature on international monetary integration holds that nation-state borders are becoming irrelevant to the commercial imperatives pursued by international banks. For this reason, offshore transactions present something of a 'hard case' against which to evaluate whether the separation of politics and markets which the market-driven model of monetary integration implies is empirically and conceptually tenable. It is important, also, to be clear about what is meant by integration in this context, for the concept is often used to refer to conditions more accurately described as openness and identity. A completely open economy or monetary system has no legal, social, political, geographical or cultural barriers to international exchange.[39] Identity refers to similarity in consumption patterns, material aspirations, and production and exchange relations across geopolitical borders. An integrated economic or monetary framework consists not of the absence of barriers but of interdependence through specialization.[40] Integration and identity are not synonymous. Neither does the presence of one presuppose the presence of the other.

Offshore banking involves lending and borrowing currencies outside their country of issue. Eurocurrencies - denominated in dollars, marks, sterling or yen, for example - predominate in offshore banking, although the markets for these are not confined to Europe. An initial condition[41] for the development of offshore banking was the establishment of currency convertibility in 1958 among leading European currencies and the yen. Previously, only US and Canadian dollars and the Swiss franc were freely convertible, with the use of the latter outside Switzerland strongly discouraged by Swiss authorities. Of greater significance, however, was the surfeit of dollars generated by US balance of payments deficits and boosted by American companies' conversion of profits into dollars outside the United States.[42] Technological innovation has also helped shape offshore markets: in increasing pressure towards regulatory changes, enabling institutions to undertake a broader range of activities, and negating the importance of spatial limitations derived from geographical location on the provision of specific financial services.[43] Offshore transactions penetrate the domestic money and banking system. They are not simply undertaken outside geopolitical borders but are played off against those borders as a condition of their commercial success. There is not a separate group of institutions involved in offshore markets and official markets respectively. Any crisis within offshore networks might consequently be transmitted into domestic monetary networks and banking systems. Offshore banking therefore presents problems to monetary administrators not simply because of the quantity of funds involved but because there is no clear regulatory framework for controlling those funds. Loans and deposits can be made in offshore centres which are not permitted elsewhere: either because of the nature, even absence, of collateral on offer, or because reserve requirements are less strict when undertaken in the absence of lender-of-last-resort facilities. These characteristics form the basis of the attractiveness of offshore transactions. When problems do occur, central banks are only indirectly involved, being based in the centre where offshore transactions are undertaken or in the country of origin of the lenders and borrowers. They will most probably engage in collective hand-wringing.

It would be erroneous, however, to imagine that offshore markets have thrived simply by evading domestic regulations, through a process in which 'market forces' aided and abetted by technological innovation have superseded leaden-footed efforts of domestic regulators and supervisors. Deregulation in international financial centres, or what I have suggested can be more accurately defined as reregulation, does not involve a straightforward loss of control on the part of monetary authorities but stems from the deliberate and reasoned abrogation of certain facets of control.[44] Indeed, government regulations have helped stimulate the growth of offshore markets. In some cases, admittedly, the stimulant in question has been generated unwittingly. For example, Regulation Q instituted in the United States during the late 1960s limited the rate of interest which domestic banks could offer to holders of dollars, not only presenting foreign banks with a competitive edge but providing an incentive to place dollars outside the United States.[45] Similarly, a mistake by the US government in the early 1970s - reducing interest rates at a time when German rates were tightening - exacerbated the outflow of funds into offshore markets.[46] In the UK, sterling parallel markets comprising unsecured loans with no lender-of-last-resort developed partly in response to the imposition of credit restrictions during the 1960s and further following the secondary banking crises of 1973–4.[47] In other instances, however, offshore transactions have been stimulated by domestic regulations with precisely this consequence in mind. For example, Japanese authorities have systematically encouraged the integration of the Japanese financial system with international markets both onshore and offshore. Reregulatory measures undertaken within the Japanese banking system during the early 1980s were directly linked to the 1979 oil price shock, with the Bank of Japan instituting a tight monetary policy and the Ministry of Finance instructing banks to offer rates as high as necessary to attract surplus OPEC funds.[48] The Ministry of Finance in particular relaxed restrictions on the capacity of Japanese banks to open offices overseas, especially in the Middle East. The Japanese government engaged in diplomatic efforts to encourage Arab governments to place funds in Japan.[49] Significantly, the development of offshore markets, far from superseding domestic regulations in Japan, partly strengthened the capacity of the Ministry of Finance to act in its own strategic interests, such as in response to unwanted current account surpluses or deficits.

The development of offshore markets does not therefore indicate in any straightforward way a process of evasion of regulatory authorities by international transactors, but has had and continues to have a clear political dimension. In so far as offshore currencies are based in national currencies, they are partly dependent on the political and institutional conditions underlying their strength. More importantly, offshore capital networks have historically comprised a high proportion of sovereign funds.[50] The Marshall Plan provided the initial political impetus behind the expansion of official international capital networks. Unilateral development aid continued to expand during the 1950s, with other developed nations formulating programmes for providing grants and low-interest loans to less developed countries (LDCs); and in the 1960s, with a sometimes unfulfilled commitment by the former to devote 1 per cent of national income to LDCs. Offshore transactions have served as a major conduit for these funds. Analyses of the relationship between government aid and offshore transaction has been dominated by a conventional wisdom exemplified by the 1977 OECD McCracken Report. This analysis holds that much of the surplus of funds made available to OPEC countries by the 1973 rise in the dollar-denominated oil price was deposited in offshore markets 'from where it was recycled by the large international banks to oil-deficit LDCs'.[51] This would amount to privatizing international aid. Spero disagrees with this version of events, arguing that the redistribution of the OPEC surplus via offshore markets had more to do with American hegemony than with the market-driven re-balancing of the international distribution of capital. He argues that a large proportion of OPEC funds was invested in US Treasury bills, while those funds which did go to LDCs, rather than being taken up by the most needy, were actually borrowed by middle income LDCs - some even oil-exporting - such as Algeria, Argentina, Brazil, South Korea, Mexico, Venezuela and Nigeria.[52] The implications of Spero's interpretation are unclear, but he does at least suggest that the intersection of commercial and political imperatives underpinning international monetary integration has been too complex to allow the kind of uncomplicated assertion of monetary sovereignty around which the debate over international monetary union tends to revolve. On the one hand, US political hegemony clearly was important to the expansion of offshore monetary networks, in terms of not only the destination of surplus funds but also their denomination in dollars. On the other hand, commercial concerns were at stake for private international banks prepared to lend the surplus dollars in the form of syndicated loans. These concerns reflect the recession under way in the advanced nations: the high profits anticipated from the process of indebted industrialization undertaken by LDCs and newly industrialized borrowers would obviously have been attractive.

One crucial difference between official and private aid concerns the demands placed on recipient states. The World Bank and International Monetary Fund (IMF), as well as Multilateral Development Banks, have been funded not merely to support specific projects but also for laying down stringent conditions regarding the economic priorities pursued, and the manner of their pursuit, by the recipients of assistance.[53] The stated aims of IMF intervention are professedly apolitical, comprising efforts to engender market frameworks where they have been absent or are considered flawed. In other words, intervention is regarded by the intervenors themselves as prising economics away from politics, not the other way around, thereby encouraging recipient states' participation in the international economy.[54] Significantly, then, in the case of both offshore transaction and IMF intervention, it could be argued that regulations are being stripped away to allow free markets to flourish unencumbered, as if the market were some kind of pre-given essence underpinning all monetary and economic relations. This interpretation is wholly consistent with the economic reasoning underlying the political economy of money discussed in chapter 1. A similarly market-focused analysis is possible in the case of private aid. Offshore loans are unaccompanied by intervention within the domestic economic and monetary arrangements of the borrowers. Gilpin, for example, argues that private aid offered those countries 'fortunate enough to be classified as 'creditworthy' ... a way around the 'conditionality' of multilateral aid agencies, the influence of unilateral aid givers, and the domination of the multinationals'.[55] In the case of both official and private aid it is impossible, however, to concur with an interpretation of the development of offshore banking as somehow superseding geopolitical boundaries. The advance of syndicated loans by international private banks to sovereign states through offshore networks was stimulated by commercial priorities, but the large anticipated profits from rapid industrialization were shored up by the identity of debtors as sovereign states, by the belief that states do not go bankrupt. Gilpin is probably more accurate in this sense when he argues that the growth of offshore funds was fuelled by a mixture of surplus OPEC dollars, eager and politically naïve international private banks sometimes assisted by national governments, and the capital hungry sovereign states of Eastern Europe and the Third World: bankers and governments locked in a curious alliance.[56]

If anything, then, transactors in offshore markets depend on the capacity of national monetary authorities to sustain the conditions and commercial incentives on which such evasive transactions draw for their competitiveness. Offshore transactors rely on the strength and consistency of the monetary and fiscal sovereignty of individual states. It is from differences between individual regulatory environments - which are based on the sovereign right of each state to legislate independently - that commercial incentives are derived.[57] Indeed, a limited suspension of sovereignty, entailing the harmonization of national laws and supervisory practices, rendering 'differences in legal approaches unimportant as incentives for movement of capital',[58] is necessary if some of the risks implied by offshore transaction, perceived from the stance of domestic regulators and supervisors, are to be avoided. As Goodhart suggests, the development of offshore markets has not wholly undermined the authority of state agencies in respect of monetary affairs, but does demand central banking flexibility, supervision as opposed to regulation. In so far as regulation tends to repel financial institutions - for 'there will always be competitive pressures among the regulated to move towards the system with the greatest degree of laxity'[59] - supervision can only be exercised effectively on a co-operative international basis, not by host and parent countries separately.[60] And as Kindleberger adds, this would require 'ganging up on the Luxembourgs, Liechtensteins, Bahamas and the like to undermine their advantage as tax havens emanating from the sovereign right to set levels of taxation and to protect business dealing within the jurisdiction with laws ensuring secrecy':[61] in other words, a reinterpretation and perhaps selective abandonment of monetary sovereignty.

The conceptual convenience of the distinction between international and national monetary systems should not be allowed to disguise its analytical weakness. Analyses of offshore transactions tend to be coupled with a mythical conception of the power of market forces derived from economic reasoning. Tsoukalis, for example, argues that a critical problem of instability stems from the shift in the organization of international monetary networks, marked by the novel absence of a central administrator. He regards this as a new kind of international monetary system altogether, a development which 'signifies a clear shift to the market ... a conscious, or unconscious, negation of the idea of a collectively managed system with a tight official control over markets'.[62] Tsoukalis contends that a system of such scale and complexity cannot operate efficiently without some form of collective management. Indeed, the system itself can be said to have emerged by default, generated by inactivity on the part of monetary administrators.[63] Two problems arise in this analysis. First, it is not at all clear that the fact of the emergence of the system as unmanaged necessarily means that this must have been a consequence of passivity on the part of state agencies, which is what 'by default' implies. State agencies have been far from inactive in the development of international monetary networks, however much their policy objectives have been compromised by this. Tsoukalis himself seems to concede that state agencies cannot straightforwardly be characterized as passive when he notes that '[e]ven a refusal to take action is a decision in itself'.[64] Second, Tsoukalis's analysis is not helped by his confused references to the concepts of 'system' and 'non-system'. He seems to associate an international monetary system only with arrangements which are collectively managed, and a non-system with the reverse. He offers no indication of what a non-system might be, however, and rather distances himself from the expression by noting that 'some prefer to call [it] a 'non-system' because of the conspicuous lack of jointly accepted rules about exchange rates and the process of adjustment, the creation of international liquidity and reserve assets'.[65] Lack of clarity in this respect is exacerbated by difficulties entailed in establishing the precise status and role of geopolitical boundaries in relation to the non-system. This particular issue is not confined to Tsoukalis's analysis, but is integral to the very nature of international monetary integration as a conceptual and administrative problem.

While the expansion of international monetary networks undeniably presents state monetary administrators with significant difficulties, the issue can only be fudged by complaints about a loss of monetary sovereignty in the face of the emergence of an unfettered international monetary system. As I have said, commercial incentives are actually generated by differences between individual regulatory environments, not the absence of regulations altogether. It is for precisely this reason that debates over EMU seem rarely to rise above the level of bluster and fancy where the loss of sovereignty is concerned. Geopolitical boundaries in relation to monetary networks have not completely disappeared. But they were never entirely secure in the first place. Confusion over the nature and importance of monetary sovereignty stems from a misconception of the characteristics of financial and monetary networks as markets. It is not at all clear that international monetary networks mark the emergence, teleologically as it were, of a market stretching across geopolitical boundaries whose operation approximates more and more closely to a perfection derived from economic reasoning. The very concept of the market, perfect[66] or otherwise, is deeply problematic when examined closely. As Unger contends, the essential characteristics of a market, 'an economic order where a significant number of units trade on their own initiative and account', is in practice compatible with 'very different systems of contract and property rights, each with its own consequences for the distribution of power and wealth and for the tenor of life in the society'.[67] In other words, the abstract idea of the market provides no exhaustive guide to the sociological conditions under which markets operate in practice. There exists no pre-given foundation to markets which will emerge as soon as political fetters are removed. Political conditions do not hold back markets in this sense, but are among those factors which are integral to the constitution of specific, historically situated markets in the first instance.

This contention was at the heart of my discussion of the financial system in Japan, Germany and Britain. In all three financial centres, the analysis of the practice of monetary administration is not merely empirically complex but methodologically problematic. In particular, it is difficult to establish whether decisions are founded on political and personal leverage or convergent interests. This makes the implications of regulatory changes difficult to assess. In principle, informal arrangements would have to change in the face of deregulation: practices based on convention and personal relationships would be exposed by competitive pressures and probably deemed inefficient. According to this reasoning, a 'free' financial regime would remain, in the absence of administrative and other fetters, approximating to a pure market. This has simply not been the case. The financial centres of Germany and Britain do not correspond to pure market frameworks to a greater extent than in Japan. Nor are they necessarily more free, which is implicitly the same point. They are on the contrary founded on qualitatively distinctive social, cultural and political practices. Markets do not pre-exist the economic activities of men and women. Nor do they emerge naturally from such activities like some kind of ahistorical social order. Just as to cast the market only as a collection of buyers and sellers is too indeterminate a characterization of a social framework whose political and cultural facets are integral to the decisions and courses of action undertaken therein, so to attempt to exhaust the framework once and for all - for example, by reference to substantive factors such as maximization and the institution of private property - provides no lasting basis for theoretical analysis. Markets consist of an ongoing series of specific historical relationships, and can only accurately be conceptualized in these terms.

The argument that international monetary networks have become disconnected from states is no more satisfactory than their portrayal as near-perfect markets. State agencies have facilitated the development of international monetary networks not through passivity or by being superseded by market forces but by fostering international business within their respective financial centres; in other words, through the furtherance of political will. It is the utilization of international monetary relations for the pursuit of political aims which underscores the paradoxical nature of the development of international monetary networks as far as state agencies are concerned, not some fluke of historical misfortune defined by the irrepressible forces of market dynamics overcoming anachronistic geopolitical borders. More subtle distinctions between regulation and supervision, deregulation and reregulation, and the role of state agencies as rule-formulators and transactors are required. It is important not to be seduced by the notion that money has been caught up in an irresistible tendency towards globalization, in which geopolitical boundaries are giving way to political, economic and cultural systems linked by international congress, monetary integration and the development of communications media. It is not credible, empirically or conceptually, to contend that money and financial systems have been globalized in such a way as to outstrip geopolitical boundaries altogether. Such an argument rests on a fundamental misunderstanding of the way in which geopolitical boundaries are chronically implicated in international monetary transac- tions as an integral component of the commercial incentives thereby pursued. Moreover, the globalization thesis glosses over the precise relationship between state agencies and international monetary networks. State agencies are not just rule-formulators. On the contrary, they intervene and transact within international markets for diffuse and sometimes inconsistent reasons. As long as monetary networks are characterized as bounded systems, with those boundaries coinciding more or less with geopolitical borders, the complexity of the relationship between state agencies and international monetary networks will be difficult to grasp: first, because the state is conceptualized in a unitary manner and thus the distinctive operations of its agencies are fudged; and second, because the unit of analysis taken up within such an approach must inevitably be transacting agents positioned inside or outside state parameters, whereas only monetary transactions, not transactors, are constitutive of monetary networks.

What emerges above all from this chapter is the importance of the entwinement, with monetary transactions and monetary networks, of forms of activity which in social and economic theory have been consigned to distinctive dimensions of society. It is this which makes the alignment of monetary systems with other types of system, or rather the alignment of their respective boundaries, so problematic. Monetary transactions do not comprise a neatly demarcated sphere of activity. Limits to money's circulation are constituted by and through the relationships between transactors which generate and sustain monetary networks, not placed around money's circulation as implied by the characterization of monetary systems. In order to understand this it is essential to reject the association of monetary transaction with a core domain of rational action separated off from the rest of society, and in relation to which political and cultural factors are a constraint rather than an integral and constitutive part. Not only economists but also sociologists have tended to commit this error. The error originates in flawed assumptions deriving ultimately from the application of economic reasoning to monetary analysis as an overarching logical framework, denoting a form of rational human activity which has causal and symbolic primacy within modern life. In the narrow sense suggested by this form of knowledge, there is no such thing as an economy.

6

Money in Postmodern Economics

The neglect by sociologists of the uses most people make of money for most of the time is indicative of an approach to economics within the discipline, in so far as sociologists approach economics at all, which is no longer tenable, and perhaps never was tenable in the first place. Sociological thinking about the economy has been somewhat obsessed with production.[1] The economic activities of individuals are largely viewed in terms of their role as producers. Finance is associated almost exclusively with production. Financial transactions undertaken for commercial ends, relying on market fluctuations rather than productive performance to make money, are rarely considered at length. The proclivities of consumers are addressed primarily as an expression of their status and capacity as producers, and consumption itself is seldom thought of as an economic activity in its own right. It seems as if attention to the use of money in any connection other than productive is regarded by many sociologists as faintly immoral. Perhaps this derives from a romantic attachment to the philosophical anthropology of Marx, even amongst those sociologists who claim to have little time for some of the less thoughtful versions of Marxist economics. This approach, which I shall refer to as the production paradigm, is characterized by a model of economic life which holds that all economic processes are conditioned by production and is manifested by the fact that sociologists seem to think about little else as far as the economy is concerned. The paradigm is flawed not because production is unimportant but because its importance should not give rise to a theoretical rigidity which obscures the study of other economic processes and activities. To argue that the operation of the economy is conditioned by production is to imply that the causal relationship between production and other economic activities is one-directional. It is doubtful whether this has ever been true. But in the light of the expansion of financial markets since the 1960s, together with the promotion, within theory, of consumption from a fact of everyday life to a defining characteristic of contemporary culture, consumerism, the assertion has never been *less* true than it is in the present day.

The expansion of international money markets, in conjunction with fundamental changes in the regulatory structure of the major international financial centres, has placed both state policy-makers and manufacturing industry under significant strain. The volume of cross-border monetary and financial transactions has been increasing at a faster rate than the transfer of raw materials and manufactured goods. This has led to a more volatile international economic environment. More seriously, it has weakened the connection between key monetary and financial indicators and real economic activity.[2] These indicators are expected to fulfil a sensitive corrective role with regard to imbalances in international trade. These developments, which were discussed in chapter 5, therefore raise doubts about the model of the economy as a whole, particularly the relationship between its real and financial sectors, from which economic policies, activities and expectations have conventionally been derived. Such doubts have most recently been expressed in postmodern commentaries on social life which focus on the phenomenon of consumerism, which I discuss in the first section of the chapter. These commentaries treat the activities of consumers as an index of their cultural lives, and are therefore significant in the light of my argument throughout this book that the cultural framework in which monetary exchange takes place is not only richer and more varied but more important than conventional economic or politico-legal theories of money have been able to convey. As I contend in the second section, postmodern theories of economic life are problematic, however, in seeking merely to overturn assumptions in economic reasoning in support of the view, implicit in the very concept of postmodernity, that something fundamental has changed in the structure of contemporary societies in the West which marks a historical disjuncture between modernity and a succeeding epoch. In the third section of the chapter, I argue to the contrary that, irrespective of whether any such disjuncture has taken place, the binary oppositions on which economic reasoning is based and which theorists of postmodernity have sought to overturn - between production and exchange, rationality and irrationality, and the material and the ideal - are misconceived. Economic reasoning should be seen for what it is and reformulated at its roots, not exploited for the advancement of questionable claims about history.

It would be helpful to provide an initial definition of postmodernity. But this is virtually impossible to do with clarity. It is also, perhaps, against the spirit of the postmodern enterprise itself. Be that as it may, most definitions of postmodernity refer to processes whereby different kinds of boundary within society are being eroded. These may be boundaries between once incompatible forms of activity such as politics and advertising; between once incommensurable aesthetic styles in art, architecture and design; between once distanciated high and low cultures; between a once distinctive reality and representations of reality on television (or in film, painting and literature); between a once unique human intelligence and replicable or artificial intelligence; and between a once separate domain of economic life and virtually every other form of life. No single definition of postmodernism contains all these elements, and few refer explicitly to the erosion of boundaries.[3] Yet while the concept of postmodernity, together with its variants, has probably outlived any usefulness it ever had within social theory, the notion of the erosion of boundaries is the one central idea in theories of postmodernity which seems worth retaining in any attempt to understand contemporary societies, though not for the reasons postmodern theorists claim. The significance of the idea of the erosion of boundaries can be grasped by opposing it to the concept of differentiation which tends to be used in one guise or another to characterize the emergence of modern societies in the West. This idea appears in Weber's work in connection with the break-up of an overarching world-view into separate dimensions of thought such as science, morality and art. For Parsons, differentiation characterizes the evolution of the social system, its development as a series of smaller, more specialized and functionally related sub-systems. In the work of Habermas, differentiation refers to the separation of the social system and the lifeworld. All three theorists focus on the emergence and development of modern societies, explicitly associating social differentiation with rationalization, with a form of knowledge which has economic reasoning at its heart. The characterization of postmodernity as the erosion of boundaries, then, implies a process of de-differentiation, not necessarily as a regression backwards towards some kind of monolithic society but as a different kind of fragmentation, less coherent in functional terms and less clear-cut with regard to the distinctiveness of different parts of society from each other. But this kind of analysis relies on acceptance of precisely that form of knowledge characteristic of the sociological understanding of modernity itself, crystallized by the application of economic reasoning to monetary analysis, which I am seeking to criticize in this book. I intend to argue here that the concept of the erosion of boundaries does not mark out a disjuncture in history, but exposes flaws in the understanding of history which has dominated sociological thinking throughout the modern age.

Consumerism

The concept of the consumer society is closely linked to the theory of post-industrialism, in which it is held that economic organization within advanced capitalism is based on post-Fordist principles. Stocks are highly sensitive to sales. Corporate budgets are knowledge-centred, focusing on research and development, marketing and advertising.[4] Production is decentralized. Advances in telecommunications enable the rapid transmission of information regarding consumption patterns. Employees must be geographically mobile.[5] Post-Fordist techniques such as small-batch production, subcontracting, outsourcing and just-in-time delivery have increased the speed of the production process, generating faster rates of turnover in the distribution, retail and consumption of goods.[6] Time has been compressed in the marketing of goods. Tastes and styles have become more ephemeral. Novelty and subsequent obsolescence have been drawn closer together, particularly in the production and consumption of gadgetry. The fogeyish follows on from the voguish more rapidly. There has been, in other words, an increase in the tempo by which commodities are bought, consumed and discarded. Theorists of postmodernity, accordingly, have written of a society increasingly characterized by instantaneity and disposability;[7] of a turbulence and transitoriness affecting not just consumption but 'personal values, relationships, life-styles, attachments, and other 'received ways of doing and being'';[8] of a postmodern culture consisting of a 'pool of constantly moving, unconnected fragments';[9] and of the *jouissance* of the consumerism of the 'full-time professional shopper'.[10] It is in this context, though arguably naive in historical terms, that Simmel, for whom an agitated tempo in social, cultural and economic life is singularly characteristic of the onset of modernity, has been adopted by postmodern commentators as a seminal social theorist of their own ilk.[11]

All these trends noted in postmodern theory can be characterized in terms of the concept of de-differentiation. The main argument in postmodern economics concerns the consequences of imitation, interchangeability and the manipulation of sign-values on the consciousness of individuals. Individual and collective identity has lost coherence in the face of advertising which fragments the symbolic systems which have traditionally reinforced group identities along the lines of class, gender and age.[12] The priorities of niche-marketing reflect a proliferation of consumer products sold on the basis of their identifiability with a particular lifestyle and social position, goods of almost infinite variety of style and design. Having traditionally been associated with a relatively small, affluent and precious minority, a central characteristic of postmodernity is the spread of pernickety consumption habits into the wider population. This implies that goods do not merely have a use-value but also what Baudrillard calls a sign-value based on their capacity to make some kind of positional statement about the consumer.[13] Sign-values are targeted by the advertising industry. They can serve as instruments of domination in so far as the signs carry ideological meanings. The consumption of sign-values has generated greater subtleties of distinction between styles, labels and designs, creating a highly specialized market for consumer goods. Specialization in consumption can involve a barrage of stylistic imitation (rather than invention) in production, often eroding boundaries between styles from different historical periods or distinctive cultures.

But the idea that goods are consumed not just for their use-value but for their sign-value is not especially novel, as reference to Thorsten Veblen's concept of conspicuous consumption, formulated during the late 1890s, readily shows.[14] Veblen's study focused on the activities of a relatively small and affluent group in society, the leisure class. The argument that the attitudes of this class towards consumption have filtered into other social groups suggests that the relationship between media forms and the marketplace for consumer goods has become the single dominating institutional factor in the process by which goods are bought and sold. Consumer demand in all areas of society is shaped in significant ways during the increasing amount of time that people spend absorbing media images, not merely through advertising hoardings and television commercials but in the actual content of television programmes, films and books where product placement has become a major source of marketing and promotion. But these developments have taken place in a rather obvious way for some time. They are neither startlingly new nor indicative of the kind of radical break between historical periods which the distinction between modernity and postmodernity would suggest. They simply reflect the systematic expansion and refinement of relationships and techniques which have been a focus of interest in the study of popular culture and consumerism since some of the earliest work of the Frankfurt School.[15] If this is all that so-called postmodern economic life amounts to, it is hardly surprising that commentators in this field have sometimes appeared merely to regurgitate the ideas of theorists such as Simmel writing about a century before. If there is anything distinctive and worth addressing in postmodern commentaries on economic life, there has to be a basis on which not merely quantitative but qualitative differences between modern society and whatever follows can be discerned. In general terms, theorists of postmodernity seem largely to have failed to discern such differences, hardly justifying the kind of epochal proclamation implicit in the very concept of postmodernity, not to mention in some of the more excitable writing devoted to the issue. The developments referred to in postmodern theories concern an acceleration in the tempo of economic life, extension of the depth and complexity of systems of signs, and blurring of the relationship between the symbolic representation of reality and reality itself. But all these issues feature strongly not only in the work of Simmel but in other theories of modernity; they indicate no fundamental historical disjuncture. Simmel's work can be used as a basis for a distinctive approach to understanding contemporary economic life, but not for the reasons postmodern theorists have claimed. Indeed, his work is most significant in the context of my argument not for what is included in his study of money but for what he could have gone on to say, for what he suggests but fails to develop.

When Simmel writes of the acquisition of money for its own sake, he refers to the sense of intoxication derived from the freedom of choice that money can provide for its holder. But like intoxication, this freedom can become an obsession, a ruling idea. It can become valued in and for itself, such that money is not spent but hoarded, idle in all but its empowering features. This is, he suggests, the rationale of the miser, characteristic of the 'avarice of old age'. The avaricious are not concerned, contrary to popular myth, with the monetary value of things. They do not look beyond money to things at all. Instead, 'the power that money stored-up represents is experienced as the final and absolutely satisfying value'.[16] This attitude to money is inherently reflexive. That is, an idea of money, of its capacity as an ultimate means, is fetishized and turned in on itself to form the basis of the desire to acquire it. Money thereby ceases to be a means to anything. Or rather, money becomes a means only to the sense of power derived from its status as a means. Money, epitomized by Simmel's concept of the pure instrument, is no longer an instrument to anything other than itself. Simmel does not claim for one moment that avariciousness is particularly widespread or definitive of modern attitudes towards money. He does however suggest that the avaricious embody an extreme form of the modern stance towards money, towards its capacity to empower. This, he maintains, is an expression of the modern trend towards the objectification of culture, 'the outstanding and most perfect example of the psychological raising of means to ends'.[17]

At first glance, avariciousness seems to be the very antithesis of the consumerism characteristic of postmodern economics. Money is static when hoarded, fluid when used as a means of consumption. Yet the appearance is deceptive, for avariciousness and consumerism generate the same basic desire for money, the same form of acquisitiveness focused on money in and of itself. The extreme form of consumerism is extravagance. The extravagant, like the avaricious, are barely concerned with things. Whereas the avaricious focus on the sense of their own capacity to acquire things, the extravagant gain pleasure from the process of acquisition itself irrespective of the nature of the things actually acquired, the pleasure being virtually lost at the moment of acquisition: 'the attraction of the moment of squandering surpasses both the proper appreciation of money as well as of the objects'.[18] In both instances, Simmel suggests, 'money has dissolved into pure desire for it'; only what 'avarice exhibits ... in material paralysis, extravagance reveals in the form of fluidity and expansion'.[19] On the face of it, then, there is nothing particularly novel in the perception of money underlying consumerism. Consumerism is the reverse side of avarice only in the way money is used, not in the way it is perceived.

Yet Simmel's analysis does in fact suggest a more fundamental distinction than this between the two forms of economic behaviour, which brings the argument back to the relationship between production and exchange. He argues that the form taken in the process by which money is objectified as an end in itself depends on the 'cultural tendencies of an epoch': more specifically, '[m]odern man and the ancient Greek have such different attitudes toward money largely because formerly it served only consumption whereas now it essentially serves production'.[20] Simmel explains this point in terms of the close proximity of consumption to what in his terms is the 'final goal' of economic life itself. Where money is involved predominantly in consumption, for example in an agrarian economy with 'its simple and traditional stationary technology', its character as primarily a medium, its emptiness and indifference, will come to the fore. By contrast, the institutionalization of money as productive capital in modern society means that 'it is both more removed from the final goal and surrounded by other means in comparison with which it possesses a totally different relative significance'.[21] It is in this light, rather than in respect of the postmodern argument that an acceleration in the tempo of economic life and the fragmentation of subjective life are especially new phenomena, that the renewed emphasis on consumerism in postmodern economics can be seen to imply that there has in fact been a distinctive shift in the cultural significance of money. This is not of course to suggest that there has been a return to the form of economic life characteristic of agrarian societies, any more than the concept of de-differentiation at the heart of theories of postmodernity implies any kind of regression towards a pre-modern condition. In order to understand exactly how such a shift might have occurred, it is necessary to examine two areas of contemporary economic life which have been closely related to the phenomenon of consumerism, namely, international money markets and the media industry. I explore these in the next two sections.

Second-Guessing

Avariciousness and extravagance can be treated as identical in their relationship to money because, in both forms of economic behaviour, the idea of money as a transparent and manipulable means to an end is turned into an end in itself, an object of desire. The concept of money, or information concerning its abstract features as an economic instrument, do not therefore serve merely as a reflection upon money's properties as an independent object. The idea of money is a motivating force conditioning the way it is used, thereby underpinning the functions money itself fulfils. In this sense, information about money cannot be said to be distinct from money itself but is integral to its features: an ideal representation of money is collapsed into its characteristics as a material object. This is a vitally important point for the critique of the binary oppositions inherent in economic reasoning that I am formulating in this book. Monetary theories in economics focus on money's role in the transmission of information, but this is invariably information about something other. The properties of money itself are taken to be independent of this information, possessing an integrity unimpaired by the process by which money itself is conceptualized. From the point of view of economic reasoning, transactors make rational decisions on the basis of the information available to them and, in some cases, on information they seek out. Their decisions, in turn, form part of the information used by other transactors. Information, according to this view, is part of the environment in which monetary transaction takes place, having a mediating but never a constitutive role in economic behaviour. But this approach will never get to the heart of the matter. Information is not merely a lubricant facilitating the efficient circulation of money but has a substantive bearing on the assumptions and decisions underlying specific monetary emissions, decisions about what actually to do with money. This argument does not apply only to supposedly marginal or allegedly irrational behaviour such as avariciousness and extravagance, but provides the key to understanding the operation of monetary and financial markets; where, one might have presumed, the approach to monetary analysis derived from economic reasoning is most likely to be confirmed.

The information available to professional transactors can take a variety of forms such as official and commissioned reports, signals issued by central banks, even rumour. In each of these instances, so-called deficiencies in the quality or quantity of information available must be accounted for in explanatory and predictive models, for example by distinguishing between 'insiders' and 'outsiders'.[22] It must be open to question, however, whether such models, which presuppose the existence of perfect information and treat any departure from this as indicative of some kind of flaw, are capable of explaining the complexities involved in the transmission, reception and interpretation of information in all activities which involve the use of money. It is not at all clear, for example, that 'market failures' can be explained solely by reference to deficiencies of information. Take the signals issued by central banks. In practice, these tend to be transmitted through transactions, discreet statements by key individuals, and more occasionally by changes in regulations or supervisory practices. It is well known, as the events leading up to Black Wednesday confirm, that the effectiveness of these signals is uneven, for it is beyond the capacity of any central bank to enforce certain actions, or induce certain conditions, merely by means of the weight of its open market transactions. For example, a higher volume of sales and purchases through open market operations would be necessary for interest rate changes to be enforced than is feasible for one central bank, or even several such banks assisting each other. For this reason, even information does not have the integrity presupposed in economic reasoning. The notion that information is simply 'transmitted' and 'received', as if its meaning remains constant and unimpaired throughout, is unsustainable. Both the meaning and effectiveness of the information transmitted by transactors, and thereby its entire character in the first place, is chronically dependent on the process by which it is interpreted. To transmit and receive information in this context is not simply to project an independent body of facts through space and time, but to bring those facts into being *as* facts.

The signals transmitted by monetary authorities are essentially pointers relying on the expectations and interpretations of other transactors in order to assume meaning and take effect. Dow, for example, contends that because of the level of uncertainty associated with the purchase of financial assets, uncertainty mostly regarding their future price, dealers in financial markets tend to have short-term gains and losses no less in mind than the long-term yield of assets. There is, moreover, an inherent reflexivity to the expectations of dealers in so far as so much depends on the opinions of other dealers. To this extent, central bank signals, even central bank interventions, are more likely to be effective as psychological 'pointers' than in any literal sense: central bank effectiveness 'depends entirely on carrying the market with them', for '[w]ere they to seek to push market rates to a level too high, or too low, to be sustainable, their power would evaporate'.[23] In other words, market failures of the kind suggested by the inside/outside model formulated by Collier and Mayer, or in Akerlof's market for lemons,[24] cannot seriously be regarded as deriving merely from informational deficiencies, for this would be to presuppose that the information which is available to transactors induces responses in them which, because they are uniformly maximizing, are both explicable and predictable; in the light of the consistent difficulties which arise in the explanation of market surprises, even *post hoc*, this presupposition is hardly robust.

A central issue in economic accounts of rational decision-making concerns the horizon of the decision-maker. But the term 'horizon' subsumes too much. In Simon's work for example, which I examine in more detail in chapter 7, the horizon refers to the way in which the rationality of the decision-maker is bounded or restricted by specific, usually limited, expectations.[25] But this argument does not go far enough: the horizon is also conditioned by the theoretical understanding of the decision-maker in so far as this is employed to interpret and act on information available. To take a straightforward example, the decision to transfer funds from one currency to another in response to a surprisingly poor or unexpectedly good set of inflation figures will not be mechanistic but will depend also on the decision-maker's theoretical understanding of precisely what the inflation figures reveal, what they say about successes or failures of government economic policy, prevailing international conditions and so on. Boltho, for example, has suggested that the relationship between government economic policy and decisions taken in different sectors of the economy may be characterized by an 'expectations trap' generated by the high political profile of financial and money markets, where 'the public sector frames its stance in the light of its perception of the short-run reactions of the private financial sector to policy changes, while the private industrial sector bases its longer-run spending decisions on how it perceived the stance of macroeconomic policies to be'.[26] But it must also be recognized that expectations in financial and money markets operate at one remove: transactors do not merely respond directly or in isolation to information, but must second-guess the responses of other transactors. In this sense, the relationship between transactors' interpretations and responses to information is reflexive. And to the extent that monetary theories are involved in this relationship, it seems difficult to envisage any framework for monetary analysis convincingly and lastingly occupying a position external to the conditions under study.

My arguments about the role of information in economic action expose once more the fundamental epistemological problem in monetary analysis. Transactors in money and financial markets routinely take decisions based on expectations informed by a theoretical understanding of how various sectors of the economy actually work, including money and financial markets themselves. This is no less true of decision-making processes in other areas of economic life such as industry and the public sector. The relationship between economic expectations and economic and monetary theories is therefore inherently reflexive. This seems more conspicuous, even more acute, in the light of the recent history of money and financial markets, for the problem posed by reflexivity in monetary analysis is not only epistemological but concerns the day-to-day operation of these markets. There are clear structural reasons why this should be so. The self-same technological developments which have been responsible for decentralized, post-Fordist production have contributed to a process of centralization in the organization of money and finance. In both cases, organizational changes have entailed specialization. But the implications of these changes for spatial and temporal organization are quite distinctive in each of these sectors, a distinction which has significant implications for understanding the role of money in contemporary society.[27]

Increased rates of turnover in consumption demand faster and easier systems for the emission of money. This has been achieved through telecommunications. The use of electronic payments and credit cards enable the virtually instantaneous transmission of information throughout the network of institutions, such as retailers, distributors, banks, financial corporations and producers, in which commodities are bought and sold. There is nothing especially new in the pre-eminence of finance capital, as reference to the early 1890s and late 1920s should demonstrate. But during each of these periods, financial crashes helped re-establish a state of affairs more akin to the production paradigm.[28] Since the 1960s, however, the increasing predominance of finance capital has derived not merely from its expansion but from proliferation and innovation in the range of financial instruments available, many of them as alternatives to money. This trend has been conceptually awkward, making it difficult to distinguish clearly between money and non-money, and consequently problematic from a regulatory point of view. Advances in telecommunications have meant that the sheer speed of the transmission of information between financial centres acts to closely (and instantly) co-ordinate price and purchasing fluctuations between them. So it is not just the quantity of money involved in international financial transactions which is important but their synchronicity. Both the sheer quantity of money caught up in international finance and the synchronicity of transactions have enhanced the opportunities to make money not through investment as such but on the basis of continuously shifting prices. This has led postmodern commentators such as Harvey to suggest that 'the financial system has acquired a degree of autonomy from real production unprecedented in capitalism's history, carrying capitalism into an equally unprecedented era of financial dangers'.[29]

The structural developments referred to just now have been significant for the relationship between production and finance, but not for precisely the reasons postmodern theorists such as Harvey claim. A greater quantity of money is being switched between financial centres with little or no relationship to real productive activity; more money, indeed, than is changing hands across geopolitical borders through trade. But this does not indicate a significant structural shift in the relationship between the productive and financial sectors of the international economy, for the principles of operation within each of these sectors, nor those governing the relationship between them, have not fundamentally changed. The switching of funds between securities, stocks or currencies is largely based on expected price fluctuations which may or may not be related to what actually occurs in the real economy. Money gained by buying into a particular stock when its price rises, or by selling when the price falls, does not suddenly become fictitious just because the information on which those buying and selling decisions are taken turns out to be false. Likewise, switching funds from one currency to another may or may not be directly responsive to the relative condition of the national economies in question, but it almost certainly will be more immediately responsive to the anticipated decisions of other professional speculators, including central banks engaged in open market operations. Ultimately of course, over the long run, the relationship between the price of securities and stocks and the relative parity of currencies is clearly discernible, as reference to the short history of the Deutschemark or the performance of so-called blue-chip stocks bears out. But over the short run, the opportunities for gain from price fluctuations alone have been multiple, wide-ranging and, since the 1960s, increasing in the major financial centres. And this suggests, more importantly, that the *reasons* behind any long-term correlation between financial indicators and the real economy cannot be characterized in the straightforward functional terms suggested by the production paradigm, for this would be to exclude the constitutive role of information. The greater quantity of money involved in these transactions is part condition but also part manifestation of these opportunities. For they could not have arisen so conspicuously, they would not be as significant as they are, without technological changes which have meant that the movement of funds has not merely been more tightly co-ordinated but more rapidly co-ordinated. These changes constitute an enhancement of the principles by which monetary and financial markets have always worked, a quantitative rather than qualitative change. No fundamental shift of conditions against those depicted in the production paradigm has occurred because the paradigm has never provided an adequate explanation of the relationship between the productive and financial sectors of the economy. This is because the paradigm makes it impossible to grasp the integral role of information not merely in what money does but in what it actually is.

Passive Enrichment

So do postmodern commentaries on economic life contain no significant insights, no indication that anything fundamental has changed? In so far as postmodern theory focuses above all, as I suggested at the beginning of this chapter, on the erosion of boundaries, the claim that a historical disjuncture has occurred in the organization of economic life in general, and in the nature and functions of money in particular, in contemporary Western societies cannot be sustained. The very concept of boundaries in this context relies on a series of binary oppositions which is integral to economic reasoning. My primary aim in this book has been to argue that these oppositions are misconceived. The thesis that the relationship between these oppositions has been inverted or even eroded is central to the idea of a historical disjuncture on which the entire meaning of the concept of postmodernity depends. Yet the assertion becomes meaningless as soon as it is clear that the form of knowledge against which postmodern theory has been positioned contains fundamental flaws. It is in the light of this argument against postmodern theory however that the question regarding what if anything is distinctive about contemporary economic life can be addressed in a more constructive way.

I have argued that the claim in postmodern commentaries on economic life that the relationship between the productive and financial sectors of the economy, and more fundamentally the relationship between the material and the ideal, has undergone a significant inversion cannot be supported. There is nothing new in the fact that information fulfils a constitutive rather than mediating role in the operation of the economy, and in the reproduction of monetary networks in particular. But reference to what postmodern theorists have said about the content of the information integral to economic life, rather than about the fact that it is important at all, does suggest that the ideas which shape the uses, functions and nature of money in contemporary society have changed significantly. This change, moreover, has been closely linked to an important development in the institutional framework in which money is transacted, namely, the role of the media industry not merely in transmitting the information integral to the use of money but, in a quite distinctive way, in giving that information its shape and meaning. Media institutions have played this role in respect of both the operation of money and financial markets and the phenomenon of consumerism. The consequences of their role in each case do not mirror each other, but are inextricably and powerfully linked.

The predominance of consumerism during the 1980s derived from an emerging set of attitudes towards money shaped at least in part by the novel pre-eminence of money and financial markets. This has been consequential in both functional and symbolic terms. The discussion of international monetary integration in chapter 5 focused on the principles of organization governing the operation of financial and monetary markets. Having come so far in this chapter, I am now able to examine more closely the relationship between these developments and the phenomenon of consumerism; a relationship which, I want to argue, has been and continues to be fundamentally shaped by the media industry. Commentators on postmodernity have consistently emphasized the close links between the media and the marketplace for consumer goods in contemporary society. These links have been addressed in such commentaries largely as promotional, identifying the role of the media in both bolstering and to some extent generating the demand for particular goods, most often those associated with lifestyle. This is certainly the view lying behind the frequently cited concept of the sign-value. But the market itself, no less than money, is not simply a mode of economic organization but an idea. Its characteristics and operation, and no less importantly its conceptualization, cannot remain in the background of the study of economic behaviour, more or less underexplored as the organizational framework through which monetary transactions are undertaken. The market has been addressed in social and economic theory largely as a basis for polemical arguments about the moral and political consequences of market economics. What is needed, on the contrary, is an examination of the assumptions underlying the concept of the market itself.

Whether classified as a political ideology or merely a set of ideas, suppositions about the market as a metaphysical entity, about how markets work and their relationship to human economic activity, have underpinned the phenomenon of consumerism. Media institutions have not merely played a part in shaping these ideas but, in their role in both depicting and expressing a form of life, have embodied them. In liberal and neoliberal philosophy, the concept of the market not only has been used to refer to a set of economic relationships but embraces an approach to social life in its entirety. The market is deemed to embody a form of social organization in which the basic imperatives of human nature can be freely expressed, both of themselves and in such a way as to generate an ordered social whole. But conceived in this way, the market is a totalizing concept, less a celebration of human freedom than a constraint upon it. As Hirschman has shown, the liberal theory of the market originated as a means of channelling the human passions into a politically manageable social whole. What Hobbes fears as the competitive tension between human passions, Smith appropriates as the foundation for a system of competing human interests, but a system to temper and control those interests none the less. In these terms, Smith's market can be characterized as a gentler version of Hobbes's Leviathan, whose function, as Jameson suggests, 'is not to encourage and perpetuate freedom (let alone freedom of a political variety) but rather to repress it'.[30] There is a world of difference between this totalizing concept of the market and the passions of the consumer which feature in postmodern studies of economic life. The elevation of shopping to a pastime has disrupted and undermined the conception of a social whole integral to the theory of the marketplace, at least once this theory is taken for what it is. Smith's prudent economic agent and the instant debtor are blatantly dissimilar. The scale of personal debt and negative equity in Britain and America during the early 1990s underlines the brutally misconceived nature of the so-called consumer boom which characterized economic life (and economic discourse) in those countries for much of the 1980s. This was no confirmation of the liberal philosophy of the market, but a travesty of it.

But the discrepancy between the form of economic activity implicit within liberal market philosophy and the consumer boom of the 1980s cannot accurately be characterized, as postmodern commentators such as Jameson have sought to do, as a contrast between the Calvinesque rationality of the world of double-entry bookkeeping and the Disneyesque extremes of shopping as entertainment and for greed. Such a contrast, pitting production against exchange, rationality against irrationality and reality against fantasy, relies on an approach to understanding the distinctive features of economic action in modern society which has not been overturned by postmodern theory but unwittingly exposed as flawed. The phenomenon of consumerism cannot even be accurately described, let alone explained, by piously indicating the differences between the consumption-driven market philosophies which prevailed during the 1980s and the wider-ranging sobriety of the ideas underpinning the theory of the marketplace in the hands of Smith. The explanation, rather, lies to a large degree in the relationship between consumerism and the media industry, a relationship in which the conceptualization of the market, particularly in the context of the expansion and predominance of international money markets, has played a significant role.

Baudrillard has claimed that sign-values rather than use-values have become objects of consumption. In this view, the media plays a vital function in both underpinning and constituting the desire for goods. But it is possible to go further. As Jameson argues, consumerism is driven by 'consumption of the very process of consumption itself, above and beyond its content and the immediate commercial products'.[31] In this sense, the market is not the backdrop to consumption, or to economic activity in general, as social and economic theorists have taken it to be, but has taken on an unprecedented symbolic pre-eminence within the cultural framework of consumerism, and must be addressed by theorists in this form. In so far as one accepts the terminology of postmodern commentaries, it could be said that the market itself has been elevated to the position of a sign-value. It is important to understand that this is not simply to reiterate Simmel's arguments about extravagance. Consumerism is more than simply an aimless expression of the perception of money as an end in itself as Simmel describes it. Consumerism is not empty of content in the sense of the monetary freedom which, in Simmel's view, people do not know how to use. It is on the contrary bloated with significance as an expression of a form of life made gargantuan within a world fattened up by the media industry.

The fluidity of consumerism depends not only on the fact that individuals are inclined to spend what they have but that they borrow to spend. A recognition of the significance of borrowing is vital. In Britain, the expansion of personal debt during the 1980s was dizzyingly oxygenated by rising property prices. This apparent increase in wealth seems ultimately to have been rootless, fictional because disconnected from real productive activity, hence the regeneration of the idea of negative equity during the early 1990s. The manifestation of this phenomenon in a breathless consumerism was the quintessential expression of passive enrichment, of empowerment by money without effort. That this phenomenon may have been checked by the sheer weight of personal debt during the early 1990s, rendered virtually unmanageable in the context of stagnant and falling property prices, should not disguise its significance. For that it could have happened at all, indeed its very ephemerality, says something vitally important about how individuals perceive money and how they use it. Indeed, the ensuing depression in consumer spending during the early 1990s, the very extremity of the contrast between this stagnation and the preceding fluidity, does not detract from but supports my argument here. The retreat from consumerism does not indicate some kind of return to the caution of the cultural type characteristic of Smith's beloved saver, for it has been no less celebrated and intensified, or rather spectacularly mourned, by, through and within the media industry than were the heights of consumerism. Attitudes towards money, that aspect of monetary analysis with which economists have had the greatest long-term difficulty, are not only inherently reflexive but chronically mediatized: not simply filtered through the media industry in the manner made notorious by Horkheimer and Adorno,[32] but formed through the media, being dependent on and constitutive of this industry as a form of life. It is this development, not consumerism as such, which is novel, distinctively *post*modern if this terminology must be used, in so far as not merely the objects of consumers' desire but the very concepts of money and markets informing consumer behaviour have become inextricably entwined. Money and market relations are no longer simply the medium for the expression of these desires. They are their object. It is in this respect that the analysis of postmodern consumerism must go further than studies of consumerism in the context of modernist popular culture.

The motivating force of ideas concerning money and markets, their capacity not merely to mediate but to generate desire, cannot be adequately explained, however, without reference to a significant shift in the relationship between the media industry and financial markets. Indeed, this relationship provides the key to understanding how consumerism, in the distinctive form this took during the 1980s, was possible. Money and financial markets, through the 1980s and since, have been placed under a media glare of the greatest intensity. Much of this has concerned reportage. Information transmitted by market signals has become the pre-eminent criterion of the prevailing success or failure of government economic policy. Speeches and statements on economic policy by ministers or officials are persistently tested by reference to the price index on international stock markets and the relative parity of major currencies. Much of this, of course, reflects developments in the presentation and packaging of news as much as significant changes in the role of monetary and financial activity within the economy itself. But it also reflects the commodification of information: first, as a basis for explanatory and predictive analysis; and second, as a lever for attaining profit by means both fair and foul, the latter being indicated by the widespread phenomenon of insider trading during the 1980s, where decisions to buy or sell particular stocks are undertaken by or on behalf of individuals who have privileged access to information.[33] The media industry has played a central role in the commodification of information. For this reason, the inherently reflexive relationship between transactors' decisions and expectations on the one hand, and the study of how markets actually work on the other, is not simply epistemologically problematic. It is pertinent to any understanding of the historical development of financial and monetary markets themselves.

Given the importance of information within money and financial markets, not merely as a transparent commentary but as a key component of their actual operation in practice, the integral role of the media industry in the commodification of information parallels the mediatization of the market in consumerism. The media glare has not simply contributed to the operation of money and financial markets in a technical sense. It has served to fetishize them. This is in Jameson's view the single 'most astonishing feature' of postmodern economics, namely, that 'the dreariness of business and private property, the dustiness of entrepreneurship, and the well-nigh Dickensian flavour of title and appropriation, coupon-clipping, mergers, investment banking, and other such transactions ... should in our time have proved to be so *sexy*'.[34] During the 1980s, money and financial markets came to be associated with the rapid accumulation of wealth: not according to a familiar pattern, but by an apparently unexpected and unexpecting sector of society in the form of a 'new' money associated not with property or inheritance but with markets. Organizational and technological developments in international money and financial markets corresponded to a sharp expansion in employment within this sector. The steady rise of stock prices during this period, even taking into account spiralling falls such as occurred in October 1987, reflected both the scale and, more importantly, apparent near-certainty of enrichment by such means.

These developments are of course important in structural terms, indicative of the fluidity of the relationship between the real and financial sectors of the economy. But they are also culturally significant, for the bullishness of money and financial markets symbolized, at one remove, the phenomenon of passive enrichment at the heart of consumerism. The attentiveness of the media industry towards money and financial markets has in this sense not merely been voyeuristic. It has been embroiled in a political drive, especially in Britain, to popularize this particular dimension of capitalism. In all the major financial centres, new share issues are now promoted largely through mass advertising. This process began with the privatization of British Telecom in November 1984, with a two-stage advertising campaign targeted towards the small-scale investor: intensive corporate promotion prior to the announcement of the offer, and subsequent promotion of the offer itself. On that occasion, the number of people owning shares in Britain immediately increased from just over 1 million to around 2 million, or 5 per cent of the adult population.[35] This widening of small-scale share ownership may have been superficial in the sense that most new investors participated no further in developing some kind of share portfolio, holding their new certificates merely as an alternative to saving with banks and other financial institutions. But there is in any case no need to celebrate these developments as a form of 'popular capitalism', nor smugly to indicate somewhat contrary developments during the early 1990s, in order to grasp their cultural significance as an indication of contemporary ideas about money. Indeed, closer analysis of the details of this phenomenon helps place it in proper perspective. By and large, individual participation in new share issues has been based not on the investment of a proportion of money-income separate from other forms of saving, but rather on the transfer of existing money from savings accounts into shares. In some cases, money has actually been borrowed in order to purchase shares in anticipation of the instant rise in price at the start of trading. For this reason, the popularization of money and financial markets does not provide a contrast to consumerism as an alternative, that is to say, productive use of money, for irrespective of the structural differences between the two activities, the ideas underlying them are in fact identical. In both activities, the abstract idea of the market is symbolically tied to the phenomenon of passive enrichment. This phenomenon is identified with the buying of stocks and shares and the international trading of currencies, and manifested largely by the sheer energy and intensity with which individuals have committed themselves to consumption. This could not have been possible without the mediatization of markets, without their being associated with the apparently effortless certainty of profit.

It is in the context of the relationship between consumerism, money markets and the media industry that Jameson characterizes the market as an ideologeme. Ideas of the market in postmodern society, he suggests, have been prised away from the way markets actually work in practice. He thereby formulates on historical grounds an argument which has, already in this book, been put forward for epistemological reasons. That is, the study of how markets work is ultimately inseparable from the analysis of market discourse: 'to get it right, you have to talk about real markets just as much as about metaphysics, psychology, advertising, culture, representations, and libidinal impulses'.[36] Jameson's argument suggests that the whole dimension of economic activity is not merely subject to discourses about economics, but in fact includes those discourses as part and parcel of the way this form of life actually proceeds. It is in this context that the relationship between markets and the media industry should be regarded not merely in functional or structural terms but as analogous, not in the obvious sense of similarity, but 'because the 'market' is as *unlike* its concept (or Platonic idea) as the media is unlike its own concept'.[37] But more than this, the distancing of the concept from its object in each of these cases has, in Jameson's view, enabled the concepts themselves to become so interdependent as to be ultimately combined, indistinguishable from each other. He refers to this combination as a process of transcoding in which 'two separate explanatory systems are combined ... by way of the assertion of a fundamental identity (about which it is always protested that it is *not metaphorical*, the surest sign of an intent to metaphorize)'.[38] Subsequently the relationship is neither clarified by re-establishing the distinction between the two systems, removing the 'figural bracket', nor resolved by 'producing a new synthesis, a new combination, a new combined language, or whatever'.[39] As a consequence, the relationship between concepts or systems is left in mid-air, suspending 'everything that used to be 'literal''.[40] This process has had fundamental implications for the relationship between markets and the media industry in practice. In the consumption of media images, for example, the pleasure derived has increasingly been based on their form, the techniques and technology used, as much as their content, what the images portray. The techniques have been commodified.[41] Likewise, the pleasures gained from and pursued in the relentless (and indebted) 'wilder forms of consumption available in the postmodern'[42] are largely derived from the commodification of the marketplace itself, of the process of consuming. The two forms of discourse, two sets of ideas about market economics and the media, have imploded in on each other: 'the media, as which the market was itself fantasized, now returns into the market and by becoming a part of it seals and certifies the formerly metaphorical or analogical identification as a 'literal' reality'.[43] The relationship between them remains confused and unresolved. This has generated a set of practices which express the relationship both structurally and, no less important, symbolically.

Simmel portrays extravagance as a purely monetary phenomenon. It is clear from his analysis that the perception of money this implies cannot have arisen outside the context of the mature money economy. Consumerism, however, is more complicated than this. It is not only a monetary phenomenon but is inextricably linked with the media industry: not merely in connection with the consumption of media images, but on the basis of the mediatization of consumption itself. The market, both as an abstract idea and in conjunction with monetary and financial activity, has irresistibly merged with the ideal of passive enrichment. The substantive point arising from this discussion concerns the possibility that a profound shift has occurred in the cultural framework in which economic activity takes place. This refers to prevailing ideas, even a prevailing ideology, about how the economy works, and more specifically about the nature and functions of money. Whether the focus is on modern or postmodern society, however, the epistemological question underlying this discussion should be clear: economic activity in general, and the transaction of money in particular, cannot be accurately understood without reference to the ideas, concepts and discursive practices in which they are always embroiled. Such ideas will always define, and more importantly always have defined, the expectations that individuals have regarding the consequences of their actions and the reasons behind the actions of others. They will inform their under-standing of what it is in their best interests to do. But there is nothing irrational about this. The depiction of consumerism as irrational, a consistent theme in postmodern commentaries, cannot be seriously sustained. Jameson is quite wrong to portray consumerism in postmodern society as a 'virtual delirium' in which the 'very idea of the market ... is consumed with the most prodigious gratification'.[44] He is no less wrong to draw a contrast between, as he conceives it, this form of acquisitive insanity and the hard-headed rationalism of industrial society, where priorities concerning production are pursued with an energy no less intense. This argument exposes moral priorities and explanatory skill of unwavering and dogmatic simplicity. As I shall argue in chapter 7, the criterion of rationality, when associated with the motive to maximize, is too restrictive to say anything meaningful about how individuals come to use money in the ways that they do. This self-same point underlines the inadequacy of the production paradigm. The distinction between production and consumption is inextricably linked with the distinction between rationality and irrationality and, more fundamentally, with the dualism between the material and the ideal. To employ these oppositions is to misconceive the nature of economic life in a modern, as well as any other, society. What I propose here is not a full-blown theory of postmodern economics. It is not an economic theory at all. I have sought on the contrary to substantiate in historical terms the analytical argument

I have been developing in this book: that the concepts and ideas, the myths and fantasies, the discourse which surrounds economic activity in general and the transaction of money in particular, will always have a substantive bearing, a shaping role, in relation to how those activities and transactions actually proceed, in relation to what those activities actually are.

7

High Modernity, Rationality and Trust

The most significant conclusion which can be drawn from postmodernism is that the form of knowledge underpinning social theories of modernity is in need of reappraisal. This is not because such knowledge has become outdated, however, but because the self-understanding of modern societies from which this knowledge is derived has always provided, on epistemological as well as substantive grounds, a flawed basis for understanding them in social theory. The claim in postmodern theories that a disjuncture has occurred between the modern and the postmodern which mirrors the break between pre-modernity and modernity is unconvincing because it relies on assumptions about that earlier break which are difficult to sustain on closer scrutiny. At the heart of these assumptions is a form of economic reasoning derived from a narrow concept of rational action. This has been of foundational significance to monetary theory, both for distinguishing between the use and operation of modern as opposed to pre-modern monetary forms, and for the question as to how networks requisite for modern, standardized monetary exchange are reproduced over time. More broadly, the emergence of the money economy has been heavily implicated in the work of theorists such as Tönnies, who addresses the onset of modernity in terms of a fundamental change in the nature of human association,[1] and Weber, who links the mature money economy to a process of rationalization right across society,[2] as well as in the later work of Parsons and Habermas on the role of money in the differentiation of modern societies. The supposition that monetary exchange primarily involves intrinsically rational, calculating action is a defining principle in economic accounts of the nature and functions of money which, as I argued earlier in the book, social theories of money have tended to take at face-value. The inadequacy of this supposition for monetary analysis is not, however, revealed by the insights of postmodern theories. It is a conclusion which follows irresistibly from exposure of their most fundamental shortcomings.

As I argued in chapter 6, a central theme in theories of postmodernity concerns the erosion of boundaries, best understood as an inversion rather than a reversal of the process of differentiation depicted in theories of the onset of modernity. Yet it is not at all clear that differentiation in modern societies has occurred in the way and for the reasons social theorists appear increasingly to have assumed without question. This possibility has vital significance not only for the substance of monetary theory but for the epistemological principles which are essential to the rigorous approach to monetary analysis I have sought to develop in this book. The contention in postmodern studies of economic life that symbolic representations have increasingly penetrated the real world of economic value relies on a serious misconception of the ideational features which economic action in general and monetary transaction in particular inherently possess. The symbolic character of money is not simply a consequence of the projection of ideas onto monetary objects as independent things but is integral to the abstract features of money in general and essential to the fiduciary dimension on which monetary networks depend. Through examining the characteristics of so-called post-industrial societies such as consumerism and the expansion of monetary and financial markets, postmodern commentators have suggested that the production paradigm no longer provides an adequate framework for understanding economic life. They ought to have added that it never has done. They instead compound the error by simply overturning the paradigm itself, relying on the opposite pole of a duality between the material and ideal which has defined economic reasoning in modern societies without providing an adequate basis for understanding economic action. In the guise of the opposition between subject and object, this duality is at the heart of the philosophical anthropology foundational to the pre-eminence of the production paradigm in social theory.[3]

As conceived in social theories of modernity, the differentiation of the economy from other dimensions of social life has enabled the relationship between society and its environment integral to economic action to operate unhindered by non-economic relationships and values and thereby to become a distinctive, specialized domain of human activity. This relationship is structured around the rational pursuit of self-interest, a form of activity which has correspondingly risen to a position of central exposure in social theories of modernity. For Parsons and Habermas, as I discussed in chapter 4, this development has been crystallized by the standardization and universalization of monetary exchange. In their work, the penetration of monetary transaction into activities formerly governed by personal forms of exchange, even into areas of social life not previously regarded as economic exchanges at all, is ascribed unquestionable significance for the emergence of modern society, both as an expression of wider developments in economic, political and cultural life and as a consequential process in its own right: loosening personal dependences in some areas of life while creating them in others; transforming the character of many human possessions and attributes into commodities to be bought and sold; and freeing individuals from the spatial and temporal restrictions associated with economic relationships such as barter or serfdom.

The principles underpinning economic reasoning do not, however, provide an adequate framework for understanding these consequences. For this reason, they can hardly serve as a basis for assessing the implications of any further shift in the developmental trajectory of contemporary Western societies. Suppositions regarding the nature and uses of money lie at the heart of the application of economic reasoning to the sociological investigation of the onset of modernity, and therefore provide a focus for discussion of its central themes. This contention underpins my argumentative strategy in this chapter. In the first section, I contend that economic reasoning does not provide an exhaustive basis on which to understand the nature of monetary transaction. This form of knowledge is therefore inadequate as a guide to exploring the implications of the standardization of monetary exchange in modern societies. In particular, as I move on to suggest in the second section, it is the fiduciary dimension inherent to the reproduction of monetary networks which places economistic accounts of money under severe strain. Trust in money is not only irreducible to economic reasoning but incompatible with it. I argue in the final section that this critique of economic reasoning in relation to monetary analysis has significant implications for understanding the latest stage, if indeed such a stage exists, of the developmental trajectory of modernity.

Rationality

Economic reasoning rests on the proposition that economic action is structured around the rational pursuit of self-interest. It is important to be clear about what this means. The pursuit of self-interest in this context does not refer to some vague idea about what is best for oneself, but to the objective of *maximum* gain. Conventionally, this proposition has been incorporated in monetary theory by means of the negative concept of minimal transactions costs, although an identical process of reasoning, driven by the goal of maximization, is involved. This concept is entailed for example in the process of substitution depicted by Goodhart's law[4] and the transmission mechanism.[5] Further analysis of monetary behaviour in economics, however, has exposed difficulties in the basic model of economic action from which these ideas have been derived. Herbert Simon, in his analysis of bounded rationality, has sought to account for these without surrendering basic tenets of economic reasoning. His arguments certainly provide a more subtle framework for understanding economic decisions. But it is open to question whether they explain how money works. Basic flaws in economic reasoning might be overcome by resorting to additional criteria for explaining economic action, for example by arguing that it contains irrational elements or normative dispositions. This would imply that economic logic simply requires extension or elaboration. This approach has been typified by economic sociology, where dissatisfaction is uniformly expressed from a sociological perspective with neoclassical explanations of economic processes. The concept of 'embeddedness' has been utilized for example to argue that economic action is constrained by non-economic factors arising from human cognition, culture, social structures and politics.[6] I want to suggest that this argument does not go far enough, for it retains at its heart those very principles of analysis with which economic sociologists have proclaimed dissatisfaction. There is no core rational domain of economic reasoning and action underlying the transaction of money. This is not because economic action is basically irrational rather than rational, but because the binary oppositions underpinning economic reasoning are unworkable. Indeed, inherent weaknesses in economic reasoning when applied to monetary analysis cannot be overcome without a fundamental reassessment of their epistemological status.

The view of human decision-making at the heart of economic reasoning is difficult to sustain even on its own terms. Logically, circumstances are conceivable where, even with adequate information, it is impossible rationally to pursue self-interest in a straightforward sense because no single course of action fits the bill. Elster writes of two such cases. In both, the maximization of self-interest is difficult because of indeterminacy regarding the choices open to the actor, providing no clear basis for a decision. First, there may exist several courses of action which would all enable the actor to maximize to an equal extent. For example, profits might in principle be open to maximization via alternative routes, such as 'by a low volume of sales with high profits per sale or a high volume with low profits per sale'.[7] Second, there may exist different actions which are neither equally maximizing nor more or less so, but simply incommensurable.[8] For example, a consumption choice - say, between buying a new kitchen and paying for a course of education - may be irresolvable by reference to differential preferences between types of satisfaction, particularly because the latter option cannot be consumed with the immediacy of the former, and may or may not yield eventual benefits (which are in any case difficult to assess). In such cases, tossing a coin would provide no worse a guide for action than rational choice. Or to express this point another way, the application of economic reasoning to the decision-making process can only generate what are equally rational choices within the terms of this form of reasoning.

A maximizing course of action can also be impossible to discern because of prevailing uncertainty. The mere existence of uncertainty need not of course place in question the proposition that economic action is structured around the rational pursuit of self-interest. Indeed, economic reasoning is commonly used as a basis for understanding how to cope with uncertainty, and this provides one type of explanation for the origins of money. But there is a fundamental analytical sense in which the concept of uncertainty undermines economic reasoning. Analytically, the concept of uncertainty refers to the difficulty of assessing the consequences of actions which are inherently speculative. This need not mean gambling, but can occur in decisions over levels of investment in research and development. Uncertainty in this context can lead to circularity rather than maximization. For example, investment in research and development is most likely to pay dividends when the firm is alone in pursuing a particular avenue of research. The inherent uncertainty relating to the outcome of the research itself is partly based on the fact that firms must double-guess each other.[9] But firms patently do not simply go in circles when making such investment decisions, although the decisions actually taken may well be incorrect. Rational techniques of assessment derived from economic reasoning are used in such cases, and it is in this context that Simon's concept of satisficing, or bounded rationality, has been formulated.

If the condition of empirical uncertainty generated by imperfect information constitutes an external limitation to the rational pursuit of self-interest, the condition of inherent uncertainty stems from limitations present in economic actors themselves, such as their capacity to attain and process information efficiently enough to make an effective decision. This may simply be a question of time: for example, where a firm takes so long to make a decision that the terms of reference have shifted, or a contract has been won by another firm using rational procedures less strictly.[10] Alternatively - and this would apply to the successful firm in the example just cited - the decision-maker in question may simply not seek to maximize gain in a perfect sense, resting content with a satisfactory outcome, an outcome which is good enough given particular aspirations. This is what Simon means by satisficing, where the decision-maker merely forms 'some *aspiration* as to how good an alternative he should find'.[11] On the face of it, Simon holds a qualified view of the decision-maker similar to that of Hayek. But whereas Hayek contends that we must learn how to maximize, Simon suggests that our perception of a good enough outcome will be based on notions of what it is reasonable to expect, how much effort seems worthwhile and so on. Rarely will our conclusions lead to the pursuit of maximum gain in any perfect sense. Simon regards the rationality of individuals and firms as inherently bounded in so far as they fulfil particular social roles which help define what is to be expected. Firms are most likely to identify, for example, a minimum acceptable profit level which avoids the possibility of takeover: management and innovation strategies are informed by the imperative to avoid big mistakes no less than by the quest to maximize.[12] Simon's account of these practices suggests not merely that levels of aspiration in this context will vary according to conditions inside and outside the firm, but also that the information on which such practices are based will rarely be unambiguous, for its interpretation also relies on internal and external conditions.[13]

Simon's arguments have significant implications for understanding the integral role of information in monetary transaction, but in this respect he undermines rather than salvages the case for applying the principles of economic reasoning to monetary analysis. The existence of a stable economic environment clearly has an important bearing on the expectations and aspirations of individuals and firms. In the form of business cycles, inflation or rigorous competition, instability 'paralyses rational action because it destroys most of the customary bases for forming accurate expectations'.[14] But expectations are formed on the basis of *perceptions* of stability and instability, in which case they are not merely a reflection of but are foundational to the very existence of a stable environment, for this depends on consistency in the expectations of firms rather than just their objective accuracy. This process underpins what I called 'second-guessing' in chapter 6. In this sense, expectations can on aggregate resemble something of a self-fulfilling prophecy in which the rational assessment of information plays an integral and constitutive rather than a detached and objective role. The attainment of full and accurate information is therefore dispensable to a stable business environment: 'Stability of expectations can be so essential for decision making that it may be more important, in some circumstances, to have *agreement* on the facts than to be certain that what is agreed upon is really fact'.[15]

As I have argued throughout this book, information does not merely mediate but helps constitute the environment to which the rational decision-making process inherent to economic reasoning is applied. This is vitally important to understanding not merely how individuals and firms handle money but how they decide which monetary form to employ where several forms are available. The second of these issues is directly pertinent to the evolutionist arguments of Hayek and White discussed in chapter 2. The application of neoclassical logic in their advocacy of free and denationalized banking relies on the assumption that perceptions of the stability of specific monetary forms will be sufficiently rational to act as the sole determinant of the expansion or contraction of their circulation. But if Simon is correct, a series of good enough outcomes for transactors with limited aspirations may in sum not be good enough; amounting in fact to the worst possible outcome as far as money is concerned, namely, the tolerance of an inflationary currency until a sudden, massive flight is triggered, perhaps by the actions of a less tolerant group of transactors. Tolerance levels may vary according to different experiences and therefore expectations of inflation: compare postwar Germany and Britain for example. If the monetary form most widely used under the conditions envisaged by Hayek and White is not by definition the most efficient and therefore the most stable, no sound basis is provided for the advocacy of the unfettered issue of competing currencies: the guarantee that bad money will be driven out by good must be withdrawn.

A further means of understanding the cautious, bounded rationality of monetary transactors is suggested by the concept of the *maximum minimorum*, or the maximin. But on closer analysis, this is no more applicable than the idea of satisficing to monetary analysis. Indeed, this particular weak version of economic reasoning further underlines its inherent flaws in a monetary context. As set out by Rawls, decision-making on the basis of the maximin principle entails two basic steps: first, the agent ranks alternatives according to worst rather than best outcomes; and second, that alternative is chosen 'the worst outcome of which is superior to the worst outcomes of the others'.[16] Rawls notes three conditions which, when present together, indicate the prudence of this process, at least as a rule of thumb. The first such condition exists when knowledge of the probability of particular outcomes is difficult or impossible to attain. The second condition prevails where the decision-maker cares insufficiently about any gain additional to the 'minimum stipend' to choose riskier but potentially more profitable alternatives. The third condition is present whenever the rejected alternatives have worst outcomes which are simply too grave to be acceptable. It is the conceptualization of best and worst outcomes in Rawls's scenario which is problematic in a monetary context. Implicit in the terminology used by Rawls is the notion that to seek the best of all outcomes, to maximize, is by definition to choose the riskiest alternative. To guard against worst outcomes, to maximin, is conversely to play safe. These assumptions are unworkable in monetary analysis. Hayek and White rely for example on the application of maximizing principles to the decision to accept and hold on to one of a range of alternative monetary forms. But it is not clear whether it is the liquidity or value of that commodity which is at stake. Liquidity rests on characteristics of stability and ease of interchangeability which indicate that specific monetary forms are safer to hold on to than others. But if the monetary form in question is addressed as an asset and its appreciation is taken into account - rather than, as is generally the case with money, its devaluation through inflation - the issue immediately ceases to concern the adoption of the most efficient, that is to say the most liquid, monetary form. Indeed, that asset most likely to appreciate over time is probably least likely to possess high liquidity. It is for this reason that investors tend to seek a balanced portfolio of assets, where liquidity is weighed against anticipated levels of appreciation. But as I argued in chapter 1, the political economy of money is characterized precisely by a confusion between the two functions of money, as a medium of exchange on the one hand and as a store of value on the other, prised apart by this dual application of the maximin. To this extent, the concept of the maximin is even less plausible than the ideas of maximizing or satisficing as a general guide to the way in which transactors' decisions underpin and help shape the development of particular monetary forms.

Simon's vision of the capacity of the *homo oeconomicus* to make rational decisions is eminently sensible as a rebuttal of narrower versions of economic reasoning which focus merely on the maximization of gain. Rational choices clearly cannot be made omnisciently. They depend on expectations bound to the specific social role of the decision-maker, and to the conditions under which any decision is made.[17] But Simon advances only a superficial understanding of the implications of this argument. He grasps that decision-makers do not merely respond to an external economic environment on the basis of a predisposition to maximize. There is in this sense a reflexive relationship between the actual nature of the economic environment on the one hand and expectations regarding that environment on the other. Simon rightly contends that aspiration acts as a limiting framework for the formation of expectations:[18] the aspirations of decision-makers will vary according to the quality of available alternatives. Yet expectations are not formed in mid-air. Nor do they depend completely on a pragmatic assessment of good enough outcomes. There is a significant sociological dimension to the process by which aspirations are formed: for example, there is a need to account for differing aspirations within particular social groups or classes where available alternatives are presumably, or at least by definition, about the same for everyone. In this context, Simon is helpful in a negative rather than a constructive sense, suggesting why there are limits to the rational pursuit of self-interest without really addressing or helping to overcome difficulties inherent within the framework of economic reasoning itself.

This is not, it should be emphasized, simply a question of projecting cultural or class-specific values onto a core domain of economic reasoning. More importantly, the sociological process by which aspirations are constituted embraces economic reasoning itself as a form of knowledge. This contention goes to the heart of my argument that there is a reflexive relationship between monetary theories and monetary practices. Economic reasoning cannot be positioned outside this relationship, held up as an overarching logical framework from which external criteria for the explanation of economic actions can be derived. Economic reasoning is integral to the environment against which and through which aspirations and expectations are formed. Simon's rejection of the narrow version of the maximizing thesis is persuasive in exposing fundamental analytical weaknesses in economic reasoning. Acceptance that such weaknesses exist need not, however, presuppose agreement with Simon's own approach. Indeed, as a basis for an alternative approach, the concept of bounded rationality is vacuous. Simon's attempt to weaken the assumptions behind economic reasoning merely reinforces the view that this logical framework is inapplicable to monetary analysis, not only on substantive grounds but because it is incompatible in epistemological terms with what monetary analysis should set out to achieve. This cannot be corrected merely by tinkering. Rigour is essential here. The argument that principles derived from economic reasoning should be applied to monetary analysis and administration cannot be advanced pragmatically as if these were the surest or best available principles by which to organize and understand the issue and transaction of money. In a monetary context, as exemplified by the proposals of Hayek and White, the argument depends on being set out in absolute terms. Once basic analytical flaws are exposed in economic reasoning, the outcome is not a contrary interpretation of the facts, an empirical counter-argument. It becomes overwhelmingly clear that the application of economic reasoning to monetary analysis cannot be sustained even in principle. This point becomes clearer still once the fiduciary dimension of monetary networks is taken into account, as I shall move on now to argue.

Trust

To pay with money is to pay up. For this to be possible, the question of trust should not arise between individual transactors as far as the validity of money itself is concerned. The identity of a currency as legal-tender, and the perception of its validity, does not depend on believing what other transactors say, nor on what they will do in the future. Monetary transaction relies on trust not between individuals but between transactors and the transacting network. This fiduciary dimension is vital to the reproduction of monetary networks, to their continuity over time. It is an abstract property of those networks which is irreducible to economic reasoning structured around the rational pursuit of self-interest. As I argued in the Introduction, trust in money is an essential property of monetary networks, and is dependent on the substantive relationship between money and the social, political and cultural conditions in which it is transacted. In the abstract form assumed by its expression in money, trust is an important feature of the restructuring of spatial and temporal principles of organization closely bound up with the phenomenon of globalization. In this sense, there are reasons connected to the wider concerns of contemporary sociology why this aspect of the operation of money in society should be clearly understood.

There is an obvious need to distinguish between the use of trust in verbal expressions ('I trust you are well'; 'Trust her to say that') and its substantive character as a component of social, political and economic relations.[19] This is not a straightforward distinction, because the use of the term in verbal expressions, although often synonymous with 'hope' or 'it is typical of', includes reference to the sense of expectancy inherent to trust as a social relationship. What is missing from such expressions of expectancy, however, is the sense of faith which trust entails, the implication that trust is blind by definition. It is this aspect of trust which takes it beyond the reach of economic reasoning, although there are additional reasons for this. In economic life, trust is integral to the maintenance of social relations in the face of two conditions in particular: uncertainty and complexity. In the analysis of economic behaviour, the characterization of trust can easily polarize. At one extreme, trust can feasibly be taken as being synonymous with rational expectation, closely equated with the reasoned taking of risk by a decision-maker on the basis of available information.[20] At the other extreme, trust can be addressed as a property of the social system, characterized and explained in terms of its functionality.[21] Although these two approaches are indeed often polarized, neither has as a corollary direct contradiction of the other.

Substantive definitions of trust - some of which begin with the *Oxford English Dictionary*,[22] while others focus on differences between trust, confidence, faith and so on[23] - commonly highlight two components of the experience of trust, namely, expectancy and reflexivity. This is clearest of all in Gambetta's definition of trust as 'a particular level of the subjective probability with which an agent assesses that another agent or group of agents will perform a particular action, both *before* he can monitor such action (or independently of his capacity ever to be able to monitor it) *and* in a context in which it affects *his own* action'.[24] Reflexivity is integral to the sense of faith which accompanies trust. To place trust in a person or event requires a leap of imagination regarding the future. But unlike prediction, trust does not only entail the possibility of being wrong. To commit oneself by trusting in something or someone and later find that trust has been misplaced is to damage oneself in some way, to become a sucker; materially, emotionally or both. What is worse, damage is partly self-inflicted. This is unavoidable: trust is necessitated by the existence of others' freedom,[25] and so by definition entails risk of disappointment, or more emotively, betrayal. Not only does the act of trusting feed back into the actions and dispositions of the dependent party. Trust is usually reciprocal, and the experience of both trusting and being trusted can be mutually beneficial to both parties. For this reason, trust can be deliberately generated by initially acting as if one trusts another, although to intermingle trust with intentionality in this way has its risks.[26]

The existence of money in society suggests that the sense of expectancy integral to trust need not be based on personal familiarity or passion. Analytically, however, the relationship between trust and rationality is complicated and uneven. If characterized as a commodity or good, trust can be expanded rather than depleted with greater use.[27] Trust can be built upon 'as if' foundations or through historical accident.[28] To seek to establish trust in some systematic way, either with another person or across a social group, can be self-defeating, making matters worse.[29] It is no easier for example to build a reputation by which one may be trusted if one is actually trustworthy than if one is in fact untrustworthy.[30] Trust entails a psychological investment which may cloud assessment of whether it has been misplaced: as when prophecy fails, falsifying instances can be explained away, and there is unquestionable motivation to do so where trust is concerned.[31] But it is precisely because of this curious mixture of psychological robustness and emotional dependence that trust, where established reciprocally within a relationship or across a social group, can be effective as a means for coping with the freedom of others, in the sense of protecting such freedom as well as protecting oneself. In economic life our sense of and capacity to cope with others' freedom is demanded by the existence of an uncertain and complex environment.

Both trust and distrust are consciously taken stances towards specified events and persons whose future outcome or actions are by definition uncertain. Uncertainty in relation to trust has two properties: first, the openness of one's own future to the freedom of others to act in ways which one may not want or be able to predict; and second, the lack of information available when assessing what might happen in the future, a lack which is both empirical and definitive. From an individual point of view, trust may be based on experience over time, both one's own and second-hand (reputation). The continuity of time is an essential component of trust in this sense, just as it is essential to the reproduction of monetary networks. Trust involves thinking backwards from projected outcomes ('what if...'), assessing the consequences of trust itself, and it is in this respect that it might seem feasible to equate trust with rational expectation.[32] Luhmann tries to define more closely the rational component of trust by distinguishing between trust and confidence: trust entails choosing between alternative courses of action; confidence is a generalized or habitual expectation that specific and probably remote kinds of dangers will not be realized, for instance that the bus driver will not be a lunatic or the doctor an imposter. In this approach, trust entails rational choice while confidence is habitual. Disappointment in trust leads one partly to blame oneself. Disappointment where there had been confidence usually allows one to blame others.[33] Giddens disagrees with Luhmann here, less because of the distinction itself than Luhmann's treatment of it. Trust, for Giddens, is no less continuous a state than confidence, suggesting that trust is a type of confidence rather than distinct from it.[34] I shall discuss Giddens's approach in more detail below, because he examines trust specifically in relation to money.

Whereas the relationship between trust and uncertainty stems from a lack of information or the existence of imperfect information, complexity generates the need for trust because there is too much information, too much to take in. In economic life, this is partly a function of scale, where the range of factors and processes which must be taken into account in making a decision is simply too broad to be manageable. Complexity necessitates the employment of symbols and signalling systems such as the price mechanism. In the work of Parsons and Habermas which I examined in chapter 4, money's transmission of information reduces complexity in the social system. It relies on abstract relations of trust in order to do this. But while it seems feasible to argue that trust helps cope with uncertainty and complexity, this is difficult to sustain as a basis for explaining the actual formation of trust. This problem is especially acute in the case of trust because, like money itself, it resists any kind of general theory based on substantive cases. Manifestations of trust vary considerably. There are blurred edges between trust and other types of expectancy such as faith and confidence, each of which seem to presuppose elements of the others. Luhmann's attempt to formulate a theory of trust, similar to that of Barber, is founded on functionalist tenets. Expressed simplistically, Luhmann argues that trust is integral to the capacity of any social system to reduce complexity. The critique of the assumptions underlying this approach formulated in chapter 4 is pertinent here, for the adhesion of trust to normative integration underpins the shortcomings of systems-theory when addressing the relationship between money and power. It is not clear in any case whether trust actually is functional in the way intended within systems-theory. Williams contends for example that, unless trust is partly derived from self-interest, a social order based entirely on trust in an altruistic sense will be inherently unstable, vulnerable to other more egoistical forms of motivation. It would seem, then, that trust must involve an element of self-interest and rational calculation.[35] Explanations of trust derived from an assertion of the importance of normative integration to the reproduction of the social system are therefore difficult to sustain: for the novel reason in social theory that trust is not always functional.

This does not mean, however, that the study of rational expectations can exhaust the analysis of what is at stake in the expression of trust; and *a fortiori* that trust can be generated by the rational pursuit of self-interest alone. As I have suggested already, trust extends beyond the parameters of economic reasoning, although it is not easy to explain how or why outside specific cases. But the problems inherent within each of these explanatory strategies, functionalism and economic reasoning, cannot be overcome simply by producing a composite theory of trust based on a combination of the most successful aspects of each. Trust in money fluctuates. This is not only because our expectations regarding the future re-exchangeability of specific monetary forms are likely to rise and fall, but also because such expectations cannot always be accurately characterized as trust. In so far as trust depends on a degree of rational deliberation, this is clearly more pertinent to monetary analysis in circumstances of instability or change, for example in the event of a shift to a single currency within the European Community, than to conditions of long-term monetary stability, in which case the habitual connotation of the term confidence is apposite. If the analysis of trust in money cannot provide a basis for distinguishing between even these cases, it is not the right concept to be using. No insights can be provided by examining trust in money if this merely refers to the fiduciary relationships on which monetary networks obviously depend. Only by distinguishing between trust as an essential feature of money in general and trust in the stability and validity of specific monetary forms can this issue be addressed in a way which is sufficiently rigorous in the light of the particular requirements of monetary analysis. For this reason, the difficulties entailed in the explanation of trust, and more specifically trust in money, are not only substantive but analytical.

Giddens characterizes money as a symbolic token on a par with other expert systems, for example systems regulating traffic flows in cities and procedures for maintaining safety in public buildings, which generate the process of time–space distanciation characteristic of modernity. This concerns the trend whereby social interaction is possible across increasing distances, differentiating out the axes of time and space: we do not need to be present together in order to talk, do business, argue and so on. Money, addressed in these terms, necessarily incorporates credit. Although, as I have argued, to pay with money is legally to pay up, the real satisfaction or utility to be gained from an exchange from the point of view of those being paid comes with the re-exchange of the money at some future date, probably in another place. In order to agree to hold money over time in this way, the transactor must trust - or even hope, expect, be confident that, pray and so on - that the tokens received will do what they are supposed to do. If it is unclear whether others will recognize the validity of the tokens in question or whether their value is stable, they are unlikely to be accepted in the first place: another form of payment will be demanded, such as another currency or an object which can be bartered. In this instance, however, the withdrawal of trust need not undermine the fiduciary character of money in general but concerns only the substantive properties of specific monetary forms. To this extent, Giddens's argument that it is in the abstract properties of money that we place trust is incomplete. As soon as one asks what these abstract properties are - or, which is what matters, how they are perceived by others - complications arise which cannot be resolved in terms of Giddens's formulation.

Trust in the validity and stability of a particular monetary form is by extension trust in the agents and agencies - for example the state, central bank and banking system - directly responsible for its administration. Because of this, Giddens argues that the nature of risk involved in monetary transaction is quite specific, and reflects the unique character of risk more generally within the modern world, namely that it derives from things which the human race itself has done. Where such risks are regarded as acceptable, one might say that we possess weak inductive knowledge regarding possible outcomes, for our perception of risk is reflexively tied to expert knowledge. In a monetary context, weak inductive knowledge entails rationally assessing information in order to make transacting decisions: for example, regarding future prices, the rate of unemployment and even the political outlook. For this reason, the response of transactors to, say, rising inflation cannot be accurately predicted without reference to their expectations or aspirations regarding the level or stability of inflation. Such expectations will not only reflect experience - high inflation in the UK is the stuff of dreams for a Peruvian - but also theoretical knowledge. As I argued in chapter 6, this type of knowledge is disseminated through commentary in news media: not merely in straightforward reports of economic events but through the organization and presentation of those reports. In this sense, as I suggested in earlier chapters, not only money but monetary theories are subject to levels of confidence and trust. This is critical to perceptions of whether to trust a particular monetary form. It is perhaps less critical however to perceptions of and trust in the essential features of money in general. This is a vitally important distinction, but one which cannot be addressed within the terms formulated by Giddens.

Giddens contends that trust has the character of a 'moral hostage to fortune'.[36] This captures the sense in which monetary transaction in general contains an element of faith, some kind of psychological investment, in a way which predictive calculations of the economic variety plainly do not, unless one goes in for theoretical sacred cows. Yet to equate trust with morality as part of a substantive theory of money would be unhelpful in addressing distinctive practical issues. The moral fabric of a monetary network based on state issue for example is quite different from those processes of reasoning entailed in the monetary arrangements advocated by Hayek and White, both of whom suggest that money and markets are amoral. I have already argued that the reduction of the fiduciary dimension of monetary transaction in general to economic reasoning is unsustainable. This does not mean, however, that this form of knowledge has no bearing on particular instances of the way individuals and firms handle money. Rational deliberation regarding the validity and stability of money is certainly more likely to occur where currencies compete than where the state monopolizes issue. By extension, transactors may be more likely to apportion some of the blame for collapse or instability upon themselves in the former instance (Luhmann's trust), whereas in the latter they will probably blame state agents or agencies (Luhmann's confidence). If trust in money is addressed only in substantive terms derived from rigid adherence to monetary theory rather than as an issue concerning the essential features of money in general, only one of these cases can be defined as trust, whereas they are equally conceivable and of equal importance to understanding the reproduction of monetary networks over time.

Greater analytic rigour is possible if the characterization of trust in the essential properties of money is not reduced to a categorical relationship between the type of confidence which helps sustain the transaction of money and particular institutional arrangements governing monetary administration: questions of the latter type should be confined to substantive discussion, not inflated as generalized statements about the abstract features of money. Where particular monetary forms are concerned, it is likely that the type of confidence entailed in their transaction, and the extent to which this merges with faith, trust or rational choice, depends on ongoing, variable and not exclusively monetary conditions. At this level, trust in money should be addressed not as a functional requirement for monetary transaction but as a varying characteristic of the way individuals handle money, subject to a sometimes awkward and uneven combination of rational decision-making and habitual expectation. Continuity in the sense intended by Giddens, on the other hand, concerns the abstract features of money in general. It is therefore vital that transactors' perceptions of money as a social institution, of money's essential features, are distinguished from their attitudes towards the performance of specific monetary forms. The sense of faith and expectancy implied by the expression of trust in money suggests the existence of abstract preconceptions regarding the essential properties of money itself. These preconceptions underpin but are none the less distinctive from the less consistent and dependable attitudes and expectations chronically involved in the transaction of particular monetary forms. It is against such abstract preconceptions, after all, that levels of confidence in actual monetary forms will be fulfilled or falsified.

Trust in money therefore operates on two levels: formally, relating to money as a social institution, to money in general; and substantively, in actual transaction, relating to specific monetary forms. Unless this distinction is drawn, there is no convincing basis for discussing what happens when the circulation of a weak or soft currency is encroached on by strong or hard alternatives. Under these circumstances, there is no doubt that one currency or monetary form is more trusted than another. But once trust in money as a social institution is conflated with trust in particular monetary forms it is difficult to avoid concluding that the withdrawal of trust in a monetary form amounts to the withdrawal of trust in money. In some cases another currency will be utilized as an object of barter; elsewhere, an unofficial, black market or parallel currency might be established, its issue being controlled by a particular figure, organization or group; in other cases, monetary transaction may cease altogether as a social activity. Failure to distinguish between trust in money as a social institution and trust in specific monetary forms threatens to take the differences between such instances beyond the reach of monetary analysis. For this reason, the substantive distinctions drawn by Luhmann and Giddens are inflexible, too rigid to encapsulate the inherent fluidity of monetary networks. It is this fluidity, after all, which has rendered monetary relations in contemporary society not only difficult to understand but chronically problematic from the point of view of theory. The argument I have developed here suggests that this problem does not derive from the substantive content of those theories so much as from the more fundamental question of their epistemological status *as* theories. This contention goes to the heart of the predicament in which contemporary social theory finds itself, as I shall move on now to contend.

High Modernity

Assumptions about the nature and operations of money are implicit in attempts by social theorists to discern and explain the distinctive features of contemporary Western societies, particularly the extension of their core principles of organization into other parts of the globe. Money's connection to these arguments does not simply stem from its causal importance but is thematic, expressing specific features of a form of knowledge, economic reasoning, which has been at the heart of the project to explain the outward expansion of modernity, whether this is described as a process of globalization or Westernization. I have sought throughout this book to criticize the application of economic reasoning to monetary analysis. The implications of this critique for the wider concerns of contemporary social theory can now be assessed. At the centre of these concerns is the series of transitions which have been under way within and across the nation-states system, and which arguably mark a fundamental shift in the developmental trajectory of modern societies into a period variously described as late capitalism, postmodernity and high modernity. The consequences of this alleged shift are globally extensive but also intensely near-at-hand, having profound economic, political, cultural and existential significance for everyday life.

Giddens characterizes this latest stage in the history of the modern West, particularly its global implications, in terms of the concept of high modernity, emphasizing its points of continuity no less than discontinuity with modernity itself. His characterization of modern society is based on four institutional clusters comprising capitalism, industrialism and the surveillance and military components of the nation-state. He contends both that these dimensions were integral to the historical imperatives underpinning the onset of modernity, and that they define a conceptual framework for the analysis of modern society itself. This approach is extended in his theory of high modernity, in which the original terminology is expanded: for capitalism now read world capitalist economy; for industrialism read international division of labour; for surveillance read nation-state system; and for military power read world military order. It seems reasonable to assume from Giddens's arguments that the new terminology does not supplant the old but underlines how existing forces underlying the development of modern societies have accelerated in velocity and expanded in scope. In other words, he is advancing two main arguments: first, that the causal imperatives which had been behind the onset of modernity are now, albeit in modified form, primarily responsible for a later stage in its development which cannot therefore be accurately conceptualized in the disjunctive sense implicit in concepts such as postmodernity; and second, that the structural and institutional forms assumed by these imperatives provide the basis for a conceptual framework through which they can best be analysed and understood.

Giddens's arguments, however, do not focus merely on how contemporary society should be theorized. He is concerned with what is in effect the process by which that society conceptualizes and understands itself. He contends that modernity is characterized by the supplanting of religious cosmology by 'empirical observation and logical thought ... focused upon material technology and socially applied codes'.[37] The reflexivity of knowledge within modern social life stems from the institutionalization of rational review procedures. In respect of what he calls the 'reflexive ordering and reordering of social relations', Giddens argues that the utilization of these procedures of review is integral to the continuing unfolding of the development trajectory of contemporary society: integral both to the process of change itself and to the unsettling sense of risk generated by the ongoing experience of change brought on by the institutionalization of reflexivity. In other words, the rational form of knowledge through which contemporary society understands itself is at the heart of the dynamic process by which the development of that society proceeds through time. High modernity is therefore characterized by the unprecedented pre-eminence and dynamism of reflexivity within social life. This provides novel opportunities to re-frame central moral and political questions. The appropriate response to high modernity is not, however, the postmodernism of Lyotard[38] but the essentially practical project of utopian realism. Giddens frames questions which might be addressed in such a project, and more specifically the way they are addressed, in the light of an ambivalent characterization of the human experience of high modernity, especially globalization, which is in some ways reminiscent of the tone of Simmel. For Giddens, the way in which globalization displaces human beings - increasing the level and frequency of impersonal contact, widening the spatial and temporal scope of social interactions - does not engulf them but generates new sources of familiarity at the local level. High modernity therefore marks both a qualitative and a quantitative shift in the nature of human relationships, 'less a phenomenon of estrangement from the local than one of integration within globalized 'communities' of shared experience'.[39]

Giddens's arguments are directly pertinent to the analysis of money. But in so far as the phenomenon of reflexivity as he describes it is crystallized by the handling of money as I have portrayed it in this book, serious analytical difficulties arise in his explanatory approach to high modernity. The implications of Giddens's argument for monetary analysis are partly indicated by his assertion that money is an abstract token based on the spatial and temporal extension of trust. Reflexivity is central to this idea, for perceptions of the abstract properties of money which are so essential to trust are chronically (though not solely) derived from monetary theories. As I suggested earlier in this chapter, it is at this substantive level that economic reasoning is so important to monetary analysis, for it is implicated in the ideas and expectations transactors have of money which inform their decisions about whether and how to use it. But these expectations are not exhausted by economic reasoning, and are therefore irreducible to economic logic as a form of knowledge. This, as I have argued, has significant epistemological implications for monetary analysis. The implications are no less significant for contemporary social theory.

Substantively, the fiduciary dimension of monetary transaction cannot be understood by reference to economic reasoning alone. Epistemologically, in so far as perceptions and theories of money are not detached from but integral to its features as an economic instrument, they do not provide an exhaustive basis for examining the essential features of money in general, nor the properties requisite to the reproduction of monetary networks over time. This is not only because the substantive characteristics of money and monetary networks vary within and across societies through time. Although this assertion is correct in itself, the reasoning behind the arguments I have been developing in this book should be set out with greater clarity: the substantive properties of money and monetary networks are specific to the sociological conditions in which particular monetary forms are transacted not despite but *because of* the essential features of money itself, because of its transparency as an economic instrument. Realization of this is vital if theoretical rigidity in monetary analysis is to be avoided; or more specifically, if substantive features of money are not to be confused with its essential properties, if contingency is not to be confused with necessity. Precisely this has been at the root of the inability of scholars to formulate monetary theories which are lastingly convincing, and the related incapacity of governments to act meaningfully and consequentially towards their citizens through monetary policy.

As I have already said, the arguments put forward in this book with regard to monetary analysis can, and indeed should, be directly applied to contemporary social theory. Economic reasoning is at the core of the form of knowledge which in Giddens's view defines not only the experience but also the *unfolding* of high modernity. It is the dual application of such reasoning which is problematic in the context of the themes explored in the preceding chapters. Where human experience within contemporary society is concerned, Giddens's characterization of the reflexivity of rational review procedures is instructive for monetary analysis. But in utilizing that self-same form of knowledge to *explain* the developmental trajectory of modernity and high modernity, Giddens conflates precisely those two levels of analysis which, as I have argued throughout this book, must be prised apart if the substantive aims and epistemological claims of theory are to be grasped with clarity. By building the concept of reflexivity at the heart of the experience of high modernity into the project of utopian realism, Giddens explicitly acknowledges the importance of distinguishing between contingency and necessity, of rejecting preconceived patterns of historical development, for 'history has no teleology, and supplies us with no guarantees'.[40] Yet a teleological conception of history is difficult to avoid once the form of knowledge which has been integral to the self-understanding of the modern West is employed as a theoretical framework for actually explaining the phenomenon of globalization itself; which is precisely what Giddens seems to suggest when he argues that '[m]odernity is universalizing not only in terms of its global impact, but in terms of the reflexive knowledge foundational to its dynamic character'.[41] Substantive investigation into the roots and consequences of this self-image is incompatible on epistemological grounds with the analytical claims implicit in the explanatory project which Giddens seeks to undertake.

Giddens's substantive arguments urge upon us a process of open-ended reflection in which 'we can envisage alternative futures whose very propagation might help them to be realized'.[42] Yet he fails to provide secure analytical grounds on which to understand the myriad potential ways in which this process might shape the developmental trajectory of contemporary societies. Giddens's theory of high modernity relies on a form of knowledge, at the core of which is economic reasoning, which has been at the heart of the self-understanding of modernity but which, as a direct corollary of this, cannot provide an adequate basis for its analysis over time. To equate rationality and reflexivity is to suggest that this form of knowledge is an artefact, a product of human creativity and desire which is historically and culturally specific. It is to suggest, as Castoriadis has argued, that 'reason and rationality [are] historical creations of humanity'.[43] But in this form, economic reasoning is an imaginative ideal, a mythology corresponding to 'attitudes, values, and norms, a ... social definition of reality and of being, of what *counts* and what does *not* count'.[44] Realization of the reach, significance and power of this ideal is of course vital: first, because of its potency in propelling and legitimating economic and technological expansion;[45] and second, because of its direct impact on the subjective lives and relationships of individuals,[46] or more abstractly, on the nature of subjectivity.[47] But *a fortiori*, realization of these facts must not conceal the incompatibility of the ideal with the criterion of analytic rigour integral to the explanatory claims of theorizing. The difference is not one of relative superiority. It is a difference in kind. Giddens emphasizes procedural aspects of rationalism: reflexivity consists 'in the fact that social practices are constantly examined and reformed in the light of incoming information about those very practices, thus constitutively altering their character'.[48] It is for this reason that he refers to modernity as 'essentially a post-traditional order'.[49] Without doubt, this assertion would be sustainable if the Enlightenment philosophy Giddens equates with reflexivity was *reducible* to the procedural principles covered by his definition of reflexivity itself. But Enlightenment philosophy contains propositions which are not procedural but substantive. For this reason, it seems untenable to characterize rationalism as transcending all traditions. The 'reflexive review procedures' that Giddens identifies as being at the heart of rationalism extend only so far. Where economic reasoning in particular is concerned, this outlook, which explicitly identifies itself as post-traditional, has largely failed to scrutinize its pivotal substantive assumptions, namely those relating to the existence of a core domain of rational human activity underpinning modern forms of association. These make up its own particular 'tradition'. Indeed, no such scrutiny is even imaginable within the parameters of an outlook which is defined, and no less importantly defines itself, in procedural terms alone. The adoption of this kind of reasoning as the basis of an explanatory strategy does not help anticipate its consequences for contemporary society but merely replicates them in the form of theoretical rigidity.

There is no requirement, however, to proceed from this argument to a form of relativism which Gellner identifies as nihilistic. He equates the argument that rationalism has no abstract epistemological superiority over any other historically and culturally specific form of knowledge with neglect of the significance of its accumulation as the foundation for massive asymmetries of wealth and power. This, Gellner contends, is the upshot of the position, which he associates with postmodernism, in which it is held that 'to set up a ranking between kinds of knowledge is morally and politically wicked'.[50] He maintains that such a position 'precludes us from even *asking*, let alone from answering, the question concerning why the world is so very unsymmetrical, why there is such a desperate wish to emulate the success of one kind of cognition, and why there is a discrepancy between fields in which the success is achieved and those in which it is absent'.[51] But Gellner's arguments are less compelling for their adherence to rationalism in particular as the foundation for theory than for their advocacy of a particular approach to the procedures of theorizing in general. Indeed, he himself seems to imply as much when he argues that, within the postmodern outlook as he calls it, '[w]hat seems to be the very devil is the supposition that a theory could be articulated, understood, assessed, without any reference to its author and his social identity'.[52] The close historical relationship between this approach to theorizing and the substantive claims of rationalism does not carry the logical force which Gellner imagines. In other words, to reject rationalism as a theoretical framework need not, as a corollary, lead to the adoption of the relativist position which Gellner condemns: to imagine so merely confuses analytical argument with moral posturing. That such confusion is unsurprising given the focus of Gellner's critique does not mean that his reasoning is sound. He argues that '[w]hen dealing with serious matters, when human lives and welfare are at stake, when major resources are being committed, the only kind of knowledge which may legitimately be used and invoked is that which satisfies the criteria of Enlightenment philosophy'.[53] But this does not sit comfortably with his summary of those criteria as entailing '*no* privileged facts, occasions, individuals, institutions or associations'.[54] The Enlightenment philosophy to which he refers cannot be accounted for by reference to procedural principles alone, for as I have already suggested, it contains substantive assumptions about human activity and association[55] which have been crystallized within economic reasoning. And as I have argued throughout this book, the role and significance of economic reasoning in contemporary society is a matter for substantive investigation in theory, not for analytical supposition about what exactly theorizing entails. To separate these types of question is not to abandon the kind of theorizing advocated by Gellner. On the contrary, it is to seek to strengthen the analytical claims of theory to be providing a secure and lasting basis on which to examine the substantive questions which Gellner himself, on largely moral grounds it would seem, regards as so important. The rejection of rationalism as the analytical foundation for theory does *not* have as its corollary the advocacy of relativism, nor the political naivety and moral abstinence which Gellner caricatures.

It is undoubtedly the case that, as Gellner argues, '[o]ne particular style of knowledge has proved so overwhelmingly powerful, economically, militarily, administratively, that all societies have had to make their peace with it and adopt it'.[56] It is no less doubtful that, as Giddens contends, '[i]n respect of both social and natural scientific knowledge, the reflexivity of modernity turns out to confound the expectations of Enlightenment thought - although it is the very product of that thought'.[57] But both substantive positions are compatible with the argument that the *analytical* shortcomings of rationalism in general and economic reasoning in particular have resulted in a persistently inadequate theoretical understanding of modernity: of the causal forces propelling modern societies in a particular direction, and of the best means to resolve whichever predicament that society happens to find itself in from time to time. This argument is as applicable to the failure of state socialism as to the continuing failure of representative democracy where the enactment of the will of citizens is concerned. It also applies to the compelling fragility of contemporary monetary networks. It must be open to analytical questioning whether we have misunderstood ourselves by resorting to a form of knowledge derived from economic reasoning, itself dependent on somewhat over-flattering ideals of rational human agency, political capability and economic organization. From this perspective, theories of globalization or Westernization derived from this self-same form of reasoning would be inadequate from an analytical point of view and pernicious from the point of view of politics. It is irrefutable that diffuse areas of the globe have been caught up increasingly in the monetary affairs of the West. But this entanglement may owe more to an expansive and avaricious clumsiness borne of human desire than to any kind of rational human agency. And to say as much need not, contrary to Gellner's claims, entail ignoring the significance and power of rationalism as a form of knowledge. But while to recognize the causal reach of economic reasoning on substantive grounds is one thing, it is another matter entirely, indeed it is a matter of epistemological rather than substantive inquiry, to unquestioningly adopt such reasoning as a foundation for the explanatory claims of theory. The transmutation of substantive arguments into analytical foundations will result only in a rigid and incomplete understanding of the predicament posed by these questions. In monetary analysis, only by breaking away from theoretical rigidity will it be possible to understand the profound ambivalence of the role of money in contemporary society: its continuity over time in the face of the structural fragility of monetary networks themselves; and the trust in money's abstract features expressed in its transaction as opposed to its symbolic and causal connection with starkly conflicting interests stemming from the persistence of fundamental social, political and economic inequalities.

An essentialist conceptualization of money and monetary practices is imperative to analytic rigour. But its epistemological status must be made explicit. The approach to monetary analysis I have sought to develop in this book is intended to resist regarding the practices, beliefs and expectations of transactors as an aspect of the environment of monetary networks, as external to a core domain of economic reasoning. The perceptions and beliefs of transactors are integral to the substantive nature of particular monetary forms. Substantive theories of money cannot claim simply to reflect or observe the practices and strategies employed in its ongoing transaction. The application of economic reasoning to monetary analysis is informed by a set of epistemological claims which cannot be sustained. The imposition of economic reasoning as a rigid theoretical framework for monetary analysis entails the implicit proposition that there is a core domain of rational action which, if external obstacles were removed, would be not only operational but intrinsically more efficient. Given the naturalistic implications of such a proposition, it would be difficult to avoid equating it with the further conviction that economic reasoning alone provides the key to a set of principles for organizing money and market networks which is not only practically feasible but politically desirable. This is the clear substantive argument implicit in monetary theories which advance unwarranted epistemological claims: they become what are in effect ideologies by default. Precisely the same issue arises, albeit on a larger scale, in the analysis of the developmental trajectory of the contemporary West. The concept of modernity, with economic reasoning at its core, has been exploited in social theory for two objectives: as a political project and an explanatory strategy. Neither objective has intrinsic superiority over the other. There is no compelling reason why they cannot be combined. But how they are combined is a matter for analytical reflection, not presumption based on a fundamental confusion about what a social or economic theory should set out to achieve. These questions are not confined to monetary analysis, but are most clearly exposed in this context because the distinctive features of money itself have persistently evaded adequate theoretical understanding; and because, no less importantly, money is symbolically and causally implicated not only in the lives and livelihoods of individuals but in the contemporary difficulties of governments. As long as the use and perception of money by individuals, firms and governments is conceptualized on the basis of a substantive form of reasoning associated with an essential domain of rational human endeavour, and thereby used as a foundational framework for theory, what we continue to think we know about money will not only be condemned to a condition of analytical confusion. It will remain a source of profoundly consequential political incapacity.

8
Monetary Analysis in Sociology

Throughout this book I have advocated the necessity of analytic rigour as against theoretical rigidity. Money possesses distinctive abstract properties which cannot be successfully incorporated with the substantive claims of extant theories, whether of society in general or of the economy in particular. In such theories attempts to formulate generalized, substantive claims about the operation of money in society have largely failed. Money does not possess qualities which condition how and why it is to be used. Money cannot in this sense embody the substantive arguments of social and economic theories regarding the nature of economic action and the institutional, political and cultural framework of economic life in general. Money's indeterminacy is its sole distinguishing feature. While no material or symbolic object conditions how and why it is to be used, only money possesses this as its defining characteristic. It is precisely because of this that money lends itself so readily to theoretical manipulation in sociology. But for the same reason, such manipulation can only ever narrow the scope of inquiry into how money works and distort understanding whenever such an inquiry is attempted. An essentialist approach to the nature of money is not simply an optional indulgence which can be safely confined to the higher reaches of philosophy and social theory. It is on the contrary a fundamental requirement for an approach to monetary analysis which is conceptually robust and empirically sensitive. Only by conceptualizing money at this abstract level can patterns, variations and inconsistencies in the way it is used and perceived in different societies be fully grasped and explained.

The approach to monetary analysis I have been advocating in this book does not therefore preclude substantive inquiry into the role of money in contemporary society. It is intended to provide a basis on which such an inquiry can proceed unhindered by the suppositions of any one theoretical explanation of the nature of social and economic life. This argument is informed above all by an understanding of the peculiar difficulties of monetary analysis: in economic and social theory, in the formulation of economic policy, and in the decision-making processes which underpin economic action more generally. But it cannot be properly formulated without following through its implications as a critique of the inclusionist objectives of much of social and more specifically grand theory. An essentialist approach to monetary analysis does imply the ambition of universal application. But there is an important distinction between seeking to widen the explanatory scope of social theory in a substantive sense and providing an analytical framework from which a wide range of explanatory projects can be derived. This distinction has been fudged in social and economic theories which conflate the formulation of analytical principles underlying an approach to their object of study with the kinds of substantive argument which can only emerge once such an approach has been made. Conflation of these two objectives can only result in the theoretical inflexibility and empirical inadequacy which so undermines the work of Parsons and Habermas. These shortcomings in their work are not confined to money. But the distinctive features of money are such that the requirement for rigour in its analysis will always be starkly exposed as soon as substantive arguments which have been formulated on the basis of a rigid adherence to a particular theory are closely scrutinized.

The abstract features of money give it a quite specific ontological status as an object of study. It is for this reason that money, like time to St Augustine, tends to become more elusive the closer it is examined. The ontological status of money derives from its transparency as an economic instrument. The particular epistemological requirements of monetary analysis can only be clarified once this is understood. Monetary theorists have been misled by a preoccupation with the material or functional characteristics of specific monetary forms. But these are characteristics which money will always share with other economic instruments. It is for this reason that a completely satisfactory definition of money has never been formulated. An essentialist characterization of money can never coincide neatly with the features of actual monetary forms. But this is not what such a characterization sets out to achieve. As I have been arguing throughout this book, the abstract idea of money as a transparent medium is at the heart of perceptions which define how and why it is used. These perceptions have a substantive bearing on how money operates. This is why the distinction formulated in the Introduction between the requirement for abstractness and the problem of generality is so important. Money, wherever and whenever it is used, is not defined by its properties as a material object but by symbolic qualities generically linked to the ideal of unfettered empowerment. This is an ideational feature of money and monetary transaction which, as Simmel has shown, has far-reaching cultural and economic consequences. There is no doubt that in practice money never does provide its holder with completely unlimited possibilities for its use. Specific monetary forms clearly are associated with more restricted forms of economic agency, more culturally specific economic goals and narrower conceptions of how and why it can or should be used. The ideal of unfettered empowerment, of complete freedom to act and assimilate at will, is none the less at the heart of the conceptualization of money in general as a transparent symbolic medium. This is the basis of the desire to possess money, of the very concept of money which is essential to any decision to accept it as payment, to work for it, to save or hoard it, and to be both repelled and fascinated by what money seems to enable people and institutions to do. Other economic instruments are associated with these ideas and activities. But only money is synonymous with them, coextensive with the very idea of economic empowerment itself. Without this symbolic feature, nothing distinguishes money at all. In so far as money is the object of study, its analysis must begin at this abstract level. Failure to do so is not merely to miss a particular aspect of money. It is to be blind to money itself.

The abstract properties of money are defined by its symbolic features. Those properties are not, however, reducible to such features. Implicit in the use of money is a set of assumptions about its re-use elsewhere and in the future. In other words, actions involving the use of money have an implicit spatial and temporal orientation. The use of money rests on the anticipation that it can be re-exchanged, not simply in the future but anywhere within a delimited territory. The concept of money's transparency would be nonsensical without reference to money's role in the on-going formation of networks of exchange, to its relationship with the continuity of time. As I argued in the Introduction, these networks depend on the existence of specific kinds of information. The symbolic features of money are inextricably linked with this information. Ideas and perceptions of money do not merely inform how it is used. They are essential to the possibility of its being used at all. In this respect, Simmel's characterization of money as a pure instrument does not go far enough. He grasps the ontological status of money without addressing the sociological conditions which make the existence and circulation of an instrument possessing such status possible. This failing must not, however, be attributed to the absence in his study of a systematic theory of modern society. Characterization of the properties of monetary networks requires an approach no less abstract than conceptualization of the features of money itself. Once again, the need to resist confusing empirically specific observations regarding the use of money with general theoretical statements about its nature and functions is paramount. This is why the incorporation of money by Parsons and Habermas into a substantive theory of modern society as a social system is unworkable, leading to conclusions which are inflexible with regard to empirical study and obstructive in respect of monetary analysis. Substantive questions about the role of money in contemporary society, about its relationship to the state and its connection with principles of normative integration, cannot be satisfactorily addressed unless the abstract properties of monetary networks are fully grasped.

For example, the empirical association of monetary networks with currency systems in contemporary society, if interpreted as a feature of monetary networks in general, will preclude inquiry about the future of the relationship between money and the state. Two issues are raised by such an inquiry to which the approach to monetary analysis developed in this book can be instructively addressed. First, to focus on the abstract features of monetary networks rather than the definite boundaries of actual monetary systems means that the fiduciary dimension of these networks, in which the modern state has thus far played such an important role, can be explored without irreversibly anchoring them to the state itself. To regard the state's issuing and validating role as an inherent requirement for the circulation of money in society, as Knapp and Weber do, makes the termination of the relationship between money and the state impossible even to conceive: *a fortiori*, their arguments cannot privide a basis on which the implications of any such termination could be explored. Second, the analytical framework of the monetary network, as opposed to the monetary system with definite geopolitical boundaries, suggests that geopolitical borders have an implicit and historically specific rather than definitive role in the reproduction of those networks over time. This enables the phenomenon of monetary integration to be examined without having to resort to the crude juxtaposition of politics and markets. As a result of this, as I argued in chapter 5, the consequential role of sovereign funds in the constitution of offshore markets can be acknowledged without fear of contradiction, and in particular, without losing grasp of the potentially destabilizing features of those markets. Those features derive not from the fact that offshore markets have overwhelmed the sovereign capacity of nation-state governments, but for reasons which can only be fully understood by addressing their structural, institutional and informational properties as monetary networks.

The development of offshore markets has been part of broader structural developments in the relationship between the real and monetary or financial sectors of the Western economy. But these cannot be fully understood by reference to a political economy of money derived from the production paradigm. To suggest that the expansion of international monetary and financial networks has been destabilizing because of a major departure from this paradigm would be tautologous, simply expressing the fact that it is in the productive sphere that the consequences of the destabilizing features of these networks are found. To mourn the passing of the production paradigm, whether in economic theory or in economic activity more generally, is adequate only as a description of contemporary political economy based on assumptions about how that economy should best be organized. Such an approach explains nothing. International monetary and financial networks are potentially destabilizing because the inherent role of information in these networks has assumed a pre-eminence and rate of transmission which, when unimpeded by the connection between money and real goods, means that the objectives of commercial capital transactions rely on market fluctuations which will inevitably disrupt the real economy. Expansion and technological innovation within these markets has exacerbated this effect. But this does not amount to a fundamental restructuring of their principles of organization and operation. On the contrary, it is simply an enhancement of the way they have always worked. Theories of money based on the production paradigm provide no basis on which to understand these principles of operation either in the past or in the present. It is not the case therefore that the production paradigm has become outdated, but rather that it has never provided an adequate basis for explaining and understanding uses and perceptions of money. I argued in chapter 1 that puzzlement as to the basis and nature of the demand for money, linked to the negation in economic theory of money's function as a store of value, has long been a central source of difficulty in mainstream monetary theory. The pivotal role of information in the reproduction of monetary networks over time has a fiduciary function which theories of money focusing on its character as a commodity, the basis of its value in utility, or its relationship to a historically specific mode of production simply cannot grasp. Information plays a substantive role in the constitution of monetary networks which cannot be reduced to the function of a lubricant within a pre-existing monetary order. The role of information in the transaction of money is not confined merely to observation about an external and independent economic environment. Information is on the contrary the defining feature of monetary networks, for they are networks of, not just containers of, information.

Monetary networks have a fiduciary dimension irreducible to the orientation of individuals and firms to pursue economic self-interest, to the role of the state in issuing and validating specific monetary forms, or to the normative principles by which particular societies, communities and social groups are integrated. Any or all of these phenomena can and will play a vital part in the constitution and reproduction of monetary networks in specific societies at specific points in time. But on no account can any one or even a combination of them be regarded as defining the sociological conditions requisite for the existence and circulation of money in society at all. Substantive ideas about the nature and functions of actual monetary forms are specific to particular cultures and vary over time. These ideas are no less important than the institutional framework in which money is transacted for explaining how it works. This point is vital to the understanding of the epistemological status of monetary analysis which lies behind my call for analytic rigour. I do not suggest that ideas have causal primacy in economic life. On the contrary, the juxtaposition of the real and the ideal in the conceptualization of economics on which such a contention would depend is untenable. In the discussion of consumerism in chapter 6 I did not maintain, as postmodern theorists are inclined to do, that the phenomenon of passive enrichment was merely a triumph of fantasy over fact, of media obfuscation over economic prudence, of irrationality over rationality. These distinctions derive from a dualism in the conceptualization of economic life, and of social life more generally, which I have sought to reject. The concept of the 'real' economy, against which the 'monetary' economy has so often been defined, relies on a juxtaposition of material and symbolic dimensions of economic activity which cannot be separated and should not be separated even in principle. Ideas, expectations and symbolic associations play an integral role within, rather than simply being a reflection upon, real economic activity; on the way in which individuals in fact use and handle money, on the way in which money in fact works in society, on the way it is in fact administered by governments, and on the consequences its operation in fact has right across society. Information does not inform or express aspects of real economic activity as a series of ideas mediating the material world with more or less objective accuracy. Information is part of that world, which is therefore neither material nor symbolic but something other; an other which cannot be grasped within the language of economics, nor indeed within any language which derives its structure from the dualism of the material and the symbolic, of concepts and the reality they are supposed to depict.

Theories regarding the operation of money should not therefore be regarded as neutral, detached processes of reflection. The use and operation of money are driven by perceptions of how and why it works. These perceptions are chronically informed by the explanatory project of theorists. It is vital that this reflexive relationship between monetary theory and monetary practice is incorporated within money analysis. This can only be achieved through an essentialist approach to the abstract properties of money and monetary networks, an approach which relies on an explicit distinction between analytical statements about the essential properties of money in general and substantive arguments about the features of specific monetary forms. No claim should be made, as far as the first objective is concerned, to be providing an empirically accurate account of the operations of money in particular societies. Indeed, the essentialist approach can never provide an exhaustive description of how money actually works in practice. It is intended to provide an analytical framework through which such a substantive investigation can be undertaken. Because of its self-conscious indeterminacy with regard to the object of study, the essentialist characterization of money and monetary networks proceeds on an analytical level quite distinct from the substantive monetary theories which are reflexively tied to monetary practices. The arguments I have developed in this book concern, first and foremost, an approach to monetary analysis which has a qualitatively different epistemological status to substantive monetary theories. This is not, however, intended to avoid reflexivity as a problem, but rather to embrace it as an operational feature of all monetary networks. Once the distinctive ontological status of money is grasped, and the abstract properties of monetary networks are adequately conceptualized, examination of specific monetary forms and the operation of actual monetary networks can be undertaken without losing sight of the epistemological status of this form of inquiry. The reflexive relationship between monetary theories and monetary practices can then be incorporated within the object of study, not marginalized as an irritant to the claims of theory. No substantive theory of money can ever provide a lastingly convincing explanation of precisely how money works in different societies and at different points in time. The ontological status of money precludes this. By making explicit the specific analytical requirements generated by the distinctive features of money, monetary theorizing can be undertaken self-consciously, in full awareness of what can and cannot be achieved. No confusion need arise about the claims and objectives of monetary theory if the conflation of abstract principles of analysis with the formulation of substantive arguments, which has been the object of my critique throughout this book, is avoided.

The abstract properties of money are defined by its inherent transparency as an economic instrument. Money does not merely embrace but embodies essential features of the empowerment of the human will, of the capacity and desire of individuals to acquire what they do not have, to possess and assimilate objects of desire. This is at the heart of the demand for money, irrespective of precisely how and why it is used. Money's empowerment of its holder derives from the freedom it provides for the expression of needs and desires. Trust in money's abstract properties is, at the same time, trust in its stability and continuity over time and in its validity across a particular, delimited space. It is for this reason that information plays such an integral role in the reproduction of monetary networks, and why the fiduciary component binding those networks together is so important. It would be a fundamental misreading of this argument, however, to suggest that the relationship between money and asymmetries of wealth and power in society is somehow coincidental or even accidental, an unfortunate contingency in the way monetary networks have been organized in modern societies. It is undeniably the case that money has been bound up with the unequal distribution of wealth and property wherever and whenever it is used. No less importantly, money has been chronically implicated in the economic, cultural and political processes which have ensured that social inequality is not merely sustained but institutiona- lized. Money has been and will continue to be the focus, in both causal and symbolic terms, of massive conflicts of interest in society, and of fundamental structural schisms in the production and distribution of wealth in the global economy. These issues are of compelling significance to the analysis of money. It is therefore vital that the precise nature of money's role in the reproduction of asymmetries of wealth and power is understood.

In chapter 1, I argued that the concept of political neutrality employed in economy theories of money is sustainable in principle but unworkable in practice. This point should now be made with greater clarity and its implications drawn out. The inherent transparency of money in relation to the will of its holder is, by definition, non-discriminating. The possession of money is empowering irrespective of the wealth, property, class position and social and political status of its holder. These are essential features of money which form the basis of the desire to possess it. In practice, however, these features are almost invariably obscured. A monetary income which barely meets the purchase of subsistence goods presents a starkly different set of choices to its holder than money held over and above this requisite level. Money acquired in the form of a windfall or gift can give rise to a series of possibilities which are markedly distinct from money routinely gained in the form of income, where most if not all of its potential uses may already have been accounted for by regular economic obligations or commitments. What can be achieved through money can also depend on pre-existing networks of relationships, on differential degrees of access to the acquisition of goods and services not accounted for by the price mechanism alone. Price may not be the sole determinant of access to art, property and the services of others. The capacity to repay is rarely the sole determinant of access to credit for individuals, firms and governments. These inconsistencies in the empowering features of money are structurally interconnected with the distribution of wealth and power in society and across the global economy. There is, then, a clear incongruity in the transparency of money as conceived in principle as opposed to the empowering features it actually possesses in practice. This does not mean, however, that these two sets of features should be aligned or collapsed into each other for purposes of theoretical discussion. To do so would not help but hinder any attempt to explain the role of money in the production and distribution of wealth and power. Indeed, the very incongruity between these two characterizations of the transparency of money provides the key to explaining the relationship between money and power.

I argued in chapters 3 and 4 that the incongruity between money's fiduciary yet divisive character defines its profound ambivalence as a symbolic medium and economic instrument in contemporary society. It must be possible to hold what seem to be two contradictory positions at the same time if this ambivalence is to be grasped: money depends for its existence and circulation in society on a generalized level of trust in its abstract properties; money none the less symbolizes and is structurally interconnected with massive conflicts of interest based on the unequal distribution of wealth and power in society. Monetary theorists tend to negate this contradiction, or at least diminish its significance, either by emphasizing one proposition at the expense of the other or by ordering them sequentially so as to suggest that the role of money in society has undergone a fundamental transformation. Classical and neoclassical economists, albeit in different ways, tend to reduce the first proposition to a set of narrow principles concerning the nature of rational economic action; these principles are then inflated in the form of a set of logical imperatives which suggest that conditions described by the second proposition are exceptional, that they can only arise by virtue of a departure from those imperatives; the departure, rather than the imperatives themselves, is then given the status of the problem to be explained. Marx's approach to the political economy of money transforms the first proposition into a foundational philosophical anthropology brutally at odds with the fundamental asymmetry, defined in terms of the second proposition, inherent in the capitalist mode of production. Like Habermas after him, Marx combines the two propositions only in diachronic terms, speculating that the first can only fully emerge in society once conditions depicted in the second are overcome. Parsons, finally, diminishes (rather than denies) the importance of the second proposition by submerging money in a sea of analogies which, constrained by self-imposed rigidities of theoretical consistency, serves merely to conflate instrumental rationality and normative integration and turn the first proposition into a founding principle of social theory rather than treating it as a phenomenon to be explained.

Only Simmel makes it clear that both propositions must be addressed side-by-side, indeed as mutually dependent. By focusing only on the abstract features of money, however, and not on the essential properties of monetary networks, he provides only a limited basis on which to do so. As I suggested in chapter 3, the absence of the latter theme in Simmel's work reflects a problem of scale. His arguments concerning the ambivalence of money in modern society are concentrated on an essential but inexhaustive feature of the relationship between money and power. Simmel's analysis persuasively captures the sheer motivating force of money's inherent capacity to empower. He underlines how money's transparency can lead to profound dissatisfaction if it comes to be desired as an end in itself. He also suggests how the reciprocity implicit in the essential features of money can be compromised by structural characteristics of the society in which it is used, particularly as a consequence of differential levels of wealth and income. But in focusing solely on the character of money as an abstract economic instrument and referring only implicitly to the abstract spatial and temporal relationships necessary for its existence and circulation in society at all, relationships I have characterized as basic properties of monetary networks, Simmel fails to extend his analysis in a way which could help explain not merely how the use of money is affected by the broader asymmetries of wealth to which he refers but, no less importantly, the role played by money in their reproduction over time. He argues that the features of money which make it a transparent or neutral means for the expression of the human will in principle are those which, in practice, serve as an irresistible basis of the desire for money in general. It is a significant corollary of his concept of the essential transparency of money that it is, at this level, indeterminate with regard to the organization of wealth and power in society. But likewise, the features of money which make its abstract features unconnected with power in principle are those very same features which make its interconnection with power virtually inevitable in practice. This is not a contradiction which prevents an understanding of how money works but on the contrary is vital to its explanation.

Money's symbolic features as an empowering economic instrument do not derive from its capacity to acquire wealth and property. They are the source of that capacity, and rest on the abstract properties of monetary networks. Money's essential features do not concern its power over particular goods and services, for example by symbolizing their specific value, but rather express the power of acquisition and assimilation in its ideal form. This is only possible because of money's relationship with the spatial and temporal properties of monetary networks, not the other way around as a commodity or utility theory of monetary value would suggest. As soon as this is understood, the economic, political and social consequences which ensue from the organization of monetary networks in practice can be examined without building those consequences into the conceptualization of monetary networks as one of their essential features. Money's symbolization of abstract relations of trust and its substantive role in the reproduction of asymmetries of wealth and power are not incongruous; they should not be conceptualized on the same analytical level. Trust in money's abstract properties is an essential feature of monetary networks, inherent to the ideational properties of money which are so important to its status as an object of desire. In fact, as I suggested in the second part of this book, trust tends to be sustained through an awkward combination of habitual expectation bolstered by a set of institutional arrangements which are often inefficient and sometimes downright unstable. But trust fundamentally depends on symbolic or ideational features of money which are not projected onto it as an independent entity but, as I argued above, are integral to its very nature as an economic instrument and foundational to the desire to possess it. Without these symbolic features no amount of institutional adjustment or normative support could ensure that money's existence is sustained, for the very idea of money which is so essential to its use would be terminally compromised.

It is the symbolic features of money which make it such a powerful facilitator of the reproduction of asymmetries of wealth and power. Money's inherent capacity to empower is the source of conflicts of interest over its distribution. This is bound to be so. Money's nature as a quantitative means for the comparison and distribution of qualitatively different goods and services, based on the role of the standardized accounting system in the constitution of monetary networks, ensures that money will not simply mediate but will crystallize inequalities in the distribution of wealth, income and property. The price mechanism is not only a means of access to goods but a basis of exclusion, preventing access precisely because prices help equilibrate the (real or contrived) scarcity of goods and services with a scarcity in the possession of money, in the possession of its capacity to empower. This is the one significant sociological conclusion which should be gleaned from the truism at the heart of the Quantity Theorem. In conditions of scarcity, irrespective of how these conditions come about, money serves to reproduce and indeed exacerbate real asymmetries in the distribution of wealth and power. Its capacity to do so rests not merely on the essential features of money in general but on the abstract properties of monetary networks which underpin those features. It is vital, however, to maintain the distinction between the principles of monetary analysis and substantive monetary theories when addressing this issue. How and why money contributes to the reproduction of asymmetries of wealth and power is a form of inquiry which must be dealt with in the substantive investigation of the operation of monetary networks in different societies and at different points in time. This fundamental requirement of monetary analysis should not be dispensed with just because politically incisive issues are at stake. My argument that the relationship between money and power is not a question of monetary analysis but an issue for substantive monetary theory is not informed by a denial of the significance of that relationship. It is on the contrary informed by the need for clarity as to exactly what is entailed in, what are the aims and objectives of, and what claims can be made in respect of such an investigation. The question of significance has no part in this demand for clarity. My argument here does not concern whether the relationship between money and power is important, but rather how that relationship can best be understood.

The substantive relationship between money and inequality is more than simply a question of the possession and non-possession of money itself. The institutional practices and organizational principles essential to the reproduction of monetary networks over time play an integral role in the perpetuation of inequality. There is no need to employ a crudely functionalist idea of geopolitical causality to understand the crucial part played by governments in the production and validation of money to the structural difficulties which now exist in the administration of Third World debt. As I argued in chapter 5, fundamental misconceptions of the status of governments as debtors were at the heart of the build-up of a network of intolerable obligations between Third World governments, First World banks and OPEC countries. But these were not just technical miscalculations derived from flawed financial practices. The decisions of creditors in this context have an inherent symbolic dimension based on the political as opposed to economic status of governments, not to mention a substantive component concerning the prudence and stability of particular governments. The role of these decisions in the development of offshore markets has been inexorably linked to the regulation and supervision of banking, to a set of practices bound up with the policies and ideologies of governments. Central banks are inherently political institutions because the administrative objective most of them pursue, monetary stability, is a politically consequential issue in its own right. The independence from government of one central bank as opposed to another does not negate this fact but gives it a different complexion. The institutionalization of monetary stability as an objective which must be pursued prior to or independent of the substantive policies of governments does not prise the objective away from the play of political pragmatism and ideological supposition. On the contrary, it politicizes the goal of monetary stability all the more intensely, turning it into an overwhelming priority, an ideology veiled as a purely technical question transcending all matters of mere politics.

But the objective of monetary stability is inherently political not just because it affects what governments are able to do. Its pursuit is bound up with the interrelationship between the regulatory and supervisory practices of central banks and the organization of monetary networks themselves. There is no single or neutral method of pursuing monetary stability where the organization of wealth and power is concerned. Alternative approaches to the methodology of monetary control have in common an inherent relationship with money's role in the reproduction of inequality. The choice between a policy focused on interest rates as opposed to direct credit controls is at the same time a choice about how the effects of such a policy will filter into society, about which sectors of the economy are affected, about when, and about how. It is irrelevant whether such issues play a major part in the deliberations of monetary administrators. The consequences of their decisions will be the same. But more than this, the administrative framework in which those deliberations take place, the regulatory and supervisory practices themselves, are implicitly consequential for politics. Banking practices are not derived from a neutral set of rules, not only because no such rules could ever exist but because their interpretation and implementation have an inherent sociological dimension. Relations between banking and financial institutions, and between those institutions and official monetary administrators, make up a network with its roots in the organization of class and power in society. Irrespective of whether this network is a self-perpetuating élite, its intersection with other major constellations of political and economic power in society has a critical role to play in the way money is administered and controlled. These relationships do not constitute the structure and organization of banking, but neither should they be added onto that structure as marginal or facilitating features. They are components of the structural principles by which monetary networks are organized in society, no less than the rules and regulations formally in place. They are not latched onto the implementation of technical procedures derived from abstract financial and monetary theories. They are integral to the forms of reasoning on which such theories are based. This is not only politically significant but underpins the reflexivity of substantive monetary theories in relation to monetary practices.

As I have argued throughout this book, decision-making processes underlying how money is handled in society have a vital fiduciary dimension in which information plays a substantive role. Information does not merely form the basis of economic decision-making but is integral to it as a form of reasoning. The principles of economic logic are part and parcel of the social and cultural framework on which money's existence and circulation in society depend. They are products of those very social, political and cultural conditions to which, in neoclassical economics, they tend to be juxtaposed. As I argued against Habermas in chapter 4, the principles of instrumental rationality on which the received efficiency and self-sufficiency of market systems depend do not stand opposed to what he calls the lifeworld as core features of economic life. On the contrary, they are generated through and within the processes of normative integration and communicative reasoning that he associates with a separate dimension of society. The passions may, as Hirschman suggests, have been subsumed by the interests in economic reasoning. But more importantly, they are constitutive features of the sociological conditions which made the process of subsumption conceivable in principle and feasible on retrospection. This is not to suggest that contemporary economic life is dominated by the passions rather than the interests, that economic decisions are in fact basically irrational as opposed to basically rational. It is to suggest that the conceptualization of economic activity, and of social action more generally, on which such distinctions depend is deeply flawed. I do not contend, either, that social and economic action contains elements of both rationality and irrationality, both passions and interests. This way of characterizing what people do and why does not work because the very idea of rationality, and alongside it the very idea of irrationality, cannot be sustained even on their own terms. These are not neutral, free-standing and prior descriptions of possible forms of action. They are, as descriptions, forms of action in themselves, integral to economic activity as a form of life. To suggest that economic action in general and the handling of money in particular are irreducible to rationality or irrationality but contain elements of both is to seek to criticize economic reasoning in a way whose meaning depends on that process of reasoning itself. The argument I have sought to develop in this book, on the contrary, is that economic reasoning has no meaning other than as part of the fiduciary character of economic life, that it offers no external criterion by which this form of life can be examined. It is rather part of its content, part of the frameworks of meaning and discursive practices chronically implicated in the reproduction of monetary networks over time. To seek to theorize about those frameworks and practices within the terms of economic logic is not merely to formulate a substantive argument about them. It is to commit a fundamental epistemological error. Economic reasoning excludes the epistemological principles necessary to conduct an analysis of its role in society, of the significance of such reasoning for the operation of money. Economic reasoning is in this sense the quintessence of theoretical rigidity. It should be the object, not the foundation, of the project to explain how money works, to understand its nature and account for its existence in society. The analytically rigorous approach to money I have argued for in this book stems not from the conviction that economic logic is inadequate or substantively flawed. It is informed by the requirement to understand more exactly what that logic is. I have not formulated a critique of the substance of that logic. I have not advanced an alternative logic of my own. I have sought to attack the epistemological claims on which its significance for the role of money in contemporary society fundamentally depends.

Notes

Introduction: On the Nature of Money

1 The second figure is an estimate, *The Financial Times*, 17 September 1992.
2 Ibid.
3 *The Financial Times*, 24 September 1992.
4 The somewhat less morbid title, Golden Wednesday, has been employed by those whose political convictions suggest that the withdrawal of sterling from the ERM was a matter for euphoria, not mourning. But this merely reinforces my point.
5 See Einzig, *Primitive Money*, pp. 29–37.
6 *Money and the Mechanism of Exchange*, pp. 32–40.
7 For both sides of this argument, see Melitz, who contends that 'there can be no harm in ascribing the label 'money' to a properly circumscribed class of goods', 'The Polanyi school', p. 1026; and Codere, who suggests that reference to physical properties only indicates whether certain objects can serve efficiently as money, 'Money-exchange systems', p. 559.
8 See Malinowski, *Argonauts*, p. 511; and Mauss, *The Gift*, pp. 93–4 n.25.
9 See Codere, 'Money-exchange systems', p. 60; and Humphrey, 'Barter and economic disintegration', p. 49.
10 *Primitive Money*, p. 15.
11 The list is sometimes expanded to include two further functions, means of payment and standard of deferred payment. The content of the functional definition varies throughout the monetary literature, but usually only in subtle ways. For examples of the application of this approach to different contexts, see Malinowski, *Argonauts*, p. 511; Einzig, *Primitive Money*, p. 323; Bohannan, 'The impact of money', p. 491; Dalton, 'Primitive money', p. 50; Mauss, *The Gift*, pp. 93–4 n. 25; Codere, 'Money-exchange systems', p. 558;

Melitz, 'The Polanyi school', pp. 1020–1; and Crump, *The Phenomenon of Money*, pp. 53–64.

12   See Christian, *Caroline Islands*; Price, *Japan's Island of Mystery*; and Borden, *South Sea Islands*.

13   As for example by Einzig, *Primitive Money*, p. 38, and Herskovits, *The Economic Life of Primitive Peoples*, pp. 215–16.

14   See his *Primitive, Archaic and Modern Economics*, p. 122; and more generally, 'The economy as an instituted process'. Polanyi's critique of contemporary economics derives from a historical account of the differentiation of the modern economy in *The Great Transformation*. For a summary of this, see Dalton, 'Primitive money' and 'Economic theory and primitive society'; and also Holton, *Economy and Society*, pp. 36–44.

15   See 'The semantics of money-uses'.

16   Melitz, 'The Polanyi school'.

17   The relationship is also dynamic. Failure to grasp the complexity of this has been one of the central problems in monetary theory throughout its history. This issue is discussed in more detail in chapter 1.

18   See Thurow, *Dangerous Currents*, p. 67, for a more sophisticated application of this line of reasoning.

19   *Oxford English Dictionary.*

20   This description suggests that the most appropriate bodily metaphor for money is not blood but semen. No doubt much could be made of this in psychoanalytic terms.

21   Cencini, *Money, Income and Time*, p. 74.

22   For discussion of the difficulties which arise from this approach, see Tobin, 'Liquidity preference', p. 166, and 'Financial intermediation', p. 185; Goodhart, *Money, Information and Uncertainty*, p. 2; Gowland, *Modern Economic Analysis*, p. 98; and Freeman, 'Banking as the provision of liquidity'.

23   See the Radcliffe Report, HMSO.

24   Goodhart, *Money, Information and Uncertainty*, p. 100 n.1; see also Gowland, *Controlling the Money Supply*, p. 5; and Thurow, *Dangerous Currents*, p. 67.

25   Tobin, 'Financial intermediation'.

26   Clarke, *Inside the City*, pp. 203–4; and Little, 'Higonnet', p. 54.

27   For discussion of the practical difficulties of monetarism in a contemporary context, see for example Dow and Saville, *A Critique of Monetary Policy*; Laidler, *Taking Money Seriously*; and Lawson, *The View From No. 11*, chs. 8, 33 and 36.

28   For a more detailed account of these changes and their implications for monetary policy, see Goodhart, 'Carli', p. 103.

29   The need to match requirements is often referred to as the 'double coincidence of wants'.

30   For an example of such an explanation in these terms, see Menger, 'On the origin of money'.

31   See *Economy and Society*, pp. 19–22.
32   For an explanation of this concept, see *The Social System*, pp. 169–70.

Chapter 1 The Political Economy of Money

1   For purposes of this discussion, 'classical economics' will refer to work
      instigated by and following on from Adam Smith, undertaken by Jean-
      Baptiste Say, David Ricardo and John Stuart Mill. (It is worth bearing in
      mind that Marx defines classical economics as beginning before Smith,
      meaning 'all the economists who, since the time of W. Petty, have
      investigated the real internal framework of bourgeois relations of
      production', see *Capital*, vol. I, pp. 174–5 n. 34.) 'Neoclassical economics'
      refers to an approach, stemming from the so-called 'marginal revolution'
      generated by the work of Stanley Jevons, Carl Menger and Léon Walras
      during the 1870s, which has developed into something of an orthodoxy
      within contemporary mainstream economics. There are a number of ways of
      distinguishing between classical and neoclassical economics. One is to define
      the neoclassical approach as more individualistic and subjective than
      classical economics, see Hausman, 'Economic methodology', p. 92. Another
      is to regard classical theory as the analysis of the dynamics of capital
      accumulation and economic growth, and neoclassical theory as the study of
      the statics of allocating given means in the face of competing given ends, see
      Blaug, *Economic Theory in Retrospect*, p. 295. Yet another is to regard
      neoclassical theory as virtually synonymous with the principles of economic
      logic, and classical economists as tending to concentrate on practical
      problems arising in the real domain of economic policy. This contrast
      between economic logic and the economics of the real world is drawn out by
      Blaug, for example, when comparing the invisible hand theorem of Smith
      with the general equilibrium framework of Walras; see his *The Methodology
      of Economics*, ch. 8.
2   To recall the discussion in the Introduction, the persistence of this problem in
      monetary analysis provides further cause for suspecting that the definition of
      money in terms of its functions is inadequate.
3   See Blaug, *Economic Theory in Retrospect*, pp. 22, 635–6.
4   Cited in Hirschman, *The Passions and the Interests*, p. 17.
5   Ibid., pp. 100–13.
6   For discussion of this point, see Holton, *Economy and Society*, ch. 4.
7   See, for example, Gray, 'Hayek, the Scottish school, and contemporary
      economics', pp. 62–5.
8   *The Wealth of Nations*, Book 1, ch. IV, p. 127.
9   'On the origin of money', p. 250; see also O'Driscoll, 'Money: Menger's
      evolutionary theory', p. 609.
10   While on the face of it Hayek's approach to money is identical to that of
      Menger, it should be noted that Hayek contends that maximization must be

learnt, culturally transmitted, for it is an imperative, necessitated by imperfections in the information available to economic actors, which runs contrary to basic human drives. These drives are first, 'to serve the visible ends of our known friends', and second, 'to join in a common effort for common ends', see 'The reactionary character of the socialist conception', p. 38. This warns against comparing classical and neoclassical approaches in terms of a broader debate over human nature.

11 Marx, for example, notes that money does not necessarily evolve indigenously out of barter exchange, but can emerge as peripheral to a community, *A Contribution to the Critique of Political Economy*, p. 50. See also on this point, Weber, *Economy and Society*, pp. 191–2, and Hasebroek, *Trade and Politics in Ancient Greece*, pp. 70–1.

12 On the primacy of money's exchange function, see Jevons, *Money and the Mechanism of Exchange*, p. 2, and Crump, *The Phenomenon of Money*, pp. 53–8. On the primacy of the unit of account function, see Menger, 'On the origin of money', p. 250; Keynes, *A Treatise on Money*, p. 12; and Cassel, *The Theory of Social Economy*, p. 47. On the primacy of the store of value function, see Rist, *History of Monetary and Credit Theory*, pp. 66, 325.

13 *Primitive Money*, pp. 334–7; see also Humphrey, 'Barter and economic disintegration', pp. 50, 68 n. 4.

14 Schumpeter's distinction between historical and logical origins has some validity in this context, *History of Economic Analysis*, p. 64.

15 *The Wealth of Nations*, Book 1, ch. II, p. 117.

16 Cited in Blaug, *Economic Theory in Retrospect*, p. 56.

17 Specie refers to money consisting of actual pieces of metal, and is in this context virtually synonymous with bullion.

18 *The Wealth of Nations*, Book 2, ch. II, p. 391.

19 See, in particular, *Essays on Some Unsettled Questions of Political Economy*, Essay Two.

20 See his *Treatise on Political Economy*.

21 Blaug, *Economic Theory in Retrospect*, p. 43.

22 *Elements of Pure Economics*, p. 224.

23 Ibid., p. 225.

24 See Jaffé's notes in ibid., pp. 600–2.

25 Ibid., p. 330, Walras's emphasis.

26 See Blaug, *Economic Theory in Retrospect*, pp. 633–5.

27 *The Wealth of Nations*, Book 2, ch. III, p. 437.

28 Ibid., Book 2, ch. III, pp. 437–8.

29 Ibid., Book 2, ch. III, p. 438.

30 This idea is implicit both in Smith's contention that money saved 'is immediately employed as a capital', and in his assertion that money's worth, whether in the form of specie or paper, is properly understood only with reference to 'what can be purchased with it', rather than to any intrinsic value embodied by the monetary form itself. See ibid., Book 2, ch. III, p. 438, and ch. II, p. 386, respectively.

31   Ibid., Book 2, ch. III, p. 441.
32   Blaug, *Economic Theory in Retrospect*, p. 633.
33   Ibid., p. 634, Blaug's emphases.
34   This, in simplistic terms, is the 'direct mechanism' of transmission from *M* to *P* initially formulated by Cantillon and Hume; see Blaug, ibid., p. 633.
35   Although, as I shall argue in chapter 3 when discussing Simmel's work on money, a definition of money which holds that money has no consequences for the organization of power in society is conceivable in principle, this has nothing whatsoever to do with economic logic in the sense examined here.
36   *A Contribution to the Critique of Political Economy*, pp. 87–107; *Grundrisse*, pp. 203–18; and *Capital*, vol. I, pp. 247–57.
37   Elster, *Making Sense of Marx*, pp. 10–15.
38   *Grundrisse*, pp. 117–238; see also Jameson, *Postmodernism*, p. 260.
39   *The Wealth of Nations*, Book 1, ch. V, p. 133, and Book 1, ch. VI, p. 155. See also Schumpeter, *History of Economic Analysis*, p. 188 n. 20; Roll, *A History of Economic Thought*, p. 187; and Blaug, *Economic Theory in Retrospect*, p. 52.
40   As Blaug concludes, for example, *Economic Theory in Retrospect*, p. 39.
41   *Capital*, vol. I, p. 128.
42   *Making Sense of Marx*, pp. 139–40.
43   Ibid., pp. 140–1.
44   *Capital*, vol. I, p. 185.
45   *Grundrisse*, p. 165.
46   Cohen, *Karl Marx's Theory of History*, p. 348.
47   *Grundrisse*, p. 166.
48   *The Wealth of Nations*, Book 2, ch. II, p. 397.
49   *Essai sur la nature du commerce en général*.
50   *The Wealth of Nations*, Book 2, ch. III, p. 435.
51   Credit can be created, for example, through a positive Public Sector Borrowing Requirement, through the repurchase of debts by the public sector from the non-bank private sector, and through non-bank private sector borrowing from banks. In addition, the transmission of money across geopolitical boundaries has an important role to play in the quantity of money circulating within those boundaries; see Gowland, *Controlling the Money Supply*, pp. 22–5.
52   Principles derived from the Quantity Theorem are implicit for example in neoclassical arguments over central and free banking, particularly in the work of Hayek and White. These arguments are more closely connected to discussion of the legal status of money, which I examine in chapter 2.
53   Hence Cohen's definition of Marx's view of capital as 'exchange-value exchanged with a view to increasing the amount of exchange-value possessed by its owner', *Karl Marx's Theory of History*, p. 351.
54   *Capital*, vol. II, p. 49.
55   See Mandel's introduction to *Capital*, vol. I, p. 77 n. 81.
56   *Capital*, vol. I, p. 236 n. 50.

57 See *Capital*, vol. III, p. 338.
58 Ibid., pp. 321–2.
59 Ibid., p. 280.
60 See Elster, *Making Sense of Marx*, pp. 127–41.
61 Cohen, *Karl Marx's Theory of History*, p. 353.
62 *Capital*, vol. I, p. 179.

Chapter 2   Money and the State

1   It is not entirely clear, regarding particular cases, which institution possesses this monopoly. Constitutionally, as I discuss later with regard to central banking, monopoly may rest with the government or another state agency such as the central bank, or both. In practice, the regulation and supervision of money and banking tends to fall to a not always comfortable or consistent alliance of individuals and institutions.
2   *The Nation-State and Violence*, p. 17; see also *The Constitution of Society*, pp. 163–4.
3   Pelczynski, *Hegel's Political Philosophy*, p. 4; Avineri, *Hegel's Theory of the Modern State*, pp. 40–1; Habermas, *Legitimation Crisis*; Poggi, *The Development of the Modern State*; Perez-Diaz, *State, Bureaucracy and Civil Society*, p. 92; Giddens, *The Nation-State and Violence*, p. 17; Jordan, *The State*, p. 1; Smith, 'State-making and nation-building', p. 235; and Hall, *States in History*, pp. 232–3.
4   Weber, *Economy and Society*, p. 56, and Mann, 'The autonomous power of the state', p. 112.
5   The monopoly of violence was seldom, if ever, fully characteristic of traditional states, but is critical to the extent of the infrastructural penetration of the nation-state. The latter development is closely related to the institution of money.
6   Knapp argues, for example, that the numismatist 'knows nothing of currency, for he has only to deal with its dead body', *The State Theory of Money*, p. 1.
7   Numéraire: The function of money as a measure of value or unit of account; a standard for currency exchange rates, *Oxford English Dictionary*.
8   On this point, see also Keynes, *A Treatise on Money*, p. 5.
9   *The State Theory of Money*, p. 2.
10 Ibid., p. 45.
11 *The Legal Aspect of Money*, p. 28.
12 *The State Theory of Money*, p. 2.
13 *Economy and Society*, pp. 166–7.
14 Ibid., p. 169.
15 See Ingham, *Capitalism Divided?*, p. 257 n. 30.
16 *The State Theory of Money*, p. 148.
17 This is the line taken by von Mises, *The Theory of Money and Credit*, p. 73.

18 *Economy and Society*, pp. 164–5, 199–200.

19 Ibid., p. 199.

20 Ibid., pp. 161–2.

21 *The Nation-State and Violence*, pp. 172–97.

22 'The autonomous power of the state', pp. 128–9.

23 The other three logistical techniques posited by Mann are the division of labour, literacy, and communications and transport; each of these are, of course, of key significance in relation to the institution of a monetary system; ibid., p. 116.

24 *States and Social Revolutions*, p. 29.

25 The fact that the inner court of the absolutist state comprised not the higher household but 'favoured nobles and attendants', argues Giddens, 'helped make possible the creation of bureaucratic administration in principle, and in some part in practice, directly responsible to the ruler'. For example, Ministers under Louis XIV were mostly drawn from nobility, reporting to local government councils 'occupied by salaried, vocational officials', *The Nation-State and Violence*, p. 95. The link between such councils and the sovereign is characterized by Hintze as 'a concomitant of that process of political organization in which a conglomerate of separate territories becomes fused into a unitary political structure', 'The formation of states', p. 173.

26 Poggi, *The Development of the Modern State*, p. 73; Giddens, *The Nation-State and Violence*, pp. 98–101.

27 Skocpol, *States and Social Revolutions*, p. 53; Giddens, *The Nation-State and Violence*, p. 96.

28 Mann, *The Sources of Social Power*, vol. I, p. 479.

29 Weber, *Economy and Society*, p. 967; Giddens, *The Nation-State and Violence*, pp. 102–3; Kennedy, *The Rise and Fall of the Great Powers*, pp. 101–3.

30 However, Mann rejects the notion that absolutist states were straightforwardly weaker than nation-states. For Mann, there are 'two principal meanings of a strong regime: power over civil society, that is, *despotism*; and the power to coordinate civil society, that is, *infrastructural* strength'. Where money is concerned, infrastructural strength is primary, *The Sources of Social Power*, vol. I, p. 477, Mann's emphases; see 'The autonomous power of the state', p. 113.

31 Wallerstein, *The Modern World System*, vol. I, pp. 137–8; Weber, *Economy and Society*, p. 968.

32 Giddens, *The Nation-State and Violence*, pp. 89–90.

33 Hintze, 'The formation of states', p. 161.

34 Hintze, ibid., p. 161; Wallerstein, *The Modern World System*, vol. I, p. 147; Giddens, *The Nation-State and Violence*, p. 90.

35 The relationship between the military capacity of a state and its monetary system was not of course unique to or without precedent under absolutism. For example, the monetary system under the Roman empire came to be

centralized largely because money itself fulfilled such a vital logistical role in the manoeuvres of the Roman legions; see Mann, *The Sources of Social Power*, vol. I, p. 274, and Hopkins, *Conquerors and Slaves*, p. 94. Where absolutism is concerned, however, several important differences exist from the Roman case. For the absolutist states, military movements were oriented less to the extension of borders than to their consolidation. Moreover, whereas the Roman legions combined military and monetary expansion, under the absolutist system military activity outwards helped shape the internal administration of the monetary system; see Kennedy, *The Rise and Fall of the Great Powers*, pp. 90–1.

36 Giddens, *The Nation-State and Violence*, p. 112; Skocpol, *States and Social Revolutions*, p. 285.

37 Giddens, *The Nation-State and Violence*, p. 192.

38 Hont, 'Free trade', p. 42.

39 Mann, *The Sources of Social Power*, vol. I, p. 512.

40 See Hont, 'Free trade', p. 43.

41 Pocock, 'The political limits', pp. 132–8.

42 Hont, 'Free trade', pp. 43–4.

43 'The political limits', pp. 138–9.

44 *The Sources of Social Power*, vol. I, pp. 483–90; see also Kindleberger, *A Financial History of Western Europe*, p. 165.

45 *The Sources of Social Power*, vol. I, p. 512.

46 *The Nation-State and Violence*, p. 115; see also Kennedy, *The Rise and Fall of the Great Powers*, pp. 89–111. Uncertainty fostered by the identity of state creditors was exacerbated, according to Hont, by prevailing suspicions as to the 'soundness' of credit itself as a basis for public accounting, 'Free trade', pp. 49–50.

47 Wallerstein, *The Modern World-System*, vol. I, pp. 159–61.

48 Kennedy, *The Rise and Fall of the Great Powers*, ch. 3; Kindleberger, *A Financial History of Western Europe*, ch. 9.

49 *The Sources of Social Power*, vol. I, p. 516.

50 Ibid., p. 515.

51 'Kinds of rationalism', p. 97; 'Coping with ignorance', p. 19.

52 *Denationalisation of Money*, pp. 117–21.

53 Ibid., pp. 119–20.

54 Ibid., pp. 23, 37.

55 *Free Banking in Britain*, p. 36. Kindleberger, however, has questioned White's characterization of the Scottish banking system between 1775 and 1845 as free, *International Capital Movements*, pp. 71–2.

56 *Free Banking in Britain*, pp. 20–1.

57 Ibid., p. 17.

58 Ibid., p. 17.

59 Ibid., p. 18.

60 Hayek, however, seems defiantly sceptical as to the likely immediate political influence of his proposals, see *Denationalisation of Money*, p. 17. Wood adds,

in the Introduction to the Third Edition, that Hayek's arguments have had 'little apparent practical impact', p. 19. Some solace seems to have been gained, on Wood's part at least, from the espousal of an evolutionary, open and competition-based currency system based around independent central banks within the EC by Chancellor Lawson's Treasury team in 1989: 'A few years ago the notion that a British Chancellor of the Exchequer would propose freeing the Bank of England from the authority of the Treasury would have seemed totally unbelievable', pp. 19–20. Given that the Lawson proposals entail maintaining the role of central banks as issuers, albeit independently of government, rather than instituting a system of private issuers, the parallel with Hayek's programme is hardly exact. See Lawson, *The View From No. 11*, ch. 69, on his proposals for an independent Bank of England.

Chapter 3   Cultural Aspects of the Mature Money Economy

1   Simmel repeatedly states in *The Philosophy of Money* that his work is not about money as such, but that money expresses facets of contemporary social and cultural life which he takes to be essential: money has no intrinsic content to be analysed, but expresses the content of everything else. Simmel's treatment of money as an object of analysis exactly mirrors his characterization of money as a pure instrument of exchange. In the concluding paragraphs of his study, Simmel characterizes the paradoxical character of money as a pure instrument of exchange: money 'is nothing but the vehicle for a movement in which everything else that is not in motion is completely extinguished', *The Philosophy of Money*, p. 511. In the Preface to his study, likewise, Simmel clarifies his philosophical treatment of money, drawing on precisely those characteristics which define its role as a tool of exchange: 'money is simply a means, a material or an example for the presentation of relations that exist between the most superficial, 'realistic' and fortuitous phenomena and the most idealized powers of existence, the most profound currents of individual life and history', *The Philosophy of Money*, p. 55.

2   Ibid., p. 121.

3   Ibid., p. 511.

4   Ibid., p. 121.

5   Ibid., p. 236.

6   Ibid., p. 238; see also Frisby, *Sociological Impressionism*, p. 108.

7   Levine 'Simmel and Parsons reconsidered', pp. 190–3; see also his Introduction to Simmel, *On Individuality and Social Forms*, p. lviii n. 104.

8   *The Philosophy of Money*, p. 60.

9   Ibid., p. 67.

10   Ibid., p. 65.

11 Ibid., p. 6.
12 'Review article', p. 137.
13 See Frisby, *Simmel and Since*, pt. II, ch. 5. In his discussion of 'economic aspects' of *The Philosophy of Money*, Frisby highlights three points of departure in Simmel's work from the marginal utility theorem: relating to the law of indifference, the state of equilibrium, and differential coefficients. Frisby adds that Simmel's characterization of exchange as a 'sociological phenomenon *sui generis*', rather than as an economic phenomenon, further distances his work from the neoclassical economists. But other than to take the meaning of 'economic' in its narrow disciplinary sense, Frisby does not make clear what he (or Simmel) might mean in this sense. Simmel's own assertion, that '[n]ot a single line of these investigations is meant to be a statement about economics' (*The Philosophy of Money*, p. 54), begs rather than answers this question. If it is simply meant that Simmel treats exchange as a broader phenomenon than the neoclassical economists do, that is, as synonymous with interaction rather than as confined to actions involving money or goods, the contrast seems obvious and uninsightful. It is doubtful whether neoclassical economists, or indeed any economist at all, would deny that various kinds of behaviour involve exchange of some kind; they merely choose not to study them or arrive at unsatisfactory conclusions when they do, largely because of the assumptions underlying their understanding of human behaviour. I would suggest that it is with regard to these assumptions that the more interesting questions regarding Simmel's departure from neoclassical economics are raised. Such questions require investigation into the substance of Simmel's arguments, not protracted inquiry into his various disciplinary associations.
14 *The Philosophy of Money*, p. 66.
15 Ibid., p. 68.
16 'Introduction' to Simmel, *Individuality and Social Forms*, p. xv; see also Weingartner, *Experience and Culture*, p. 47.
17 *The Philosophy of Money*, p. 78.
18 Frisby, *Simmel and Since*, pp. 90–1.
19 *The Philosophy of Money*, p. 174.
20 *Georg Simmel*, p. 11.
21 *The Philosophy of Money*, p. 79.
22 Although Simmel does not refer explicitly to a price mechanism, it seems reasonable to assume that this is precisely what he means when he states that the relationship between values 'exists as something objectively appropriate and law-determined', adding that '[t]he phenomenon of a completely developed economy, at least, would appear in this light', ibid., p. 79. In any case, having characterized value as the epigone of price, Simmel is perfectly explicit in his assertion that 'the statement that they [value and price] must be identical is a tautology', ibid., p. 94.
23 Ibid., p. 79.
24 *Soziologie*, p. 41; translation cited in Coser, *Georg Simmel*, p. 11.

25 Simmel draws the distinction between human purpose and instinctual drives common to other beings in terms of the contrast between, respectively, actions defined by their consequences and those defined by their causes; see *The Philosophy of Money*, p. 204.

26 Ibid., p. 211.

27 Ibid., p. 177.

28 See Bottomore and Frisby's Introduction to *The Philosophy of Money*, p. 28.

29 Frisby, *Fragments of Modernity*, p. 55.

30 Translation cited in ibid., pp. 55–6.

31 Although this is not a straightforwardly linear development, see Frisby, ibid., p. 42.

32 *The Philosophy of Money*, p. 345.

33 Ibid., p. 457, Simmel's emphasis.

34 Ibid., pp. 309–10.

35 The importance and analytical difficulty of money's character as a pure instrument in this respect is reinforced by Simmel's contention that money may reinforce coercion to no less an extent that its possession gives to its holder the capacity to resist coercion, ibid., p. 398.

36 Ibid., p. 402, Simmel's emphases.

37 Ibid., pp. 402–3.

38 Ibid., p. 401.

39 Ibid., p. 325.

40 Ibid., p. 328.

41 Ibid., pp. 228–57.

42 Ibid., p. 403.

43 Ibid., p. 403.

44 Ibid., p. 403.

45 Ibid., pp. 403–4.

46 Ibid., p. 469.

47 This resembles the 'internal' component of Habermas's internal colonization thesis, where agents' capacity for self-expression is distorted by means of a narrow, lop-sided perception of their interests generated by the colonization of the lifeworld by repellant principles of system integration. I discuss this in more detail in chapter 4.

48 *The Philosophy of Money*, p. 484.

49 Ibid., p. 298, Simmel's emphasis.

50 Ibid., p. 298.

51 Ibid., p. 454.

52 Ibid., p. 455, Simmel's emphasis.

53 Perhaps it is with this in mind that Durkheim dismisses Simmel's study as *spéculation bâtard*; see his 'Review', pp. 326–8.

54 *The Philosophy of Money*, p. 84.

55 See Frisby, *Sociological Impressionism*, p. 127.

56 This reflects the emphasis Simmel places on interaction as the core of social life, arguing for example that, when two subjects interact, 'only when the

other is absolutely indifferent and a mere means for purposes which lie beyond him is the last shadow of any sociating process removed', *The Philosophy of Money*, p. 97.

57 *Simmel and Since*, p. 97, Frisby's emphasis.

58 Frisby does not, however, go as far as to suggest that Simmel's approach is subjectivist in the sense associated with neoclassical economics. He argues, on the contrary, that Simmel's conception 'of society as a constellation of interactions, as dynamic, individual and supra-individual...contradicts the subjectivist presuppositions of marginalism', even to the extent that, in Frisby's view at least, Simmel ultimately undermines the economic suppositions with which his own theory of value sets out, *Simmel and Since*, p. 97. Frisby seems to have changed his position on this question, having earlier argued that Simmel's preoccupation with the 'world of appearance', stemming from his prioritization of exchange, is a major weakness of Simmel's work in comparison with Marx; see *Fragments of Modernity*, p. 107.

59 *The Philosophy of Money*, p. 54.

60 Ibid., p. 54.

61 Ibid., p. 54.

62 Ibid., p. 87.

63 It is perhaps most accurate to say that Simmel's work is of rather than about his own contemporary world: he expresses diffuse aspects of modernity in his writing, but he advances no systematic theory of the emergence and development of modern society. As Frisby notes, even to write of a 'mature money economy' is hardly to base one's work on a definite historical constellation, *Fragments of Modernity*, p. 41.

64 Accidental: non-essential to the existence of a thing, not necessarily present, incidental, subsidiary. *Oxford English Dictionary*.

65 Lea, Tarpy and Webley, *The Individual in the Economy*, p. 328; see also Melitz, 'The Polanyi school'.

Chapter 4 Money and the Social System

1 *Social Systems and the Evolution of Action Theory*, pp. 206–7.

2 Ibid., pp. 198–9.

3 *Sociological Theory and Modern Society* p. 357.

4 Cybernetics: The theory or study of communication and control in living organisms or machines. *Oxford English Dictionary*.

5 *Sociological Theory and Modern Society*, p. 208.

6 Ibid., p. 229.

7 For detailed discussion of Parsons's characterization of money as a symbolic medium, see Alexander, *Theoretical Logic in Sociology*, vol. IV. For a more critical but less thorough account, see Ganßmann, 'Money - a symbolically generalized medium of communication?', pp. 285–316.

8   'The use of knowledge in society', p. 88.

9   See *The Structure of Social Action*, vol. I, pp. 698–702.

10   *Economy and Society*, p. 306.

11   Ibid., p. 71, their emphases.

12   This is not self-evident. While it is clear that Parsons places money first among the media of interchange in historical terms, it is a matter of interpretation whether such primacy holds schematically. If it does, the sub-systems do not have equal status at all; see *Sociological Theory and Modern Society*, p. 115. For a critical discussion of this point, see Habermas, *The Theory of Communicative Action*, vol. II, pp. 258–9.

13   *Theoretical Logic in Sociology*, vol. IV, p. 134.

14   See also Ganßmann, 'Money - a symbolically generalized means of communication?'.

15   'Social structure', p. 101.

16   For a critical discussion of this point, see Alexander, *Theoretical Logic in Sociology*, vol. IV, p. 257.

17   The lecture is included in *Knowledge and Human Interests*, pp. 301–17.

18   Ibid., pp. 351–86.

19   Ibid., p. 317.

20   Ibid., p. 380.

21   *Communication and the Evolution of Society*, pp. 1–68.

22   *The Theory of Communicative Action*, Vol. II, p. 276.

23   Ibid., pp. 259–60.

24   In other words, entirely substitutable with language.

25   *The Theory of Communicative Action*, vol. II, p. 262.

26   See ibid., pp. 268–70.

27   Ibid., p. 268.

28   Holton has argued that the utilization of money, for example between household and firm via consumption (**Lg** to **Ag**), is not actually mediated by **I**, the social integration sub-system. This suggests, in his view, that consumption goals are less stable than their characterization solely in terms of value consensus would allow: '[i]f value-choices expressed in consumption cannot be reduced to individual atomistic preferences, it is equally misleading however to regard them as the outcome of some stifling value-consensus'. But this interpretation is difficult to sustain if Parsons's thesis that the sub-systems act as environments for one another is taken seriously. Holton himself concedes this implicitly, noting that '[n]either 'status' nor 'prestige' can be expressed in consumption without some shared basis by which evaluation may take place'. It might well be the case that any such link between money and value commitment is indicative of a generalized commitment to consumer freedom as a value in itself. This would mean that value-consensus is generated only by 'the emergence of generalized enabling mechanisms permitting maximum variation in individual action', thereby linking '[v]alue-commitment to consumer sovereignty ... as a key component of modernity'. But even this, if Habermas's thesis is accepted,

must be open to empirical question. See Holton, 'Talcott Parsons and the theory of economy and society', p. 57.

29   *The Theory of Communicative Action*, vol. II, p. 267.
30   *Sociological Theory and Modern Society*, p. 508.
31   Ibid., pp. 508–9.
32   *The Theory of Communicative Action*, vol. II, p. 287.
33   Ibid., p. 287.
34   The distinction between the system and lifeworld is in the first instance methodological, designed to grasp in systematic form parallel processes of societal development which Habermas characterizes initially in terms of the distinction between labour and interaction, and later in terms of the distinction between strategic action and communicative action. He does not, however, leave the concepts of system and lifeworld in this abstract form, but confuses the issue by identifying specific institutions with each domain. The system, for example, integrates different actions and processes so as to ensure economic and political survival, and includes the economic system - such as industry, financial corporations, and wage-labourers - and the administrative system, i.e. state institutions, regulating the unintended consequences of strategic action through market or bureaucratic mechanisms.
35   In writing of a logic of development rather than of actual evolutionary trends, Habermas seeks to avoid the teleological trap which hampers conventional evolutionary theories, namely, the implication that a society or species is bound to evolve towards a particular end-state. A logic of development depicts an order of stages which should take shape as societies move through history, given existing modes of organization and structures of communication. A dynamic of development concerns what actually takes place, variations on or departures from the logical model depending on empirical conditions.
36   For example, in the form of political and organizational stratification.
37   *The Theory of Communicative Action*, vol. II, p. 271.
38   Ibid., p. 272.
39   Ibid., p. 270.
40   Ingram, *Habermas and the Dialectic of Reason*, p. 129.
41   With regard to the basis of the transaction, not its outcome.
42   *The Theory of Communicative Action*, vol. II, p. 263.
43   Ibid., p. 272.
44   Ibid., p. 272.
45   *Habermas and the Dialectic of Reason*, p. 145.
46   Ibid., p. 145.
47   Ibid., p. 145.
48   Ibid., p. 145.
49   *The Theory of Communicative Action*, vol. II, p. 320.
50   Ibid., p. 321.
51   Ibid., p. 362.

52 Ibid., p. 367.
53 Ibid., p. 343.
54 Compare this with ibid., p. 337.
55 Ibid., p. 374, Habermas's emphases.
56 See Honneth et. al., 'The dialectics of rationalization', p. 22.
57 *The Theory of Communicative Action*, vol. II, p. 155.
58 Ibid., p. 264.
59 Ibid., p. 125.
60 Ibid., p. 262.
61 'Critical hermeneutics versus neoparsonianism?', p. 71, Misgeld's emphasis.
62 Ibid., p. 72.
63 Ibid., p. 72, Misgeld's emphasis. However, the term 'ordinary' - used repeatedly in Misgeld's argument - suggests that he (Misgeld) does not penetrate deeply enough into all forms of monetary transaction. The expression implies that, while money is subject to lifeworld perceptions when utilized in everyday circumstances, this may not be the case where transactors possess specialist or professional knowledge regarding how the economy works. Indeed, it is unclear whether Misgeld himself regards the economy as self-contained, for he merely notes that 'from the perspective of the lifeworld ... the economy will only appear as a self-contained sphere of activity *under certain circumstances*', ibid., p. 73, Misgeld's emphasis.
64 Ibid., p. 74, Misgeld's emphasis.
65 Parsons writes of the freedom given over to the holder of money by virtue of its possession in strictly functional terms, specifying its four aspects as (i) the freedom to purchase any item; (ii) the freedom to shop around; (iii) the freedom to do so in one's own time; and (iv) the freedom to weigh up the terms of the transaction; see *Sociological Theory and Modern Society*, p. 307. Habermas simply reiterates these points, adding none of his own, see *The Theory of Communicative Action*, vol. II, pp. 264, 427 n. 56.

Chapter 5   The Politics of International Monetary Integration

1   Central banks commonly fulfil seven core functions: issuing money, usually a limited, targeted issue of notes and coin, allowing for seasonal fluctuations in the demand for cash; the control of credit creation, which involves regulating liquidity in the economy, typically through open market operations; providing banking services to the government, for example settling government debts to the private sector, issuing and redeeming Treasury bills, and issuing government stock as registrar of the national debt; providing banking services to other banks, for example holding cash balances of specified banks in respect of clearing-house operations and the statutory obligation of primary banks to hold reserve deposits with the central bank as a proportion of their liabilities; acting as an external agent to

the government, for example by holding and administering bullion and foreign currency reserves and liaising with other central banks and international financial institutions; acting as the lender-of-last-resort to the banking system, which involves lending indirectly to banks through discount houses (overnight balances) or directly with liquid reserves, perhaps responding to a run on deposits; and acting as overall supervisor to the banking system, principally by providing informal guidance which usually reinforces government directives. For more detailed discussion of these points, see Hanson, *Monetary Theory and Practice*, pp. 153–9, and Struthers and Speight, *Money: Institutions, Theory and Policy*, pp. 18-19.

2   Throughout the discussion which follows, particular reference will be made to current arrangements and recent developments in Japan, Germany and Britain.

3   This contention is often reflected in accounts of central banking practices, but rarely discussed at length. In a brief account of the constitutional independence of central banks, for example, Macesich argues that '[i]n the United States and Germany, central bank control rests with a board composed of the heads of the several regional banks, thereby allowing for greater 'independence' from the central government', *Monetary Policy and Rational Expectations*, p. 10. The very fact that Macesich places the concept of independence in quotation marks suggests that this formal constitutional position is in some sense variable, perhaps even negotiable according to circumstances. Yet he fails to elaborate, although to do so would seem to be essential to his distinction between rule-governed and discretionary monetary policy systems; see ibid., pp. 48–55.

4   For studies of the German banking and financial systems, I have drawn principally on Schneider, Hellwig and Kingsman, *The German Banking System*; Coulbeck, *The Multinational Banking Industry*; Francke and Hudson, *Banking and Finance in West Germany*; Spindler, *The Politics of International Credit*; Kennedy, *The Bundesbank*; and Holtfrerich, 'Relations between monetary authorities and government institutions'.

5   In section 3 of the Federal Bank Act of 1957 (as amended), the function of the Bundesbank is defined as regulating 'the circulation of money and the supply of credit to the economy with the aim of safeguarding the currency' and providing 'for normal banking clearance of payment transactions within the Federal Republic of Germany and with foreign countries'. This is confirmed in section 12 of the Bundesbank Law. However, there it is also stated that 'while maintaining its functions, it [the Bundesbank] has the duty of supporting the general economic policy of the Federal Government'. See Kennedy, *The Bundesbank*, pp. 31–2.

6   See Holtfrerich, 'Relations between monetary authorities and governmental institutions', pp. 145–8.

7   See Hutton, 'Inside the ERM crisis'.

8   See Kennedy, *The Bundesbank*, chs 4 and 5.

9   This view is supported by a Bundesbank report on the history of the Deutschmark, where it is noted that '[a]fter the unhappy experience - twice in a lifetime - of a central bank bound by instructions from a government, the principles of central bank autonomy and the primacy of monetary stability were hardly in dispute' during the period of the foundation of the Bundesbank, *Monthly Report of the Deutsche Bundesbank*, May 1988, p. 15.

10 For studies of the banking and financial systems in Britain, I have drawn especially on Hanson, *Monetary Theory and Practice*; Coulbeck, *The Multinational Banking Industry*; Ingham, *Capitalism Divided?*; Clarke, *Regulating the City*; Struthers and Speight, *Money: Institutions, Theory and Policy*; Hall, *Financial Deregulation* and *The City Revolution*; Lomax, *London Markets after the Financial Services Act*; Cairncross 'The Bank of England's relationships with the government'; and Reid, *All-Change in the City*.

11 See, for example, *Bank of England Quarterly Bulletin*, vol. 26, no. 2, May 1986, p. 226.

12 The Bank of England's supervisory role may be traced to the 1844–5 Bank Charter (or Peel's) Acts, see Gilbart, *Currency and Banking*; Peel, *Speeches on the Renewal of the Bank Charter*; Tooke, *An Inquiry into the Currency Principle* and *On the Bank Charter Act*; Fullarton, *On the Regulation of Currencies*; Mill, 'On the currency question'; Torrens, *The Principles and Practical Operations of Sir Robert Peel's Act of 1844, Explained and Defended*; Read, *Peel and the Victorians*; Hilton, 'Peel: a reappraisal'; and Ingham, *Capitalism Divided?*, pp. 236–8. The Acts tied the Bank of England's fiduciary policy to gold, chiefly as a means for curtailing its power, but unwittingly provided the Bank of England itself with greater autonomy; see Adie, 'English bank deposits before 1844', p. 286, and Sayers, *The Bank of England 1891–1944*, pp. 1–2.

13 Clarke, *Regulating the City*, pp. 16-18.

14 See Ingham, *Capitalism Divided?*

15 Reid, *All-Change in the City*, p. 210.

16 For more detailed discussion of this point, see Cairncross, 'The Bank of England's relationships with the government', pp. 48–53.

17 See Gilpin, *The Political Economy of International Relations*, p. 378.

18 For studies of the Japanese financial and banking systems, I have drawn particularly on Ishi, 'Financial institutions and markets in Japan'; Emery, *The Japanese Money Market*; Coulbeck, *The Multinational Banking Industry*; Viner, *Inside Japan's Financial Markets*; papers by Murakami, Hamada and Horiuchi, Muramatsu and Krauss, and Kosai from the collection edited by Yamamura and Yasuba, *The Political Economy of Japan*, vol. I; and further papers by Inoguchi, Hamada and Patrick, Shinkai, and Pyle from the collection edited by Inoguchi and Okimoto, *The Political Economy of Japan*, vol. II.

184 NOTES TO PAGES 90–96

19 The Bank of Japan is Japan's sole issuing authority. Its open market operations are carried out by six *Tanshi* companies (the *Tanshi Kyokai*) which act mostly as brokers. They are supervised by the Ministry of Finance. Issue levels are generally fixed by the Ministry. The Ministry drafts, while the Bank implements, legislation. Both institutions determine interest rates. Their relationship is not consistently harmonious, however.

20 Spindler, *The Politics of International Credit*, p. 106.

21 Viner, *Inside Japan's Financial Markets*, p. 145.

22 Muramatsu and Krauss, 'The conservative policy line', pp. 521–2.

23 See Muramatsu and Krauss, 'The conservative policy line', p. 537.

24 'The Japanese model of political economy', p. 70.

25 See Shinkai, 'The internationalization of finance in Japan', p. 253.

26 Spindler, *The Politics of International Credit*, p. 112.

27 This implies that deregulation, itself an upshot of increasing international integration, entails homogenization between financial centres, eradicating political and cultural differences. Such an interpretation is problematic: as I shall later contend, homogenization amounts to greater identity between financial systems, which is not necessarily the same as increasing integration.

28 *Bank of England Quarterly Bulletin*, vol. 27, no. 1, March 1987, p. 241.

29 *Bank of England Quarterly Bulletin*, vol. 29, no. 2, May 1989, p. 255.

30 See Shinkhai, 'The internationalization of finance in Japan', p. 253; Viner, *Inside Japan's Financial Markets*, p. 189; and Ishi, 'Financial institutions and markets in Japan', pp. 120–1.

31 Emery, *The Japanese Money Market*, p. 99.

32 From 7 per cent of GNP in 1974 to around 35 per cent by 1982; the subsequent growth of the secondary market in bonds was from 5 per cent of total volume in 1977 to 62.3 per cent in 1982; see Hamada and Horiuchi, 'The political economy of the financial market', pp. 247–9.

33 See Muramatsu and Krauss, 'The conservative policy line', p. 538.

34 Spindler, *The Politics of International Credit*, p. 32.

35 *Financial Deregulation*, p. xi.

36 *Bank of England Quarterly Bulletin*, vol. 29, no. 4, November 1989, pp. 516–28.

37 *Bank of England Quarterly Bulletin*, vol. 26, no. 2, May 1986, pp. 225–9.

38 Ingham, *Capitalism Divided?*

39 Gilpin, *The Political Economy of International Relations*, p. 145.

40 Panić, *National Management of the International Economy*, p. 4.

41 An important event in the development of offshore banking was the Soviet withdrawal of balances from New York in 1957, and their subsequent placement - as dollars - with the Moscow Narodny Bank in London and the Banque Commerciale pour l'Europe (with its telex, Eurbank) in Paris; this was reputedly undertaken through fear of an American freeze on Soviet assets; see Higonnet, 'Eurobanks, eurodollars and international debt', p. 27.

42 See Clarke, *Inside the City*, p. 203; Ingham, *Capitalism Divided?*, p. 52; and Davis, *The Management of International Banks*, p. 21.

43 See Davis, *The Management of International Banks*, p. xiii.

44 This offers a basis for distinguishing between 'control' and 'supervision', where the latter implies rational acknowledgement of the impossibility of sustaining the former in any absolute sense.

45 See Clarke, *Inside the City*, pp. 203–4; and Little, 'Higonnet: 'Eurobanks: policy analysis'', p. 154.

46 Kindleberger, *International Capital Movements*, p. 46.

47 Ingham, *Capitalism Divided?*, p. 51; Clarke, *Inside the City*, p. 131.

48 Emery, *The Japanese Money Market*, p. 110.

49 Spindler, *The Politics of International Credit*, pp. 150–1.

50 See Gilpin, *The Political Economy of International Relations*, pp. 310-11. This possibly terminally undermines any attempt to distinguish between *de facto* and *de jure* integration.

51 Gilpin, *The Political Economy of International Relations*, p. 315; see also, *Bank of England Quarterly Bulletin*, vol. 26, no. 3, September 1986, p. 375.

52 *The Politics of International Economic Relations*; see also Gilpin, *The Political Economy of International Relations*, p. 316.

53 Gilpin, *The Political Economy of International Relations*, pp. 310–14.

54 Ibid., p. 314.

55 Ibid., p. 316.

56 Ibid., p. 317.

57 As Aliber suggests, where such a regulatory stimulus is not provided by the monetary authority in question, offshore markets grow at no faster rate than domestic wholesale monetary markets, 'Eurodollars: an economic analysis', p. 94; see also Goodhart, 'Carli', p. 164.

58 Kindleberger, *International Capital Movements*, p. 73.

59 Goodhart, 'Carli', p. 167.

60 For more detailed discussion of this issue, see Shafer, 'The theory of the lender of last resort'.

61 *International Capital Movements*, p. 73.

62 'The new international monetary 'system'', p. 289.

63 Ibid., p. 293.

64 Ibid., p. 303.

65 Ibid., p. 289.

66 Gilpin provides some idea of what perfection in this context might mean: 'a perfect or self-regulating market is one that is open to all potential buyers or sellers and one in which no buyer or seller can determine the terms of the exchange. Although such a perfect market has never existed, it is the model of the world implicit in the development of economic theory', *The Political Economy of International Relations*, p. 18.

67 *Plasticity into Power*, p. 126.

Chapter 6 Money in Postmodern Economics

1 See, for example, Callinicos, *Against Postmodernism*; and by contrast, Warde, 'Introduction to the sociology of consumption'.

2 See Clements, 'Money in international trade'.

3 Harvey writes of 'time–space compression' in the organization of social and economic life as characteristic of the postmodern condition; with regard to economics in particular, he argues that the organization and technology of flexible accumulation, which is his version of post-Fordism, has diminished spatial barriers locking production into specific places, yet with the paradoxical result that relative differences between locations have taken on greater importance in decisions about where business should locate: 'the less important the spatial barriers, the greater the sensitivity of capital to variations of place within space, and the greater the incentive for places to be differentiated in ways attractive to capital', *The Condition of Postmodernity*, pp. 295–6. Bauman portrays postmodernity more as a state of mind characterized by 'its all-deriding, all-eroding, all-dissolving *destructiveness*', suggesting that the main feature of postmodernity is 'the permanent and irreducible *pluralism* of cultures, communal traditions, ideologies, 'forms of life' or 'language games'', *Intimations of Postmodernity*, pp. vii–viii, 102, Bauman's emphases.

4 See Bell, *The Coming of Post-Industrial Society*; and Kumar, *Prophecy and Progress*, pp. 219–30.

5 See Smart, *Modern Conditions, Postmodern Controversies*, p. 54; and Harvey, *The Condition of Postmodernity*, p. 159.

6 Smart, *Modern Conditions, Postmodern Controversies*, p. 55; Harvey, *The Condition of Postmodernity*, pp. 284–5.

7 Harvey, *The Condition of Postmodernity*, p. 286.

8 Smart, *Modern Conditions, Postmodern Controversies*, p. 56.

9 Bauman, *Intimations of Postmodernity*, p. 31.

10 Jameson, *Postmodernism*, pp. 269–71.

11 See for example Bauman, *Intimations of Postmodernity*, p. 31; and Weinstein and Weinstein, 'Simmel and the theory of postmodern society'. While these commentators assess the 'relevance' of Simmel's work to the study of postmodernity, Stauth and Turner oddly attempt a wholesale appropriation by claiming Simmel as 'the first sociologist of post-modernity', *Nietzsche's Dance*, p. 16. To assess the relevance of Simmel's work for the study of postmodernity might throw up some intriguing parallels; to characterize him as a theorist *of* postmodernity, on the other hand, merely threatens to reduce the concept itself to a contradiction in terms.

12 Lash and Urry, *The End of Organized Capitalism*, p. 299.

13 See his *The Mirror of Production*, *For a Critique of the Political Economy of the Sign*, *Simulations*, *The Ecstasy of Communication* and *Seduction*.

14 See *The Theory of the Leisure Class*.

15 See, for example, Horkheimer and Adorno, *The Dialectic of Enlightenment*; and for an overview, Held, *Introduction to Critical Theory*, ch. 3.
16 *The Philosophy of Money*, p. 245.
17 Ibid., p. 235.
18 Ibid., p. 248.
19 Ibid., p. 251.
20 Ibid., p. 232.
21 Ibid., p. 233.
22 See Collier and Mayer, 'Financial liberalization'.
23 *Lloyds Bank Review*, no. 166, p. 23.
24 Collier and Mayer, 'Financial liberalization'; Akerlof, 'The market for 'lemons''.
25 See *Models of Bounded Rationality*.
26 'Is Western Europe caught in an 'expectations trap'?', p. 11.
27 See Harvey, *The Condition of Postmodernity*, pp. 284, 295–9.
28 Ibid., p. 194.
29 Ibid., p. 194.
30 *Postmodernism*, p. 273.
31 Ibid., p. 276.
32 See *The Dialectic of Enlightenment*.
33 See Clarke, *Business Crime*.
34 *Postmodernism*, p. 274.
35 Source: British Treasury figures.
36 *Postmodernism*, p. 264.
37 Ibid., p. 275, Jameson's emphasis.
38 Ibid., p. 270, Jameson's emphasis.
39 Ibid., p. 275.
40 Ibid., p. 270.
41 Ibid., p. 276.
42 Ibid., p. 269.
43 Ibid., p. 277.
44 Ibid., p. 269.

Chapter 7   High Modernity, Rationality and Trust

1 See, in particular, *Community and Association*.
2 As well as *Economy and Society*, see *The Protestant Ethic*, *The City*, *General Economic History*, and 'Georg Simmel as sociologist'.
3 Production in this context should not, it must be emphasized, be interpreted in its narrow empirical sense as referring simply to the process by which goods are made. It has a much richer meaning concerning the relationship between individuals and their material environment.
4 See the Introduction above.

5   See Friedman and Schwartz, 'Money and business cycles', for an original formulation of the transmission mechanism; see also Laidler, *Taking Money Seriously*, pp. 31–7, and Dow and Saville, *A Critique of Monetary Policy*, pp. 206–11, for less outdated discussion of liquidity preference.

6   See in particular Zukin and Dimaggio, *Structures of Capital*, and Holton, *Economy and Society*.

7   *Nuts and Bolts*, p. 32.

8   Ibid., pp. 32-3.

9   See Elster, ibid., p. 34.

10 See Elster, *Ulysses and the Sirens*, p. 57.

11 *Models of Bounded Rationality*, vol. II, p. 484, Simon's emphasis.

12 See the discussion of the *maximum minimorum* below for an application of this line of reasoning in a monetary context.

13 Riker and Ordershook suggest that, in any case, if perfect information is not assumed, the concept of satisficing is compatible with the absolute version of the maximization thesis, with information costs taken into account, *An Introduction to Positive Political Theory*, pp. 21–3. As Hindess notes, however, this can lead to regress, for one must first decide which method of evaluating costs and benefits to employ, which in itself requires information, and so on; see his *Choice, Rationality, and Social Theory*, pp. 70–1.

14 *Models of Bounded Rationality*, vol. II, p. 398.

15 Ibid., p. 399, Simon's emphasis.

16 *A Theory of Justice*, p. 153

17 *Models of Bounded Rationality*, vol. II, pp. 390–1.

18 See also Elster, *Nuts and Bolts*, p. 36.

19 Dasgupta, 'Trust as a commodity', p. 51; Giddens, *The Consequences of Modernity*, pp. 29–30.

20 See Dasgupta, 'Trust as a commodity'.

21 See Luhmann, *Trust and Power* and 'Familiarity, confidence, trust'; and Barber, *The Logic and Limits of Trust*.

22 See for example Good, 'Individuals, interpersonal relations, and trust', and Giddens, *The Consequences of Modernity*.

23 See for example Barber, *The Logic and Limits of Trust*; Luhmann, 'Familiarity, confidence, trust'; Dunn, 'Trust and political agency'; and Gambetta, 'Can we trust trust?'

24 'Can we trust trust?', p. 217, Gambetta's emphases.

25 Ibid., pp. 218–19.

26 See Gambetta, ibid.

27 Dasgupta, 'Trust as a commodity'.

28 Gambetta, 'Can we trust trust?'

29 Elster, *Sour Grapes*; Dunn, 'Trust and political agency'; and Williams, 'Formal structures and social reality'.

30 Dasgupta, 'Trust as a commodity'.

31 Good, 'Individuals, interpersonal relations, and trust'.

32 Dasgupta, 'Trust as a commodity'; Gambetta, 'Can we trust trust?'

33 Luhmann, 'Familiarity, confidence, trust', pp. 97–9.
34 *The Consequences of Modernity*, p. 32.
35 'Formal structures and social reality', p. 11.
36 *The Consequences of Modernity*, p. 35.
37 Ibid., p. 109.
38 See *The Postmodern Condition*.
39 *The Consequences of Modernity*, p. 141.
40 Ibid., p. 154.
41 Ibid., p. 175.
42 Ibid., p. 154.
43 'Reflections on 'rationality' and 'development'', p. 198.
44 Ibid., p. 184, Castoriadis's emphases.
45 See, in particular, Castoriadis, ibid.; and Gellner, *Postmodernism, Reason and Religion*, especially pp. 58–63.
46 See Giddens, *Modernity and Self-Identity* and *The Transformation of Intimacy*.
47 Cascardi argues for example that 'the modern subject not only legitimizes itself but 'rationalizes' the status of its own beginning by transforming the difference between history and theory into the self-justifying, homogeneous, and ostensibly coherent narratives of human progress, self-improvement and growth', *The Subject of Modernity*, p. 70.
48 *The Consequences of Modernity*, p. 38.
49 *Modernity and Self-Identity*, p. 20.
50 *Postmodernism, Reason and Religion*, p. 38.
51 Ibid., p. 62.
52 Ibid., p. 25.
53 Ibid., p. 92.
54 Ibid., p. 81.
55 Gellner seems to acknowledge this much at least when he contends that Enlightenment philosophy 'does absolutize some formal, one might say procedural, principles of knowledge, and perhaps also (especially in its Kantian version) of moral valuation', ibid., p. 80.
56 Ibid., pp. 60–1.
57 *Modernity and Self-Identity*, p. 21.

Bibliography

Adie, D. K. 1970: 'English bank deposits before 1844', *Economic History Review*, 23, pp. 285–96.

Akerlof, G. A. 1970: 'The market for 'lemons': quality uncertainty and the market mechanism', *Quarterly Journal of Economics*, 84, pp. 488–500.

Alexander, J. C. 1984: *Theoretical Logic in Sociology*, vol. IV. London: Routledge.

Aliber, R. Z. 1985: 'Eurodollars: an economic analysis', in P. Savona and D. Sutija (eds) *Eurodollars and International Banking*. Basingstoke: Macmillan, pp. 77–98.

—— (ed). 1987: *The Reconstruction of International Monetary Arrangements*. Basingstoke: Macmillan.

Avineri, S. 1972: *Hegel's Theory of the Modern State*. Cambridge: Cambridge University Press.

Barber, B. 1983: *The Logic and Limits of Trust*. New Brunswick: Rutgers University Press.

Baudrillard, J. 1975: *The Mirror of Production*. St Louis: Telos Press.

—— 1981: *For a Critique of the Political Economy of the Sign*. St Louis: Telos Press.

—— 1983: *Simulations*. New York: Semiotext(e).

—— 1988: *The Ecstasy of Communication*. New York: Semiotext(e).

—— 1990: *Seduction*. New York: St Martin's Press.

Bauman, Z. 1992: *Intimations of Postmodernity*. London: Routledge.

Bell, D. 1973: *The Coming of Post-Industrial Society*. New York: Basic Books.

Blau, P. (ed.) 1976: *Approaches to the Study of Social Action*. London: Open Books.

Blaug, M. 1962: *Economic Theory in Retrospect*. Cambridge: Cambridge University Press (4th edn., 1985).

—— 1980: *The Methodology of Economics*. Cambridge: Cambridge University Press.

Bohannan, P. 1959: 'The impact of money on an African subsistence economy', *Journal of Economic History*, 19, pp. 491–503.

Boltho, A. 1983: 'Is Western Europe caught in an 'expectations trap'?', *Lloyds Bank Review*, 148, pp. 1–13.

Borden, C. A. 1961: *South Sea Islands*. Philadelphia: Macrae Smith.

Cairncross, A. 1988: 'The Bank of England's relationships with the government, the civil service, and Parliament', in G. Toniolo (ed.) *Central Banks' Independence in Historical Perspective*. Berlin: Walter de Gruyter, pp. 38–72.

Callinicos, A. 1989: *Against Postmodernism*. Cambridge: Polity.

Cantillon, R. 1755: *Essai sur la nature du commerce en général*. London.

Cascardi, A. J. 1992: *The Subject of Modernity*. Cambridge: Cambridge University Press.

Cassel, G. 1932: *The Theory of Social Economy*. London: Ernest Benn.

Castoriadis, C. 1991: *Philosophy, Politics, Autonomy*. New York: Oxford University Press.

—— 1991: 'Reflections on 'rationality' and 'development'', in C. Castoriadis, *Philosophy, Politics, Autonomy*. New York: Oxford University Press, pp. 175–98.

Cencini, A. 1988: *Money, Income and Time*. London: Pinter.

Christian, F. W. 1899: *Caroline Islands*. London: Methuen.

Clarke, M. 1986: *Regulating the City*. Milton Keynes: Open University Press.

—— 1990: *Business Crime: Its Nature and Control*. Cambridge: Polity.

Clarke, W. M. 1979: *Inside the City*. London: George Allen & Unwin (reprinted 1983).

Clements, A. W. 1989: 'Money in international trade', in D. T. Llewellyn (ed.) *Reflections on Money*. Basingstoke: Macmillan, pp. 139–66.

Codere, H. 1968: 'Money-exchange systems and a theory of money', *Man*, 3, pp. 557–77.

Cohen, G. A. 1978: *Karl Marx's Theory of History: A Defence*. Oxford: Clarendon.

Collier, P. and Mayer, C. 1989: 'The assessment: financial liberalization, financial systems, and economic growth', *Oxford Review of Economic Policy*, 5 (4), pp. 1–12.

Coser, L. A. (ed.) 1965: *Georg Simmel*. Englewood Cliffs: Prentice-Hall.

Coulbeck, N. 1984: *The Multinational Banking Industry*. London: Croom Helm.

Crump, T. 1981: *The Phenomenon of Money*. London: Routledge.

Dalton, G. 1965: 'Primitive money', *American Anthropologist*, 67, pp. 44–65.

—— 1968: 'Economic theory and primitive society', in E. E. LeClair and H. K. Schneider (eds.) *Economic Anthropology*. New York: Holt, Rinehart & Winston, pp. 143–67.

Dasgupta, P. 1988: 'Trust as a commodity', in D. Gambetta (ed.) *Trust*. Oxford: Basil Blackwell, pp. 49–93.

Davis, S. I. 1979: *The Management of International Banks*. London: Macmillan (reprinted 1983).

Dow, J. C. R. and Saville, I. D. 1988: *A Critique of Monetary Policy*. Oxford: Clarendon (reprinted 1990).

Dunn, J. 1988: 'Trust and political agency', in D. Gambetta (ed.) *Trust*. Oxford: Basil Blackwell, pp. 73–93.

—— (ed.) 1990: *The Economic Limits to Modern Politics*. Cambridge: Cambridge University Press.

Durkheim, E. 1979: 'Review of Georg Simmel's *Philosophe des Geldes*', *Social Research*, 46 (2), pp. 321–8.

Einzig, P. 1949: *Primitive Money*. Oxford: Pergamon Press (reprinted 1966).

Elster, J. 1983: *Sour Grapes*. Cambridge: Cambridge University Press.

—— 1984: *Ulysses and the Sirens*. Cambridge: Cambridge University Press.

—— 1985: *Making Sense of Marx*. Cambridge: Cambridge University Press (reprinted 1987).

—— 1989: *Nults and Bolts for the Social Sciences*. Cambridge: Cambridge University Press.

Emery, R. F. 1984: *The Japanese Money Market*. Lexington, Ma: Lexington Books.

Francke, H.-H. and Hudson, M. 1984: *Banking and Finance in West Germany*. London: Croom Helm.

Freeman, S. 1988: 'Banking as the provision of liquidity', *Journal of Business*, 61 (1), pp. 45–64.

Friedman, M. and Schwartz, A. 1963: 'Money and business cycles', in M. J. C. Surrey (ed.) *Macroeconomic Themes*. Oxford: Oxford University Press, 1976, pp. 279–94.

Frisby, D. 1981: *Sociological Impressionism*. London: Heinemann.

—— 1985: *Fragments of Modernity*. Cambridge: Polity.

—— 1992: *Simmel and Since*. London: Routledge.

Fullarton, J. 1844: *On the Regulation of Currencies*. London: John Murray.

Gambetta, D. (ed.) 1988: *Trust*. Oxford: Basil Blackwell.

—— 1988: 'Can we trust trust?', in D. Gambetta (ed.) *Trust*. Oxford: Basil Blackwell, pp. 213–37.

Ganßmann, H. 1988: 'Money - a symbolically generalized medium of communication? On the concept of money in recent sociology', *Economy and Society*, 17 (3), pp. 285–316.

Gellner, E. 1992: *Postmodernism, Reason and Religion*. London: Routledge.

Giddens, A. 1984: *The Constitution of Society*. Cambridge: Polity.

—— 1985: *The Nation-State and Violence*. Cambridge: Polity.

—— 1990: *The Consequences of Modernity*. Cambridge: Polity.

—— 1991: *Modernity and Self-Identity*. Cambridge: Polity.

—— 1992: *The Transformation of Intimacy*. Cambridge: Polity.

Gilbart, J. W. 1941: *Currency and Banking*. London: H. Hooper.

Gilbert, F. (ed.) 1975: *The Historical Essays of Otto Hintze*. New York: Oxford University Press.

Gilpin, R. 1987: *The Political Economy of International Relations*. Princeton: Princeton University Press.

Good, D. 1988: 'Individuals, interpersonal relations, and trust', in D. Gambetta (ed.) *Trust*. Oxford: Basil Blackwell, pp. 31–48.

Goodhart, C. A. E. 1985: 'Carli: 'Eurodollars: policy analysis' - comment', in P. Savona and G. Sutija (eds.) *Eurodollars and International Banking*. Basingstoke: Macmillan, pp. 161–5.

—— 1989: *Money, Information and Uncertainty*. London: Macmillan.

Gowland, D. H. 1979: *Modern Economic Analysis*. London: Butterworths.

—— 1982: *Controlling the Money Supply*. London: Croom Helm.

Gray, J. 1988: 'Hayek, the Scottish school, and contemporary economics', in G. C. Winston and R. F. Teichgraeber III (eds.) *The Boundaries of Economics*. Cambridge: Cambridge University Press, pp. 53–70.

Habermas, J. 1976: *Legitimation Crisis*. London: Heinemann.

—— 1979: *Communication and the Evolution of Society*. London: Heinemann.

—— 1984: *The Theory of Communicative Action*, vol. I. London: Heinemann.

—— 1987: *The Theory of Communicative Action*, vol. II. Cambridge: Polity.

—— 1987: *Knowledge and Human Interests*. Cambridge: Polity.

Hall, J. A. (ed.) 1986: *States in History*. Oxford: Basil Blackwell.

Hall, M. 1987: *Financial Deregulation*. Basingstoke: Macmillan.

—— 1987: *The City Revolution*. Basingstoke: Macmillan.

Hamada, K. and Horiuchi, A. 1987: 'The political economy of the financial market', in K. Yamamura and Y. Yasubo (eds.) *The Political Economy of Japan*, vol. I. Stanford: Stanford University Press, pp. 223–60.

—— and Patrick, H. T. 1987: 'Japan and the international monetary regime', in T. Inoguchi and D. I. Okimoto (eds.) *The Political Economy of Japan*, vol. II. Stanford: Stanford University Press, 1988, pp. 108–37.

Hanson, J. L., revised by E. W. Orchard. 1983: *Monetary Theory and Practice*. Plymouth: MacDonald & Evans.

Harvey, D. 1989: *The Condition of Postmodernity*. Oxford: Basil Blackwell.

Hasebroek, J. 1933: *Trade and Politics in Ancient Greece*. London: Bell.

Hausman, D. M. 1988: 'Economic methodology and philosophy of science', in G. C. Winston and R. F. Teichgraeber III (eds.) *The Boundaries of Economics*. Cambridge: Cambridge University Press, pp. 88–116.

Hayek, F. 1945: 'The use of knowledge in society', in F. Hayek, *Individualism and Economic Order*. London: Routledge, 1949, pp. 77–91.

—— 1949: *Individualism and Economic Order*. London: Routledge.

—— 1967: *Studies in Philosophy, Politics and Economics*. London: Routledge.

—— 1967: 'Kinds of rationalism', in F. Hayek, *Studies in Philosophy, Politics and Economics*. London: Routledge, 1967, pp. 82–95.

—— 1976: *Denationalisation of Money*. London: Institute of Economic Affairs (reprinted 1990).

—— 1983: *Knowledge, Evolution and Society*. London: Adam Smith Institute.

—— 1983: 'The reactionary character of the socialist conception', in F. Hayek, *Knowledge, Evolution and Society*. London: Adam Smith Institute, pp. 38–44.

—— 1983: 'Coping with ignorance', in F. Hayek, *Knowledge, Evolution and Society*. London: Adam Smith Institute, pp. 17–27.

Held, D. 1980: *Introduction to Critical Theory*. Berkeley/Los Angeles: University of California Press.

Herskovits, M. J. 1940: *The Economic Life of Primitive Peoples*. London: A. A. Knopf.

Higonnet, R. P. 1985: 'Eurobanks, eurodollars and international debt', in P. Savona and G. Sutija (eds.) *Eurodollars and International Banking*. Basingstoke: Macmillan, pp. 15–52.

Hilton, B. 1979: 'Peel: a reappraisal', *Historical Journal*, 22 (3), pp. 585–614.

Hindess, B. 1988: *Choice, Rationality, and Social Theory*. London: Unwin Hyman.

Hintze, O. 1902: 'The formation of states and constitutional development: a study in history and politics', in F. Gilbert (ed.) *The Historical Essays of Otto Hintze*. New York: Oxford University Press, 1975, pp. 159–77.

Hirschman, A. O. 1977: *The Passions and the Interests*. Princeton: Princeton University Press.

HMSO. 1959: *Report of the Committee on the Working of the Monetary System* (Radcliffe Report). London: HMSO.

Holtfrerich, C.-L. 1988: 'Relations between monetary authorities and governmental institutions: the case of Germany from the nineteenth century to the present', in G. Toniolo (ed.) *Central Banks' Independence in Historical Perspective*. Berlin: Walter de Gruyter, pp. 105–59.

Holton, R. J. 1986: 'Talcott Parsons and the theory of economy and society', in R. J. Holton and B. S. Turner (eds.) *Talcott Parsons on Economy and Society*. London: Routledge, pp. 25–105.

—— 1992: *Economy and Society*. London: Routledge.

—— and Turner, B. S. (eds.) 1986: *Talcott Parsons on Economy and Society*. London: Routledge.

Honneth, A., Knödler-Bunte, E. and Widmann, A. 1981: 'The dialectics of rationalization: an interview with Jürgen Habermas', *Telos*, 49, pp. 5–31.

Hont, I. 1990: 'Free trade and the economic limits to national politics: neo-Machiavellian political economy reconsidered', in J. Dunn (ed.) *The Economic Limits to Modern Politics*. Cambridge: Cambridge University Press, pp. 41–120.

Hopkins, K. 1978: *Conquerors and Slaves*. Cambridge: Cambridge University Press.

Horkheimer, M. and Adorno, T. 1947: *The Dialectic of Enlightenment*. New York: Herder and Herder (reprinted 1972).

Humphrey, C. 1985: 'Barter and economic disintegration', *Man*, 20, pp. 48–72.

Hutton, W. 1992: 'Inside the ERM crisis', *The Guardian*, 30 November – 2 December.

Ingham, G. 1984: *Capitalism Divided?* Basingstoke: Macmillan.

Ingram, D. 1987: *Habermas and the Dialectic of Reason*. New Haven: Yale University Press.

Inoguchi, T. 1988: 'The ideas and structures of foreign policy: looking ahead with caution', in T. Inoguchi and D. I. Okimoto (eds.) *The Political Economy of Japan*, vol. II. Stanford: Stanford University Press, pp. 108–37.

—— and Okimoto, D. I. (eds.) 1988: *The Political Economy of Japan*, vol. II. Stanford: Stanford University Press.

Ishi, H. 1982: 'Financial institutions and markets in Japan', in M. T. Skully (ed.) *Financial Institutions and Markets in the Far East*. London: Macmillan, pp. 84–129.

Jameson, F. 1991: *Postmodernism Or, The Cultural Logic of Late Capitalism*. London: Verso.

Jevons, W. S. 1875: *Money and the Mechanism of Exchange*. London: Henry S. King.

Jordan, B. 1985: *The State*. Oxford: Basil Blackwell.

Kennedy, E. 1991: *The Bundesbank*. London: The Royal Institute of International Affairs/Pinter.

Kennedy, P. 1988: *The Rise and Fall of the Great Powers*. London: Fontana (reprinted 1989).

Keynes, J. M. 1930: *A Treatise on Money*, 2 vols. London: Macmillan.

Kindleberger, C. P. 1984: *A Financial History of Western Europe*. London: George Allen & Unwin.

—— 1987: *International Capital Movements*. Cambridge: Cambridge University Press.

Knapp, G. F. 1905: *The State Theory of Money*. London: Macmillan (reprinted 1924).

Kosai, Y. 1987: 'The politics of economic management', in K. Yamamura and Y. Yasubo (eds.) *The Political Economy of Japan*, vol. I. Stanford: Stanford University Press, pp. 555–92.

Kumar, K. 1978: *Prophecy and Progress*. Harmondsworth: Penguin.

Laidler, D. 1990: *Taking Money Seriously*. New York: Philip Allan.

Lash, S. and Urry, J. 1987: *The End of Organized Capitalism*. Cambridge: Polity.

Lawson, N. 1992: *The View From No. 11*. London: Bantam.

Lea, S. E. G., Tarpy, R. M. and Webley, P. 1987: *The Individual in the Economy*. Cambridge: Cambridge University Press.

LeClair, E. E. and Schneider, H. K. (eds.) 1968: *Economic Anthropology*. New York: Holt, Rinehart & Winston.

Levine, D. N. 1991: 'Simmel and Parsons reconsidered', in R. Robertson and B. S. Turner (eds.) *Talcott Parsons: Theorist of Modernity*. London: Sage, pp. 187–204.

Little, J. S. 1985: 'Higonnet: 'Eurobanks: policy analysis' - comment', in P. Savona and G. Sutija (eds.) *Eurodollars and International Banking*. Basingstoke: Macmillan, pp. 153–7.

Llewellyn, D. T. (ed.) 1989: *Reflections on Money*. Basingstoke: Macmillan.

Lomax, D. 1987: *London Markets After the Financial Services Act*. London: Butterworths.

Luhmann, N. 1979: *Trust and Power*. Chichester: Wiley.

—— 1988: 'Familiarity, confidence, trust: problems and alternatives', in D. Gambetta (ed.) *Trust*. Oxford: Basil Blackwell, pp. 94–107.

Lyotard, J.-F. 1979: *The Postmodern Condition*. Manchester: Manchester University Press (reprinted 1984).

Macesich, G. 1987: *Monetary Policy and Rational Expectations*. New York: Praeger.

Malinowski, B. 1922: *Argonauts of the Western Pacific*. London: Routledge.

Mann, F. 1938: *The Legal Aspect of Money*. Oxford: Clarendon (5th edn., 1992).

Mann, M. 1984: 'The autonomous power of the state: its origins, mechanisms and results', in J. A. Hall (ed.) *States in History*. Oxford: Basil Blackwell, 1986, pp. 109-36.

—— 1986: *The Sources of Social Power*, vol. I. Cambridge: Cambridge University Press.

Marx, K. 1956: *Capital*, vol. II. London: Lawrence & Wishart.

—— 1959: *Capital*, vol. III. London: Lawrence & Wishart.

—— 1973: *Grundrisse*. Harmondsworth: Penguin.

—— 1981: *A Contribution to the Critique of Political Economy*. London: Lawrence & Wishart.

—— 1982: *Capital*, vol. I. Harmondsworth: Penguin.

Mauss, M. 1966: *The Gift*. London: Cohen & West.

Melitz, J. 1970: 'The Polanyi school of anthropology on money', *American Anthropologist*, 72, pp. 1020–40.

Menger, K. 1892: 'On the origin of money', *Economic Journal*, 2, pp. 239–55.

Mill, J. S. 1844: *Essays on Some Unsettled Questions of Political Economy*. London: John W. Parker.

—— 1844: 'On the currency question', *Westminster Review*, 41, pp. 579–98.

Mises, L. von 1912: *The Theory of Money and Credit*. London: Jonathan Cape (reprinted 1953).

Misgeld, D. 1985: 'Critical hermeneutics versus neoparsonianism?', *New German Critique*, 35, pp. 55–82.

Murakami, Y. 1987: 'The Japanese model of political economy', in K. Yamamura and Y. Yasubo (eds.) *The Political Economy of Japan*, vol. I. Stanford: Stanford University Press, pp. 33–90.

Muramatsu, M. and Krauss, E. S. 1987: 'The conservative policy line and the development of patterned pluralism', in K. Yamamura and Y. Yasubo (eds.) *The Political Economy of Japan*, vol. I. Stanford: Stanford University Press, pp. 516–54.

O'Driscoll, G. P. 1986: 'Money: Menger's evolutionary theory', *History of Political Economy*, 18 (4), pp. 601–16.

OECD (Organization of Economic Cooperation and Development) 1977: *Towards Full Employment and Price Stability* (McCracken Report). Paris: OECD.

Panić, M. 1988: *National Management of the International Economy*. Basingstoke: Macmillan.

Parsons, T. 1937: *The Structure of Social Action*, 2 vols. New York: Free Press (reprinted 1961).

—— 1952: *The Social System*. London: Tavistock.

—— 1967: *Sociological Theory and Modern Society*. New York: Free Press.

—— 1975: 'Social structure and the symbolic media of interaction', in P. Blau (ed.) *Approaches to the Study of Social Action*. London: Open Books, 1976, pp. 94–134.

—— 1977: *Social Systems and the Evolution of Action Theory*. New York: Free Press.

—— and Smelser, N. 1956: *Economy and Society*. London: Routledge (reprinted 1957).

Peel, R. 1844: *Speeches on the Renewal of the Bank Charter, and the State of the Law Respecting Currency and Banking*. London: John Murray.

Pelczynski, Z. A. 1971: *Hegel's Political Philosophy*. Cambridge: Cambridge University Press.

Perez-Diaz, V. M. 1978: *State, Bureaucracy and Civil Society*. London: Macmillan.

Pocock, J. G. A. 1990: 'The political limits to premodern politics', in J. Dunn (ed.) *The Economic Limits to Modern Politics*. Cambridge: Cambridge University Press, pp. 121–41.

Poggi, G. 1978: *The Development of the Modern State*. London: Hutchinson.

Polanyi, K. 1957: 'The semantics of money-uses', in K. Polanyi, *Primitive, Archaic and Modern Economics*. Boston: Beacon, 1971, pp. 175–203.

—— 1957: *The Great Transformation*. Boston: Beacon.

—— 1958: 'The economy as an instituted process', in E. E. LeClair and H. K. Schneider (eds.) *Economic Anthropology*. New York: Holt, Rinehart & Winston, 1968, pp. 122–43.

—— 1971: *Primitive, Archaic and Modern Economics*. Boston: Beacon.

Price, W. 1944: *Japan's Island of Mystery*. New York: John Day.

Pyle, K. B. 1988: 'Japan, the world, and the twenty-first century', in T. Inoguchi and D. I. Okimoto (eds.) *The Political Economy of Japan*, vol. II. Stanford: Stanford University Press, pp. 446–86.

Rawls, J. 1971: *A Theory of Justice*. Oxford: Oxford University Press.

Read, D. 1987: *Peel and the Victorians*. Oxford: Basil Blackwell.

Reid, M. 1988: *All-Change in the City*. Basingstoke: Macmillan.

Riker, W. and Ordershook, P. C. 1973: *An Introduction to Positive Political Theory*. Englewood Cliffs: Prentice-Hall.

Rist, C. 1938: *History of Monetary and Credit Theory*. London: George Allen & Unwin (reprinted 1940).

Robertson, R. and Turner, B. S. (eds.) 1991: *Talcott Parsons: Theorist of Modernity*. London: Sage.

Roll, E. 1942: *A History of Economic Thought*. New York: Prentice-Hall.

Savona, P. and Sutija, G. (eds.) 1985: *Eurodollars and International Banking*. Basingstoke: Macmillan.

Say, J.-P. 1821: *Treatise on Political Economy*. Philadelphia.

Sayers, R. S. 1976: *The Bank of England 1891–1944*. Cambridge: Cambridge University Press (reprinted 1986).

Schneider, H., Hellwig, H.-J. and Kingsman, D. J. 1978: *The German Banking System*. Frankfurt am Main: Fritz Knapp Verlag.

Schumpeter, J. A. 1954: *History of Economic Analysis*. London: George Allen & Unwin.

Shafer, J. R. 1987: 'The theory of the lender of last resort and the eurocurrency markets', in R. Z. Aliber (ed.) *The Reconstruction of International Monetary Arrangements*. Basingstoke: Macmillan, pp. 281–304.

Shinkai, Y. 1988: 'The internationalization of finance in Japan', in T. Inoguchi and D. I. Okimoto (eds.) *The Political Economy of Japan*, vol. II. Stanford: Stanford University Press, pp. 249–71.

Simmel, G. 1907: 'Soziologie der Sinne', *Die Neue Rundschau*, 18 (2), pp. 1025–36.

—— 1908: *Soziologie*. Berlin: Duncker & Humblot.

—— 1971: *On Individuality and Social Forms*. Chicago: University of Chicago Press.

—— 1978: *The Philosophy of Money*. London: Routledge.

Simon, H. 1982: *Models of Bounded Rationality*, 2 vols. Cambridge, Ma: MIT Press.

Skocpol, T. 1978: *States and Social Revolutions*. Cambridge: Cambridge University Press.

Skully, M. T. (ed.) 1982: *Financial Institutions and Markets in the Far East*. London: Macmillan.

Smart, B. 1992: *Modern Conditions, Postmodern Controversies*. London: Routledge.

Smelt, S. 1980: 'Review article: Simmel's *Philosophy of Money* and Frankel's *Money: Two Philosophies*', *British Journal of Sociology*, 31 (1), pp. 137–8.

Smith, A. 1776: *The Wealth of Nations*. Harmondsworth: Penguin (reprinted 1986).

—— 1976: *The Theory of Moral Sentiments*. Oxford: Clarendon.

—— 1978: *Lectures on Jurisprudence*. Oxford: Clarendon.

Smith, A. D. 1986: 'State-making and nation-building', in J. A. Hall (ed.) *States in History*. Oxford: Basil Blackwell, pp. 228–63.

Spero, J. F. 1990: *The Politics of International Economic Relations*. London: Unwin Hyman (4th edn).

Spindler, J. A. 1984: *The Politics of International Credit*. Washington, DC: Brookings Institution.

Stauth, G. and Turner, B. S. 1988: *Nietzsche's Dance*. Oxford: Blackwell.

Struthers, J. and Speight, H. 1986: *Money: Institutions, Theory and Policy*. London: Longman.

Surrey, M. J. C. (ed.), 1976: *Macroeconomic Themes*. Oxford: Oxford University Press.

Thurow, L. C. 1983: *Dangerous Currents*. Oxford: Oxford University Press.

Tobin, J. 1958: 'Liquidity preference', in M. J. C. Surrey (ed.) *Macroeconomic Themes*. Oxford: Oxford University Press, 1976, pp. 164–74.

—— 1963: 'Financial intermediation and the supply of money', in M. J. C. Surrey (ed.) *Macroeconomic Themes*. Oxford: Oxford University Press, 1976, pp. 183–92.

Toniolo, G. (ed.) 1988: *Central Banks' Independence in Historical Perspective*. Berlin: Walter de Gruyter.

Tönnies, F. 1955: *Community and Association*. London: Routledge.

Tooke, T. 1844: *An Inquiry into the Currency Principle*. London: London School of Economics (reprinted 1959).

—— 1856: *On the Bank Charter Act of 1844*. London: Longmans.

Torrens, R. 1858: *The Principles and Practical Operations of Sir Robert Peel's Act of 1844, Explained and Defended*. London: Longmans.

Tsoukalis, L. (ed.) 1985: *The Political Economy of International Money*. London: Sage.

—— 1985: 'The new international monetary 'system' and prospects for reform', in L. Tsoukalis (ed.) *The Political Economy of International Money*. London: Sage, pp. 283–304.

Turner, B. S. (ed.) 1989: *Theories of Modernity and Postmodernity*. London: Sage.

Unger, R. M. 1987: *Plasticity into Power*. Cambridge: Cambridge University Press.

Veblen, T. 1934: *The Theory of the Leisure Class*. New York: The Modern Library.

Viner, A. 1987: *Inside Japan's Financial Markets*. London: The Economist Publications.

Wallerstein, I. 1974: *The Modern World-System*, vol. I. New York: Academic Press.

Walras, L. 1954: *Elements of Pure Economics*. London: Allen & Unwin.

Warde, A. 1990: 'Introduction to the sociology of consumption', *Sociology*, 24(1), pp. 1–4.

Weber, M. 1930: *The Protestant Ethic and the Spirit of Capitalism*. London: George Allen & Unwin.

—— 1958: *The City*. London: Heinemann.

—— 1961: *General Economic History*. London: Collier-Macmillan.

—— 1972: 'Georg Simmel as sociologist', *Social Research*, 39, pp. 155–63.

—— 1978: *Economy and Society*, 2 vols. Berkeley: University of California Press.

Weingartner, R. H. 1960: *Experience and Culture: The Philosophy of Georg Simmel*. Middleton, Ct: Wesleyan University Press.

Weinstein, D. and Weinstein, M. A. 1989: 'Simmel and the theory of postmodern society', in B. S. Turner (ed.) 1989: *Theories of Modernity and Postmodernity*. London: Sage, pp. 75–87.

White, L. H. 1984: *Free Banking in Britain*. Cambridge: Cambridge University Press.

Williams, B. 1988: 'Formal structures and social reality', in D. Gambetta (ed.) *Trust*. Oxford: Basil Blackwell, pp. 3–13.

Winston, G. C. and Teichgraeber III, R. F. (eds.) 1988: *The Boundaries of Economics*. Cambridge: Cambridge University Press.

Yamamura, K. and Yasubo, Y. (eds.) 1987: *The Political Economy of Japan*, vol. I. Stanford: Stanford University Press.

Zukin, S. and Dimaggio, P. (eds.) 1990: *Structures of Capital*. Cambridge: Cambridge University Press.

Index